Life is hardly ever what it seems, Thank God!

A copy of *We're All Doing Time* will be provided free of charge to anyone in prison or jail, and to other seekers who sincerely can't afford to pay for it. Simply write to:

Human Kindness Foundation
Rt. 1 Box 201-N
Durham NC 27705

All proceeds from the sale of this book go to support our free distribution of books, tapes and newsletters to many people around the world. Additional donations are always needed and welcomed. The Human Kindness Foundation sponsors the Prison-Ashram Project and other activities toward a kinder, safer, and saner world. To make donations, request more information, or to order this and other publications, write to the address above, or visit our website at:

http://www.humankindness.org

We're All Doing Time is also published...
>   in Spanish as **Todos Estamos Encarcelados**
>   in French as **Nous Sommes Tous Dans Une Prison**
>   in Italian as **Siamo Tutti in Priogione**

Other books by Bo Lozoff:

>   **LINEAGE AND OTHER STORIES** (1988)
>
>   **JUST ANOTHER SPIRITUAL BOOK** (1990)

WE'RE ALL DOING TIME

a guide for getting free

BO LOZOFF

included in this manual:

First printing, 1985, Hanuman Foundation (18,000 copies)
Second printing, 1986, Hanuman Foundation (15,000 copies)
Third printing, 1989, Human Kindness Foundation (15,000 copies)
Fourth printing, 1991, Human Kindness Foundation (10,000 copies)
Fifth printing, 1992, Human Kindness Foundation (15,000 copies)
Sixth printing, 1994, Human Kindness Foundation (5,000 copies)
Seventh [revised] printing, 1994, Human Kindness Foundation (15,000 copies)
Eighth printing, 1995, Human Kindness Foundation (15,000 copies)
Ninth Printing, 1996, Human Kindness Foundation (20,000 copies)
Tenth Printing, 1997, Human Kindness Foundation (20,000 copies)

Editors: Sita Lozoff, Howard Rubin
Proofreading: Catherine Scott, Mho & Mho Publishers
Hatha Yoga Chapter co-written by C.J. Kamer, yoga instructor
Design & Lay-out: Bo, Sita, & Josh Lozoff
Cover design: Doug Cruickshank / Shannon Dancy
Cover artwork: Cristine Mortensen / Herb Bresky
Back cover photo: Steven R. Miller
Typesetting: Liberated Types, Durham , NC
Photo Lab: Graphic Reproductions, Durham, NC
Printing: Edwards Brothers, Ann Arbor, MI / Lillington, NC

Graphics:
Rick Morgan: All of books one & two except as listed below, plus the following pages:
226, 252, 276, 305.
Gururam Kaur Marini: pp. xi, 18, 26, 37, 59, 75, 118, 119, 124, 137, 146, 147, 151,
153, 155, 158, 167, 182, 187, 196, 221, 235, 240, 252, 295, 297, 300, 301, 303.
Maury Logue: pp. 254-272; John Morris: pp. 63 & 185; Dennis Dee: pp. 179 & 228;
Renee: pp. 142 & 223; Tommy Moore: p. 286; D. Netto: p. 115; Stan Gilliam: p. 22;
Michael Ferguson: p. 293; Stephen Land: p. 136

Photos: Rameshwar Das: p. i, 60, 64, 120
        Kenny Golden: p. xii
        Jey Barbour: pp. xviii, 2, 6, 24, 112,138, 274, 298
        Russell Rigsbee: pp. 6, 56, 76, 88, 96, 168, 180, 198
        Dave Crenshaw (The Tulsa Tribune): pp. 134, 265
        Daphne Rae ("Love 'Til It Hurts"): pp. 101, 122, 125
        Omega Press: p. 164; J. Sculzewski: p. 296; Kit Green: p. 243;
        Hanu Rao: p. 297; Bob Shrager: p. 319
Calligraphy: Neily Conrad

Contents

THE DALAI LAMA

FOREWORD

The primary aim of all religions is to help people become better human beings. Therefore, whatever our personal beliefs, it is more important to try to create a safer, kinder world than to attempt to recruit more people to the religion that happens to satisfy us. From my own experience I have found the greatest degree of inner tranquility comes from the development of love and compassion. A close, warmhearted feeling for others automatically puts the mind at ease. This helps remove whatever fears or insecurities we may have and gives us the strength to cope with any obstacles we encounter. It is the ultimate source of success in life. Kindness and compassion are extremely important in every area of life, whether we are prisoners, prison guards or victims of crime. It is futile to harbour hatred and ill-will even toward those who abuse us. Cooperation, trust and consideration are far more constructive. The hostility and negativity of prison life will not change until both staff and inmates can improve their attitudes towards each other in this way.

What is required is a greater effort to address the real problems and to heal the wounds rather than just complaining on one side or the other. Therefore, the work of organisations like the Human Kindness Foundation is very important to everyone concerned with prison life. I trust that this practical manual *We're All Doing Time* will inspire everyone who is as concerned with helping others in trouble as with their own personal improvement.

June 1, 1994

A Word About Prisons

Although this book concerns the lives of people in many prisons, critics may point out that nothing much is said about prison reform. For clarity, I'd like to state my position right here.

Prison systems throughout the world are generally ugly, barbaric, counterproductive, and insane. Someday our descendants will look back on our time with shock that such otherwise sophisticated people could have treated prisoners the way we do. But this book is about people and their spiritual work. And as much as the prison system and the mentality which keeps it going tear my heart out, mine is a different type of work than prison reform. As director of the Prison-Ashram Project, I've often been urged to shift my gears and do something to bring an end to the present system rather than helping people to endure it. Some people think that our project (and I) are no more than "tools of the oppressors" because we don't work toward tearing down all prisons.

Meanwhile, millions of people have to live in prisons just as they are today, and I've been privileged to help them do their timeless spiritual work—the work we all have to face no matter where we find ourselves—without waiting for bigger social changes to take place.

I'm glad there are many prison-reform groups, and if there weren't, I'd probably start one. But there are no worldwide projects other than the Prison-Ashram Project which offer general common-sense spiritual friendship unattached to any particular religion, guru, or doctrine. We saw a need and so we've been trying to fill it, and it's been very happy, productive work for many years.

I invite you, through the pages of this book, to share the fruits of that work. At the same time, I certainly hope all of us do as much as we can to help our society move out of the dark ages of what is so terribly inaccurately called "corrections".

INTRODUCTION:
We're All Doing Time

Everybody just wants to feel good. Consciously or unconsciously, every living thing moves through time trying to feel more complete, more satisfied, than the moment before. From the tiniest germ's struggle for survival to the wisest being's search for enlightenment, life on Earth is a matter of doing our time according to our very best guesses.

Being human, though, *our* guesses are based not just on instinct, but also on a tremendous amount of thinking and reasoning. And because we have such a wide range of choices, many of our decisions are bound to be bad ones, that is, choices which make us feel *less* complete, *less* satisfied.

We *could* live our lives as a continuing process of adventure and discovery—that is, staying sharp enough to find the secret of making every choice a good one; one that helps rather than hurts us. But instead, we tend to bury ourselves in work or play in order to avoid facing the mystery. Or we may try to do *easy* time via booze or drugs. And many of us freak out or lash out, through self-destructive behavior ranging from mere rudeness to mass murder.

Robbing a bank or killing somebody may sound like a crazy way to go about feeling good, yet that's what lies at the root of it. The robber hopes to steal some contentment; the murderer tries to destroy his own unbearable pain of separateness. And let's face it: Societies and governments have done much the same, on a far bigger scale. Like Bob Dylan sang, "Steal a little and they throw you in jail, steal a lot and they make you King." The world of insecurity and desire shares similar motivations from the lowest ranks to the highest.

But ever since the beginning of human life on Earth—in the middle of all the jiving and bloodshed & endless quests for pleasure, wealth, and power—a few people here and there have gotten together to pursue Truth—the **big** Truth, capital "T".

This search for Truth—for the key that makes sense of life, for the deep, mysterious *something* which connects all of creation—has never stopped, never even paused, for a moment.

And here we are again. It's important to understand that this *is* who we are. You and I are seekers on a sacred, ancient path carved out by trailblazers like Buddha, Mohammed, Jesus, Mary, Moses, great yogis, gurus, medicine chiefs, shamans—countless men and women of every age, race, and land.

WE'RE ALL DOING TIME is a meeting about Truth, just as if we were sitting in a hidden cave or on a faraway mountaintop. It's a great blessing to come together like this, so let's not sell ourselves short; this meeting can change our lives forever if we'll allow that to happen.

The original idea behind this book was to help prisoners, but really, prison is completely beside the point. It's just an excuse to have brought us together again along the Sacred Way. Whoever and wherever we are, in or out of prison—we're *all* doing hard time until we find freedom inside ourselves.

Though we may seem an unlikely bunch, filled with doubts, fears, and many forms of self-hatred, we also happen to be the keepers of the precious flame of Truth in this age; it survives solely because we keep it flickering in our hearts. We're *loaded* with spiritual power. We just have to unblock our access to it. And that takes a lot of self-honesty and hard work, no matter where we live, how we spend our days, or what we've done in the past.

WE'RE ALL DOING TIME is intended as an enduring companion for the long haul, not for reading in a few evenings like a novel. **Book One**, *The Big View*, is my version of the profoundest common sense, the truths we all know deep in our bones;

Book Two, *Getting Free*, is an instruction manual; it offers a lot of simple and practical ideas for gaining control of our lives; for quieting our minds so we can see what's really going on.

Book Three, *Dear Bo*, shares some of the letters I've exchanged, mostly with prisoners, over the past eleven years. Nearly every strength, weakness, and insight of the human condition—*our* condition—from divine to demonic, can be found here. It's a rare opportunity we have, to study ourselves through such a wide range of windows to our souls.

Many books and teachings offer relief from our constant guesswork by giving clear rules on how to live. This isn't one of them. I can hardly keep up with my own range of guesses from hour to hour, let alone dictate what anyone else needs to do. Besides, to me, guessing is what keeps life juicy.

All I hope to share is a Spirit of the Great Adventure, because it's the *same* Spirit which moves us in all our different ways. **WE'RE ALL DOING TIME** is simply encouragement for each of us to look inward to find the place in ourselves which feels at peace with who we are, at peace with the guesses we make as we move through life. I think we'd all love to stop lying to ourselves, screwing things up, and feeling vaguely incomplete, so that's what the book is about. The rest all falls into place once we accomplish that; it goes beyond words and pictures.

With faith, patience, and an undying sense of humor, we can find *life* rather than mere existence. I hope this book helps you find your own Way.

Bo Lozoff
1985

This book is dedicated to everyone in the world, because that's who needs all the love and encouragement we can possibly give.

Life is what happens
While we're busy making other plans.

—John Lennon

Bo & Sita on the Restless Wind, 1969

PREFACE:

Getting Here

In the summer of 1969, Sita and I found ourselves working aboard a 41' trimaran sailboat in the Caribbean. We had been married for only three years, but in the course of that time had been students, drop-outs, activists, revolutionaries, outlaws, and finally hippies, and had lived all over the country, working at dozens of different jobs. We had fought for some good causes, taken a lot of psychedelic drugs, met some beautiful people here and there—but hadn't yet found whatever it would take for our own lives to make sense.

Now something *in*ternal was finally starting to happen. Six months earlier, we had come back to my family home in Miami to help my father die at home, as he wished. By the time he died in April, he had a tremendous amount of peace and spiritual power, and his death was really very beautiful. I think because it touched us so deeply, we found it too hard to merely drift down the road again into the world of passing sights and sounds that seemed so empty.

Trouble was, we were very young, and didn't yet know about the possibilities for people who were trying to "find themselves". We had never heard of mystics and yogis and holy people—hell, from our acid trips, we thought *we* were the only "holy people"!

So, unaware of any other options, we headed for the docks, hoping to literally sail off into the sunset. We hired on *The Restless Wind* just like in the old movies: Shook hands, got room & board, and the rules were simple—Wayne, the skipper, told us what to do and we did it, night or day. I was his first mate, and Sita the ship's cook.

We had been honest with Wayne from the start that neither of us had ever set foot on a sailboat before; but it was clear to him that we were ripe for adventure, and he was too. None of the three of us had any idea what we wanted out of life—only that we hadn't come close to finding it so far.

Wayne was a drop-out, too, although from a whole other direction. He had been born and bred a conservative southern farmboy, and had been a master electrician at Fla. Power & Light. He had never gotten into drugs or done anything illegal; he just got tired of working so hard when he really didn't understand what it was for, so he spent three years building *The Restless Wind* singlehandedly. She was truly a magnificent boat in every way.

Life seems pretty simple out on the ocean. There were only two things we ever needed to think about: The weather, and where to dive for food. We went to sleep right out on deck underneath the stars when night fell, and awakened when the sun rose. We stopped using all drugs. We never even thought about sex. We were lean, tanned, and healthier than at any other time in our lives. We weathered some ferocious storms, and noticed that the most extraordinary, peaceful sunsets seemed to follow the worst ones.

Life itself was finally beginning to make sense deep in our guts. It made sense to be alive, to be where we were, just to *be*. And as different as our backgrounds were, all three of us experienced a very strong feeling of reincarnation— specifically, that we had all been out on the ocean together, long ago. We also shared feelings of the profound mysteries we could sense behind the veil of nature. Months passed by as if in a dream.

Wayne planned to sail the Caribbean and West Indies, go through the Panama Canal, turn up the Pacific coast to California, and then head across to Hawaii—and maybe just keep going around the world. Sounded perfect to us.

But again, life is what happens while we're busy making other plans. To get up enough money for the long haul, we had to take paying passengers on cruises around the Bahamas. We'd take a group of six or eight people out from Miami, spend a week or two sailing the islands, snorkeling, soaking up the sun, and then return to port.

After several months of these cruises, Wayne was getting frazzled. Having strangers on the boat was often a drag, and the money wasn't piling up fast enough to finance our big voyage. So, one dark night, he concocted a plan with my sister's husband, Pete, to smuggle 1400 pounds of pot into Miami from Jamaica; "just one time", of course, and then we'd sail away into paradise (familiar theme, isn't it?).

Sita and I had already had enough police paranoia and jail experiences for a lifetime during our hippy and activist years; it wasn't worth it any-more, especially just for a fast buck. Trying unsuccessfully for days to talk Wayne out of it, we finally agreed to be his crew *to* Jamaica, but told him we wanted to be off the boat before the pot was loaded. Wayne agreed to get a Jamaican crew for the return trip, but our big dream—as well as the ancient friendship we had felt—was already shattered. And the cruise to Jamaica— our last trip together—seemed doomed from the start.

First we were becalmed on the Bahama Bank for nearly a week—not a trace of wind, just dead in the water. Then the wind kicked up from the wrong direction, and being out of radio range we had no way of knowing that we were about to be caught in the northern edge of Hurricane Martha, a late-season hurricane (Nov. '69) coming up from Central America.

We fought the hurricane for three days and nights—no sleep, lost all our food, had to lighten the boat by dumping most of our supplies—and finally gave up trying to get into the Windward Passage (between Cuba and Haiti) because we'd surely have been smashed to bits. Instead, we did what the weather *forced* us to do: We sailed into Cuba.

We tried to hide the boat off the coast, but we were captured, towed in, and interrogated by the Cuban Army for four days (actually not so bad, after the initial terror of being surrounded by people with machine guns who couldn't understand a word we were saying). When Cuban Army headquarters became convinced we were just "romantic adventurers", they turned us loose, and we limped into Jamaica—a few rips in the sails, storm-sick and weary, but with one more interesting tale behind us.

Sita and I flew back to Miami. Wayne and the boat made it back all right too, but a week later an informant soured the pot deal, and my brother-in-law was busted. Wayne dropped out of sight on the ocean; a few others were being hunted by the police. We went into hiding so we wouldn't be forced to testify.

After a good deal of drama, Pete got three years' probation. A few weeks later he, Wayne and a few others tried the exact same scheme again, and everyone was busted very hard. Pete got 12-40 years; Wayne & the others got 6-20 years (federal prisons). I'll never forget the sound of the judge's voice as he sentenced Pete: "I remand you to the custody of the Federal Bureau of Prisons, for a period of not less than twelve, and not more than forty years, without possibility of parole." It was devastating.

Sita and I were once again on land and footloose, but our experiences on the boat had changed us forever. We now knew that life didn't have to be as complicated as most of us make it; we could see that everything beyond shelter, weather and food is really just gravy—like the Beatles said, "nothing to get hung about."

Yet the way our lives on the boat were ripped out from under us, we also saw that *whatever* we found, if it depended on people or things outside of ourselves, it could still change in a moment. The boat, the beautiful ocean, all just props—here today, gone tomorrow. Out of our control. The task remained to find something in *ourselves* as boundless as the deep blue sea, and which can't be taken away.

We wandered again for about a year. As Wayne, Pete and the others settled into their prison time, we found ourselves (with our newborn son, Josh) living in a yoga ashram—a monastery—here in North Carolina. We spent our time in meditation practice, yoga, and long hours of farm work; no movies, parties, social life, tv, drugs, restaurants or music (except spirituals and chanting). Life on the boat had cut us loose from so many forms of leisure and entertainment, it wasn't much of a leap to enter the monastic life.

By the time we visited Pete in 1973 at the federal prison in Terre Haute Indiana, our lifestyle wasn't a lot freer than his. But ours was a matter of choice, and was in fact helping us a great deal. Just by stopping in one place long enough to face ourselves without distraction, we were beginning to glimpse an inner power that had always been lacking. As Ramakrishna said, *The musk ox searches all over the world trying to find the source of the scent which comes from itself.*

After a couple of years of ashram life, it felt like time to put some energy back into the world, and my visits with Pete made it clear to me that prisons were as much in need of help as any place I could imagine. It never dawned on me to do anything as farfetched as the Prison-Ashram Project; and since I had no degree or credentials of any sort, my idea was simply to go down and get hired as a guard at the new federal prison which was being built in Butner, N.C., about fifteen miles from the ashram. I figured a compassionate prison guard might be able to do a lot of good on both sides of the bars.

I was turned down, of course; I've got about the least likely background for prison guard as anyone alive. But the assistant warden, who was in charge of interviews, kept prodding me to tell him why I wanted the job. I didn't seem "the type," and he knew something just didn't fit.

Seeing that I had no chance for the job anyway, I figured I'd at least get a kick out of being absolutely honest with him.
I looked into his eyes and told him that actually I was a "Karma Yogi", that my spiritual path was one of service to mankind, and I thought that being a prison guard would be a good opportunity for doing service.

To my utter astonishment, this crew-cutted, cowboy-booted career prison official was suddenly all over me with questions & sincere enthusiasm, and saying things like "...And you know what I think? I think reincarnation was taken out of the Bible hundreds of years after Christ!" What a wild moment that was! I loved it.

Next, he asked me to write a proposal for doing yoga/meditation classes in federal prisons. Within a month I was flown to Washington to meet with Norm Carlson, the head of the Bureau of Prisons, and his executive staff. I can still remember sitting at that long table with all those big-shots, and marvelling that just a few years earlier, I sat around with revolutionaries arguing about how to blow up those very buildings. Life is really very funny.

I got a quick education in bureaucratic hustle. The BOP guaranteed me a job at Butner and made grand promises about "ashram units" and serious training programs. Then, before the prison even opened its doors, a friend sent me this headline from Detroit:

DETROIT · SUNDAY NEWS   4/20/75

Yoga treatment canceled at experimental prison

By BETH KANTOR

'We are not taking a hard-line approach but simply a more honest one'

NORMAN A. CARLSON

WASHINGTON — In much for standing prisoners on their heads and getting them to think unconventional thoughts at the government's new, $16.5 million experimental prison in North Carolina.

Norman A. Carlson, chief of the U.S. Bureau of Prisons, said he is reassessing what he calls some of the "far-out" rehabilitation projects that have been scheduled for the correctional center being built at Butner, N.C.

One project calls for volunteer convicts to put four hours a day into Eastern cultures and meditations and postures.

Other programs involve psychiatric-oriented, behavior-altering approaches, including one based on the "I'm O.K.-You're O.K." school of transactional analysis, pioneered by the late Dr. Eric Berne.

In a memorandum to wardens of federal prisons last week, Carlson said, "We are not taking a hard-line approach but simply a more honest one" toward rehabilitation, in the shift away from the "far-out" programs.

Carlson is making his move after getting clear signals from his boss, U.S. Atty. Gen. Edward H. Levi, who "does believe in the use of punishment as a deterrent to crime, and

doesn't believe everybody can be rehabilitated," according to a Justice Department spokesman.

As a result, Butner's warden, Dr. Martin G. Groder, a psychiatrist, has quit in what has become a bitter policy dispute between him and Carlson. In theory, Dr. Groder remains warden at the unfinished prison until next Saturday. But he and Carlson no longer are on speaking terms and Dr. Groder has been notified not to use his office.

Dr. Groder's walkout is typical of controversies that have dogged the most infamous unfinished federal prison in American history.

Construction began June 8, 1972, on the Butner project, officially named the Behavioral Research Center at that time.

The government's contract with Ranger Construction Co. of Atlanta, called for an $11.6 million job to be completed by Feb. 2, 1974.

The work is less than 75 percent finished now, and Carlson estimates it may be late 1976 before the first convicts can be moved in. The price tag on the center now is $16.5 million, just to get the doors open.

Meanwhile, stories began to circulate that a group of scientists were planning to use the Behavioral Research Center for basic, biological studies on the criminal mind.

What blueprints there were for surgical experimentation were "dropped and Butner's name was changed to the Federal Center for Correctional Research.

The plan for three years has been to establish a mental

hospital unit at Butner to care for 140 men and women prisoners who have acute psychiatric problems. In a separate activity, the center is supposed to do "research work" on 300 volunteers from within the regular hard-core prison populations of federal penitentiaries that extend as far away as Vermont, Michigan and Arkansas.

These volunteer prisoners would become guinea pigs in programs aimed at restructuring the anti-social personalities of criminals.

Dr. Groder arrived at the Butner project in 1972, after attracting national attention with a socially successful rehabilitation program he patterned after Berne's transactional analysis methods.

Dr. Groder's success came in the federal penitentiary at Marion, Ill., where he worked with hardened, violence-prone convicts.

Late last month Carlson attempted to transfer Dr. Groder to the Bureau of Prisons hospital at Springfield, Mo., where "there is a critical need for psychiatric help," Carlson said.

Dr. Groder feels the plan to transfer him was "the beginning of a short-sighted sensitivation to rehabilitation problems, which will prove to be destructive and costly."

But the bigger joke was on them, because they had unwittingly made me an acceptable figure on the national prison scene. I had now been a paid consultant to the U.S. Bureau of Prisons, and I decided to milk that respectability for all I could. I cut my hair, cleaned up my act a little, and used my new title to con my way into prisons and jails to offer classes. Like a chain letter, the more classes I did, the easier it was to get into still *more* institutions. Prison doors throughout the world suddenly flew open for me.

Around this same time, Sita and I had come across the book **BE HERE NOW** and struck up a friendship with the book's author, Ram Dass. Besides having a big impact on our lives, Ram Dass too had a soft spot for convicts and had already sent thousands of free copies of **BE HERE NOW** into prisons across the country. Together we started refining the idea of helping prisoners to use their cells as ashrams, and do their time as "prison monks" rather than convicts.

In late 1973, the Prison-Ashram Project was born. It was financed mostly out of Ram Dass' pocket until it outgrew his earnings. By word of mouth, we started receiving letters from prisoners and prison workers all over the world. In 1975, Sita and I left ashram life to devote full time to the project. We moved briefly to Colorado and California, and then we built our own home here in N.C. in 1981. In '83, we built the Prison-Ashram Project office about sixty feet behind the house. It's still just a two-person staff, funded now by hundreds of small donations.

In the past eleven years, we've been privileged to send out hundreds of thousands of booklets, tapes and books. I've done hundreds of prison workshops & classes, and we've helped spawn many other projects, study groups and various resources, not just for prisoners, but also for their families, prison workers, handicapped people, vets, and a lot of "ordinary" people who write us letters like this:

Although I'm not in a physical prison, I feel locked in by my fears, anxieties, desires, and anger. My life is getting so closed in, I don't know what to do. Please help me to escape from this prison of my own making.

At this point, the prison-as-ashram idea is no longer guesswork. In eleven years we've known a lot of "prison monks"—perfectly normal convicts who decided to go for the inner adventure as we have, and have changed the course of their lives forever. And on our part, dealing with prisons and prisoners has continually pushed us through attachments and impatience, pettiness and hypocrisy. It's too bizarre to worry about whether the granola has sugar in it when there's a letter on my desk from a young kid asking how to deal with being gang-raped.

There's an old saying, "If you want to learn something, teach it." How true! All Sita and I do is to remind people of the things we want to remember ourselves. We started out with pretty naive ideas of sharing yoga/meditation methods, but we quickly came to see all of that stuff as small potatoes.

Now we write and talk of the *bigger* things, like kindness, humor, patience, courage, and self-honesty. The "Big View" isn't the view from the widest ocean or the highest mountain, but rather from deep within each of us, and *needs* to be seen at some point in our lives, whether in Leavenworth or Beverly Hills.

About the highest compliment in prison is, "He knows how to do his own time." How many of us do? How many of us use *every moment* of our lives to get a little bit stronger, a little bit freer, no matter what's going on around us—no matter how crazy or violent it all seems to be? This is the constant opportunity we all share. It takes us awhile to cop to it, but people with wisdom have known this forever.

Isn't it hilarious that Sita and I—two lost souls who tried to escape from the world by sailing the wide ocean— have found a lot of our own freedom by helping people figure out how to discover their vastness in a 6x9 cell? The Divine Humor is truly mad, and it just doesn't quit.

Book One:

THE BIG VIEW

Now the wonderful world is born,
    in an instant it dies,
In a breath it is renewed.
    From the slowness of our eye
And the quickness of God's hand
    we believe in the world.
              --Wm. Buck

Imagine what life would be like if we didn't know how to use our arms or hands; if they just hung limply at our sides. How limited and clumsy our daily lives would be, how much we would be missing, for no good reason at all! Yet it's even more so with our Spirit. We may live, breathe, walk and talk, but most of the time we don't use more than a *fraction* of our spiritual power that would make life feel infinitely more natural and more worth living.

It's not that we're "bad" or wicked or anything like that. We're just spiritually *clumsy*; we're way out of balance because we usually see life from the view of the mouse—worrying endlessly about the terribly limited world at the tips of our whiskers. Wisdom and joy come only from learning how to see a wider, much more wondrous world; and power comes only from the Spirit within. This is why most of us end up feeling weak, lifeless, weary to the bone; we drag ourselves around just trying to make it through each day, often pausing to wonder whether the good times in life are worth all the effort and pain.

Changing our vision is what this book is about, and the change begins with a look at the two worlds we inhabit at the same time: The outer world of appearances, and the inner world of Spirit.

From the world of appearances, life may look very different from one minute to the next, one person to the next, or one age of the world to the next; but from the "Big View"—from the world of Spirit—there's only one process going on: We get born, we have good times and bad times, we experience a wide range of emotions such as desire, love, anger, and fear, we face various problems and challenges that make us feel good or bad about ourselves, we learn some things and forever wonder about other things, and then we move on into the unknown.

Life is truly just this one story, and it fits Joan of Arc as well as Adolf Hitler; primitive tribesmen as well as Harvard professors. Whether we get from place to place on foot, or oxcart, or in a Ferrari; whether we carve our messages into a stone, or type them up on a computer; whether we live in caves, huts, or three-bedroom brick ranchers, does it really change that basic spiritual storyline?

But here's a mystical secret:

Each of us has the *starring role* in this Great Movie. We're all heroes, adventurers, who have a lot of ups and downs, who may stumble and fall a million times—but we can become strong, wise, and free by the end. It's really a *very* beautiful story.

The "outer" world of appearances—what we usually call reality—is nothing more than a prop room. It contains everything that operates under the Law of Time.

Think about it: No matter what we ever get or have, we won't be able to hold on to it for very long. Our possessions, our greatest inventions, even the wonders of nature and our own bodies—merely props: We use them for awhile, but then the parts rust, the paint peels, the flesh sags, the heart stops, the Earth quakes; even the sun will eventually burn out. What time brings us, time takes away. It's all part of the deal.

But time itself is no more than a stage-prop to the "inner" world, the world of Spirit. There's a Great Mystery going on here; a Great Natural Riddle which has lain deep in the mind of every human being ever born—*including* me and you.

Because this mysterious Spirit can't be seen, heard, tasted, smelled, or touched, most of us let our curiosity slide as we grow up. Even though we're never quite satisfied in the outer world, we limit our attention to our mousy busy-ness all our lives and try to believe that's all there is to reality. Society doesn't run too well on mysteries, so the standard policy seems to be: If we don't understand it, it must not exist. Problem solved.

But living in such a limited way is bound to be a drag sooner or later, and this is what the Buddha talked about in his "Four Noble Truths", and it's what Jesus said about needing to be "born of the Spirit" in addition to being born of the flesh.

These and other masters also gave us practical tips on how to go about correcting our vision:

> *Seek ye **first** the*
> *Kingdom of God, and everything else will be added unto you.*

And when someone asked Jesus just where to find this spiritual kingdom, He said

> *Neither shall you say 'Lo, here!',*
> *or 'Lo, there!', but the Kingdom is **within** you.*

4

The advice is pretty simple. The problem is, there are some *spectacular* props in this movie, and most of us stay so busy chasing them, our lives are almost over before we start to think about how empty we feel.

Seeking "first" this inner kingdom is not so much a matter of becoming a religious fanatic nor going off to a hidden cave in the mountains, but rather to simply PAY ATTENTION spiritually as we go about our normal lives. "First" is a matter of moment-by-moment priorities, not months or years.

When our central aim is to find this "inner kingdom," then we discover how it is that everything comes to us: We see that *every person, place, and event in our lives is perfectly designed to teach us something we need to learn in order to get free.*

So we get hit by a truck or elected to office, we get sent to prison or win a million dollars, we get terminal cancer or become rich and famous—we learn spiritual lessons from all of it *equally.* We use *every* situation, *every* moment of our lives to get looser, wiser, and freer.

This is what Jesus called "being in the world but not of it," and what in the East is known as Zen, Karma Yoga and Tantra Yoga. We just have to stay open and wide awake, being students—rather than victims—of our lives. It helps a lot if we can remember this: *Life, like any other exciting story, is bound to have painful and scary parts, boring and depressing parts, but it's a brilliant story, and it's up to us how it will turn out in the end.*

The Spiritual Mystery of our true inner nature is what makes sense of it all, but it can't be found in words, books, philosophies, or even religions. We have to solve it for ourselves by being sharp and noticing all the clues. And we have to calm down quite a bit in order to do that. It may take a very long time and a great deal of effort, but as many of us have noticed by now, life makes no sense at all without diving into the wonder and challenge of that Great Mystery.

It can't be found by seeking,
but only seekers will find it.

"I know, I know, you'll prob'ly
scream & cry, that your
little world won't let you go..."
--Jimi Hendrix

From the moment we're born, something deep inside pushes us to cry out for our mother's breast, a loving touch, a strong arm to rock us and soothe us. We're always seeking. We seek to feel safe, loved, warm—in a word, we seek a state of *peace*.

At first, our mother is enough for us, but lasting peace is part of the Mystery; it can never be found in the world of appearances. Soon we come upon toys, games, friends, new kinds of food, and on and on. Everybody just wants to feel good, and we keep reaching for anything that might do the trick. Yet the more things we discover, the hungrier we seem to be for still more.

Every joint smoked, every drink drunk, every pill popped, every crime committed, is just to get some relief—just to feel good, to feel safe or powerful. It's like going crazy from a toothache without knowing what to do about it; we blindly grope around in pain, and some people do it more violently than others.

Perhaps the most important realization of our whole lives is when it finally hits us that

> *Nothing we ever get, see, taste,*
> *smell, touch, hear, or think about,*
> *is going to bring us the peace*
> *we really seek.*

This is what the Buddha called his First Noble Truth. We tend to fight against this natural law, so we suffer more and more. There are some people who get all the power, success, fame, or riches they thought they wanted, and instead of being happy, they soon destroy themselves.

We don't have to look very far for examples: Elvis Presley, Freddy Prinze, John Belushi, Judy Garland, Marilyn Monroe, Lenny Bruce, Jimi Hendrix, Billie Holliday—the list could go on for pages.

What clearer reminder do we need that if we're not at peace with ourselves, then we're all doing time in one kind of prison or another? Sitting in the hole in Attica or Joliet or Santa Fe, it's hard to imagine that some swinging millionaire in a Beverly Hills mansion could possibly be suffering as much, but it's true. In fact, that "uptown" suffering is often worse, because their minds can't come up with as many excuses for being so miserable, for why life is so unbearably painful.

But excuses are just that—excuses. Making excuses gets to be our way of life if we don't watch out. In prison, for example, most people tend to exaggerate about how wonderful life on the streets was, or else they fantasize about how great it's going to be the next time out. But truthfully, if life on the streets was so great, then why is everybody in the joint? And why do so many ex-cons wind up back in prison within a year or two?

The truth is, life everywhere is very hard, because we're holding so much pain from being out of balance. Like it or not, the BIG Truth has to be approached from all the smallest truths about ourselves; the journey into the GREAT Mystery has to begin by solving all the dull, practical mysteries of our lives, like why we keep making the same kinds of choices which hurt us time after time.

The journey into these mysteries is easy to put off for a million different reasons, but a prisoner actually has a particular head-start in a way. He or she has already had the most common reasons stripped away by the government: Can't take the time, have to work too hard, have to support my family, have to keep up my social image. For the prisoner who gets tired of making excuses, incarceration could be turned into the best spiritual break of a lifetime.

One common excuse in prison life is that the spiritual trip turns us into suckers; that if we get into peace, love, truth, we lose our street-smarts and get taken advantage of by everyone else. But actually, that couldn't be further from the truth. Whether in prison or business or college or anywhere else, we become a hell of a lot sharper when we look at life more clearly, when we can see *ourselves* more honestly. A Medicine chief said,

If you seek to understand the whole universe,
you will understand nothing at all.
If you seek only to understand your Self,
You will understand the whole universe.

Obviously, somebody who understands the whole universe is going to be pretty savvy in dealing with the dudes in the next cellblock. So it makes sense to begin looking into our own true nature—which is what every spiritual tradition has told us to do. Then no matter what happens, we've always got the house advantage, because we're living in tune with the house rules of the Universe.

To live with the house advantage, the main rule we need to appreciate is called the Law of Karma. In the Bible the way it's put is *As you sow, so shall you reap.* The way it's said in prison is: What comes around goes around.

Every thought, word, and deed is a seed which we plant in the world.
All our lives, we harvest the fruits of those seeds. If we plant desire,
greed, fear, anger and doubt, then that's what will fill
our lives. Plant love, courage, understanding, good
humor, and that's what we get back. This isn't
negotiable; it's a law of energy, just like gravity.

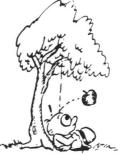

Karma is often easy to see. A Beatles song
says, "Instant Karma's gonna get you."
For example, you step on the end of a
shovel, it flips up and hits you in
the face. Or, you step on a banana peel and you fall. It's not good or bad,
it's just the way things are. It's just Karma.

At other times Karma is also immediate, but not so obvious. You flip a switch on the wall and a light goes on over your head. It's still direct cause-and-effect, but the wires are hidden.

Well, most often in our lives, the wires are hidden. Think about it.

Even *more* often, Karma is hard to follow because it's not so immediate; *time* goes by between an action and its Karmic reaction.

If I set an alarm clock for ten hours from now, I may forget all about it and then be startled when it goes off. Yet I set it with my own hand.

All through our lives, we're either slipping on banana peels, flipping switches with unseen wires, or setting alarms that we forget about or don't even know about as we're setting them. A kindness that we think went unnoticed, or something rotten that we hoped would disappear—nothing ever falls through the cracks. What comes around goes around.

OH, MOAN!

In Truth, we (everybody and everything in the Universe) are all connected; most of us just can't see the glue. Because of this basic connection, anything we think or do which creates a feeling of *separateness* causes more karma, because we're going against Truth, against the natural flow of reality. Working out karma is simply the process of undoing our own ignorance in order to get back into step with Nature.

For example, let's say I make fun of somebody who's crippled. The only way I could do that is if I felt no connection between us. So at some time in the future, my karma might be to become crippled, or to marry or give birth to someone crippled — *not as punishment*, but simply to allow me to open my heart to someone in a crippled body; to allow me to undo the separateness *I* created in the first place. It's as if I ran an ad in the "Teachings Wanted" section of the Spiritual Classifieds for an experience to show me that we're all just "us"; there's no "them".

Because Karma works this way to help each of us gain wisdom and compassion, it *looks* a lot like punishment reward, but it really isn't. It's more like magnetism — it's just the way energy works. The Golden Rule — Do unto others as you would have them do unto you — gets to be more of a scientific truth than a moral preaching. When Christ says, **Love thy neighbor as thyself**, He's simply telling it like it is:

We're all connected, and He can see the glue.

The world we live in is really not very big; it's a closed space. Just as our pollution doesn't disappear or "go away", neither do our actions or even our thoughts, whether good or bad. Each moment counts. Each of us has total responsibility for lightening the Karmic load of this sweet, pretty little planet. And each of us has the *power* to do so, every moment of every day.

Everything that happens to us in life has two purposes at once. For example, going to prison is paying karmic dues for things we came here to learn or things we've done in the past (not necessarily the crime itself). But going to prison is also one more *opportunity* to come closer to Truth, God, Self, Freedom—whatever we want to call it.

Prison life is so negative and intense, prisoners sometimes get the chance to work out karma and build strength in a period of months that might have taken fifty *years* on the streets, if they could have done it at all. What a blessing!

The bottom line is that **we create our own curses or blessings**. Every experience comes to us spiritually neutral, no matter what it looks like from the mouse's view. If we can accept our karma without shame, pride, bitterness, or regret, then some old dues get paid, and at the very same time we've been given a chance to increase our strength, love, and wisdom.

It's not important to waste our time trying to *analyze* the karmic causes and effects of things that happen to us; too many of the wires and switches and alarms are hidden. If I get a big package in the mail from some company thousands of miles away, and I have no idea how they got my name or what they're all about, the only sensible thing to do is to open the package and do whatever feels right at the time.

Same thing with karma. No need to look into a crystal ball or go to a psychic to see why such-and-such happened and then such-and-such, and so on. We just have to look through every day's "mail"—all the experiences of our lives—and handle it all without getting lost in speculation over the past. Once we understand karma, we begin to have more understanding and compassion for other people's trips. We see that we're all just beautiful children of God who have developed these stash-bags of karma by the choices we've made, and we're all working through our karma as best we can. Our stash bags are each unique—no two people have exactly the same karma. Yet the journey (working it all out) is basically the same for us all. As we become more aware, or conscious, of the whole process, we tend to *cooperate* more and more with the law of Karma, and our stash-bags get noticeably lighter. We become "conscious beings"—people who act in harmony with the truth in everything we do, from brushing our teeth to planning our lives. We do what feels *right* rather than what feels *easiest*. It's quite a relief!

The very *end* of our karmic journey—when we've completely lightened the burdens in our karmic stash—is called **enlightenment**. We become like God walking around in a body. Every thought, word and deed is in Truth, and creates no sense of separateness in the world. Christ, Buddha, and many others reached this state. They became so united with Truth, they ceased to create any karma at all—they were 100% part of nature with no resistance to the way life works best.

But the punch line of it all is that we *all must become enlightened.* Saint or murderer, president or bank robber, each of us is on the same journey, the same process of wholeness, and we will eventually go all the way to the end.

Whether today, next year, or a hundred thousand lifetimes from now, each of us will come to a point where we're tired of exploiting and being exploited, tired of "looking out for number one," slipping on banana peels, setting alarms; tired of constantly creating more karma.

At that point, help magically arrives. It may come through spiritual practices like yoga and meditation, or by meeting friends-on-the-path, or seeing an inspiring sunset, or just reading something like this. But in whatever form it comes, help does come. (It may not be help for what we *want*, but it'll help bring us the tools and experiences we *need*.)

From that moment on, our lives may seem much the same as ever, yet there's an added feeling of peace or security that comes from playing with the house advantage. We may still have fears and lusts and toothaches and hemorrhoids and all the stuff of this world, but there's a tiny part of us that *knows* it's all right, and that makes all the difference.

Amidst all the old stuff and craziness of our normal lives, we begin to focus our energy on the things that help to lighten our karma—quieting our minds, serving others, remembering not to get so lost, having faith in the way life works.

In prison, the daily dramas can get very heavy. Somebody comes up to start a fight, for example. If your own mind is centered and quiet, you see that they're just creating more karma for themselves, and that you're experiencing karma from your own balance sheet.

If you get sucked up into the whole drama, your part will live on just like theirs. But if you can handle the whole thing without so much anger or fear—whether you talk them out of it, defend yourself, or whatever you need to do—then you've finally broken the cycle, and have come one step closer to your enlightenment.

Neem Karoli Baba used to say,

*Do **whatever you must** with people;*
but never shut anyone out of your heart,
even for a moment.

When we truly understand karma, we see that one of us can never really gain from another's loss. If it looks like we can, then we're caught in the illusion of separateness. We'll cause ourselves to suffer again and again until we get it right. That's why Gandhi looked at his assassin with tremendous compassion after the guy shot him in the head; and why Jesus, after being nailed to the cross, said *Forgive them Father; they know not what they do!* Those who see the Truth don't get lost even in the heaviest scenes of the movie.

16

As we look around, it's easy to see that most of us aren't yet playing with the house advantage. We haven't yet gotten tired enough of the hustles and hypes; we haven't yet reached upward and inward for the truth of how life works, or why we struggle so hard. So much fear! So much desire! Do we really have anything to lose by going after bigger stakes? *Truth upholds the fragrant Earth and makes the living water wet. Truth makes fire burn and the air move, makes the sun shine and all life grow. A hidden truth supports everything; find it and win.*

All these words—love, truth, power, spirit—they're all the same thing. There's no single word for it because it's way beyond the mind, way beyond thoughts or concepts. That's why Jesus said,

> ...*my own peace, which **surpasses** understanding*...

It's like an old Indian story of five blind men who were placed before an elephant and asked to describe it. One felt the trunk, one the ears, one a foot, one the huge belly, and one the tail; so when they reported back to the king, they argued over what this creature was like. But the elephant was actually all they could describe and much more.

Likewise, our spiritual elephant is much more than gathering up a few laws like Karma and thinking we've got it covered. Instead of touching one little part of the elephant; instead of collecting information and facts and memorizing them; it's a matter of *emptying* our minds of all assumptions, all attitudes and limitations and definitions, so that we can see life fresh in each moment. This is what the Zen Master Suzuki Roshi called "Beginner's Mind."

It's the same principle as in the martial arts: A mind which is open, free of fear, free from unwanted thoughts, will be clear and powerful enough to deal with *anything.*

It's important to remember that such power doesn't need to be "developed"; rather, it's *discovered* as we gradually work through karma and get free from habitual ways of living. When we let the Big View sink in, the ordinary becomes miraculous, and miracles seem quite ordinary and acceptable. Life in the fast lane is replaced by life in the VAST lane.

See, I shall make all things new!

Nothing outside of us has to change. Sure, it might be fun to try a different role in the movie: to be out of prison, to be handsomer or prettier or richer or healthier or taller, skinnier or smarter; but all those conditions still come and go with time; they belong to the world of appearances; the world of birth and death. Look at an aging beauty queen sometime and see how pitiful she looks, her heavy make-up and tight girdles, trying to hold on to her passing beauty for just one more year, just one more day...

The beginner's mind is always living in the very moment of creation.

If we're not trying to hold on to the past, and not jockeying into a position for the future, then we finally *belong* in the world as it exists in the present moment, the eternal "Now". No power exists anywhere else.

All that we usually call "real" keeps slipping through our fingers, so how real can it be?

This is where the spiritual path goes way beyond religion, psychology or education. True reality has to include the mad, the mystical, the *unspeakable* which puts all the rest into proper perspective.

And it will only come from a one-to-one connection with the forces of creation; That's why Jesus called it the *NARROW Way*.

In the Hindu and Buddhist traditions, there's a word used to describe the world of appearances, of constant change: **MAYA**. It means "illusion"; it means that *the whole world of karma—of birth, growth, decay and death—is just one big dream*; a magic trick which *seems* real, but doesn't actually exist. It seems real only because of "the slowness of our eye, and the quickness of God's hand..."

Every now and then, as an act of Grace or good fortune or whatever, God's hand slows down a little, and even if it's just for a moment, we see behind this magic veil of Maya. It happens to people in every walk of life. For some, it changes their whole lives. Others freak out or try to forget what they saw as soon as possible.

...Strawberry fields, nothing is real; and nothing to get hung about...
—*John Lennon*

It may happen in a flash, or after years of faith, patience, and effort. Some of us have touched these higher realities when we've been stoned or tripping, and then we wanted to *stay* stoned, because life made so much more sense that way. Problem is, drugs are just one more part of the *maya* we're stuck in. They may provide very valuable spiritual experiences in the short run, but if we keep using them, even our highest insights will get all twisted around, and eventually just turn into more painful illusion.

What we have to appreciate about *maya* is that we can never hold on to an illusion no matter how solid or promising it seems.

In India, monkey-hunters hollow out a hole in a coconut and put sweet candies inside. The hole is just big enough for the monkey to squeeze his empty hand into, but not big enough to get a fistful of candies out. Then they stake the coconut into the ground. The monkeys find it and reach in to get the candy, but then they're stuck. They have only two alternatives: Hang on to the candy and be captured, or let go and be free. Time and

time again—even though they *never get to eat it anyway*—the monkeys refuse to let go of their *attachment* to the candy, to the *illusion* of how good it would taste, and so they get caught. How many times in our lives do we do the same? How many times in a *day*?

A guy goes to a psychiatrist and says, "My brother needs some help, doc. You see, he thinks he's a chicken." The doctor says "Well, bring him in to see me." The guy says, "I'd do that, but the problem is, frankly, we need the eggs."
—Woody Allen

The whole "spiritual path" is nothing more than being a simple realist about how life works; how the universe operates. We'll always be walking around in maya, but the trick is to *remember* that we're walking around in maya and to honor the rules of the game. We act out our script, but we don't have to forget we're merely actors, and that the whole movie's just a fictional story anyway, taking place only on the screen of God's Mind. Where else *is* there?

WHY ARE YOU UNHAPPY?

BECAUSE 99% OF THE THINGS YOU DO, THINK, AND FEEL

*ARE ABOUT YOURSELF. AND THERE **ISN'T** ONE!*

—*Wei Wu Wei*

Serious questions arise when the truth about Maya begins to sink in: If life is just illusion, then why care about Karma? What's the big deal about good and evil or right and wrong? Why put any effort into the parts we play? Why not just say, "Hell, if nothing is real then nothing matters, and I'm just gonna grab what I can, while I can. Screw everyone else. Screw the hungry, the poor, the oppressed. They're not real anyway!" But here's another mystical secret:

Nothing really matters at all. But those who truly know this carry out their lives as though EVERY MOMENT has a sacred meaning and importance.

> *"... Don Juan, what exactly is 'controlled folly'?"*
> *"I am happy that you finally asked me about my controlled folly after so many years, and yet it wouldn't have mattered to me in the least if you had never asked. Yet I have chosen to feel happy, as if I cared that you asked, as if it would matter that I care.* **That** *is controlled folly!"*
> —*A Separate Reality, by Carlos Castaneda*

It gets back down to acting out the movie. At a theater, what's up on the screen is illusion in the sense that if we tried to touch the actors, they're not really there. The experience isn't what it seems to be, but there's still a plan, plot, and design. The story makes sense and expresses a message. It's an illusion, but it's a carefully crafted one; like life.

All of existence (*including* death) is indeed an illusion, but it's a precisely designed, *lawful* illusion. The physical laws include energy, space, time, gravity, and evolution. There are emotional laws—the causes of happiness, depression, anxiety, and so forth. Then there are the *spiritual* laws, like karma, reincarnation, astrology, and the workings of other realms (astral bodies, spirit-guides, etc.).

The One GREAT Law covering all the other laws has been called by many names: Tao ("dow"), Torah, The Way, Medicine Wheel, and Dharma (**dar**ma), to name a few.

In the East, the word *Dharma* is used in two ways: *Dharma* (capital "D") is the flow of the whole Universe; our own personal *dharma* (small "d") is whatever we need to do in order to live in harmony with the *big* Dharma. It's still just a movie, but that's the basic plot. And Enlightenment is like the Academy Award; It's a gift directly from the Producer to those of us who stop struggling against the details long enough to see *exactly* what role we were born to play, and then play it with all our hearts.

There are as many *dharmas* as there are people. Some people find their destinies in tiny caves hidden away from society; others by selling shoes, raising children, pumping gas, building houses, etc. Some may become great teachers or leaders. Some may learn the Ancient Wisdom in a prison cell. Some people naturally touch the hearts of others through their music or performing skills. Some find their lives fulfilled by serving the poor and needy.

What ties us all together is the Big Dharma Law: **It is our basic nature to care for the well-being of every person, creature, plant, rock, and mole-cule of this Great Illusion.** That's all the Masters have tried to tell us. It's what Karma and all the other laws are based on.

We can be as greedy, cruel, or violent as we wish. But a life like that stems from the mouse's view, where the petty things seem all-important, and we're always worried that we're not getting enough or that we're going to die too soon. That's not *controlled* folly; it's just folly. It makes a lot more sense to seek our unique place in the Great Harmony, and to soar joyfully through life with the Big View of the eagle—the Spiritual Warrior.

god, sir... YES?

Book Two: GETTING FREE

Is it not written in your law,
"I said, You are Gods"?
--Jesus

INTRODUCTION:

Real Change

Most of the changes we make in our lives are no more than gestures. We lose 10 pounds when we really need to lose 20, we keep ourselves just on the edge of good health instead of feeling terrific, we wage lifelong battles against bad habits like smoking, drinking, drugs, etc. It's easy to *want* to see the big, clear view of life, but time after time we find ourselves prisoners of our old habits and limitations.

Book Two shares some of the most basic methods for real change which have been handed down through the ages. These are very straightforward, practical techniques which can gradually change who we are right down to our cells, atoms, and thought waves; *genuine* transformation, not just head-trips.

But no matter how old or powerful it may be, any method will only benefit us depending on what we want to get out of it. As Hari Dass Baba said, **When a pickpocket meets a Saint, all he can see are his pockets.** Two people can use the same meditation technique, and one may merely get better grades in school, while the other's entire life may be transformed by strength, compassion, and joy.

What's the secret for real change? How can we escape the general truth of Paul Simon's "Boxer"?: (*After changes upon changes, we are more or less the same.*)

Picture this scene taking place deep in an underground nuclear weapons center: The command has been given to release the big bomb. Three engineers come together in the control room, each opening a different small safe containing a single key. The keyholes are placed so that one or two people can't possibly insert them all. The engineers go to the control panel and insert their keys all at the same time. It takes all three, working together, to set this enormous power in motion.

We're designed in a similar way. The three keys which activate spiritual transformation are Grace, Spirit, and Effort—known in Christianity as the Holy Trinity: The Father, Holy Ghost, and the Son. The combined effect of these three forces is enough to heal the sick and raise the dead; so it's surely enough to set your life or my life in order.

The Grace of God is hardest to talk about. It's the key which comes from Beyond. We don't need to worry about it, and there's no point in trying to "get" it; we only have to keep a space open in our vision, hearts and souls to accept it when it comes.

The second key, the Holy Spirit, is the "Force" that the Star Wars movies were about. *All* energy is Spirit. Nothing happens anywhere except by this force, because no other power exists. Being aware of this is an important step in working *with* it rather than against it or feeling separate from it. Spirit is *our* raw energy; ours to use in all we do.

But the *third* key—ah, that's the tricky one.

You and I *are* the mysterious "Son" in the Trinity. Jesus tried to tell us this, but it was easier just to worship Him than to accept our own responsibility and power. He called Himself both "Son of God" *and* "Son of Man" to get his point across: *We* are the third key to the control panel; it's human effort that crystallizes the focus of Grace and Power.

We can waste our lives by fighting against the truth or by waiting to be "saved", but we won't get free that way. Genuine transformation requires all three keys.

The Holy Trinity doesn't belong to one religion over another; it's a profound mystical formula for getting straight. Knowing about Grace reminds us not to get so cocky; knowing about Spirit reminds us our power is unlimited; and knowing about the important role of our own effort encourages us to start clearing away all the petty weaknesses, self-created limits, old habits, and other qualities of our lives which keep us from being absolutely free—truly Gods on Earth, like all the masters have become.

These spiritual practices can't help us predict or control Grace; that's always the wild card. But they do help us to put forth what the Buddha called "Right Effort"—sincere, patient and good-humored effort to give up our weaknesses and blind spots so we can come into harmony with the Grand Design.

The methods work on body, mind, and Spirit all at once, so pick and choose which ones appeal to you the most, and try them out for a long enough time to see the subtle effects. Genuine change takes time.

There are hundreds of spiritual practices that could have been included here, but I've chosen those which have had the strongest effects on my own life—not because they're better than any others, but because I can pass them on to you with more power. This is what's called a "transmission of the Living Spirit," if you're open to receiving it.

Be open also to the guiding force of all the millions of people throughout history who have used these same practices. A lot of strange and beautiful things happen as we go beyond words and images, and plunge deeper and deeper into these sacred traditions.

ASK, and you shall receive. Knock, and the door will open.
Seek, and you shall find.

Dear Bo and Sita,

Well, it's been a year now and I finally went to trial. I've been sentenced to life imprisonment (which is only 25 years here in Canada); however, I am eligible for parole after ten years. I thought the "wait" would never end, but it has and my heart is full of joy... I feel as though I'm finally going somewhere.

Even so, my time in this small building has served a great purpose: I've seen a lot of faces come and go, I've learned a lot about myself and others. I've learned the meaning behind your phrase "Inside-Out". Indeed, my soul has finally been set free from the barriers I had trapped myself within.

I am actually glad (although I'm sure some see me as "mad") for the time I've received. Society is giving me a gift I would never have given myself: A chance to find my true self. Not only that, but they are giving me time; time... Society has always seemed to me to be a mad rush of tension. Now I have ten years to sit back and learn about what life is really all about. Each day my Spirit becomes stronger as it reaches the heights found in becoming one with God...Love...the Universe.

My hatha yoga is coming along so smoothly; my body is as flexible as a rubberband. I was having trouble meditating, but I believe the problem was being too caught up in the future. Slowly but surely I am simmering down. It's true: Suffering is a part of the great awakening. When I get to the Women's Prison, I certainly hope to find others involved with these things. It would be just excellent to have or share fellowship; thus far the climb has been alone.

This Earth is just one physical plane of many.... of an eternity of life after life again and again. God bless you.

Love and Peace, Susie/Canada

"If it were just a matter of playing football with the Firmament, stirring up the ocean, turning back rivers, carrying away mountains, seizing the moon, moving the Pole-star or shifting a planet, I could manage it easily enough," said the monkey.

"But if it comes to sitting still and meditating, I am bound to come off badly. It's quite against my nature to sit still."

1. Meditation—Just Sitting Still

It's easy to get so wrapped up in the spiritual "search" that we lose sight of the fact that it's an *inner* journey. Our greatest discoveries are gained simply by learning how to sit still. That's all meditation is when you get right down to it: Sitting perfectly still—Silence of body, silence of speech and silence of mind. The Buddha called this "The Noble Silence." It's just a matter of STOPPING.

Meditation practice has been a central focus of every religion and spiritual tradition, but because it takes place in silence, alone, it's always been set aside in favor of more social/religious practices like preaching and singing. For most of us, with our monkey-minds, it'd be easier to slice bread with a sledgehammer than to sit quietly and do "nothing" at all. When we first try a meditation technique, we think "Maybe other people can do this, but not me; I guess it's just not my nature."

But that's a crock. Meditation is hard for *everybody*, because we've all allowed our minds to run wild for many years. It takes time and effort to regain our rightful control, but it's well worth the discipline. An uncontrolled mind—no matter how much it knows, how smart it becomes, or how many pleasures it experiences—will never find peace or satisfaction. As soon as we fulfill one part of it, it'll hit us with another demand, another question, another passing thought. No wonder we spend about a third of our lives sleeping! The mind can be a great servant, but a cruel and exhausting master.

Because meditation practice is so hard to get into at first, many different methods have been handed down through the ages so that we can find one that feels best to our individual needs. It's important to understand that meditation itself is a state of mind; it's not a method or exercise. Meditation is beyond words; it's our deepest natural state, which we open into once our minds stop being busy.

Another way of looking at it: Meditation *practice* is learning *how* to use our key in the Holy Trinity; Meditation itself happens when we finally *use* our key in harmony with Grace and Spirit. It's also important to remember that just about any meditation method is as good as any other; we just have to choose one and then stick to it with a lot of patience and self-discipline.

Many people spend tremendous amounts of time and energy looking for a Guru or a master who can reveal to them the deepest secrets of the Universe. Such beings do exist, and it's wonderful to meet them, but the desperate search for them is usually just one more way of avoiding doing what we really need to do. There aren't any shortcuts on this path.

Besides, the very best that such a being can do is to inspire us to look within *ourselves* for the "secrets". Wisdom can't be put into words; it has to be experienced. That's the main difference between wisdom and knowledge.

The secrets of the Universe are only secrets to the noisy mind. So, meditation practice is simply about making enough quiet space inside to allow all the wisdom of the ages, all the peace that surpasses understanding, to flow through us freely. It's a slow, steady process of opening and emptying, in the faith that when we make ourselves ready, our own completeness will be right here—and has been here within us all our lives.

Of course, it's not an easy process. Besides all the noise of our conscious minds, we also have some pretty heavy **sub**conscious baggage we carry around with us.

Meditation practice is like turning on a light with a dimmer switch in a big room filled with furniture and clutter. At first we can only see a few things right around where we're starting from, but as the light brightens, we begin to see many vague shapes and shadows that may frighten us. Or we may get depressed when we realize just how far we have to go before this big room is empty—before the mind is really quiet, even for a moment.

But in order for us *ever* to get quiet, we have to begin right where we are. We may have to sit through intense periods of terror, lust, perversion, fantasy, grief, guilt, greed, pride, loneliness,—whatever furniture happens to be stored away in here, collecting cobwebs and taking up our peace.

In order to clear it all out, we have to learn the delicate art of allowing a thought or feeling to be whatever it is, but without getting sucked into it; we can't let it control us. We have to be able to watch the movie of our minds without getting too lost in what's happening on the screen.

That's why all the various meditation methods have a similar approach: By having *one point of attention*, no matter what comes up in our minds, we can notice it honestly and then get back to the one-point. Then something else comes up, we notice what it is, and get back to the one-point. Then something else, something else... That's meditation practice.

The process sometimes gets frustrating, but frustration is just one more thought; one more type of noise to notice and then let go of.

There's an old story about Milarepa, one of the great ancient Tibetan masters. Before his enlightenment, he once moved into a secluded cave to do some intensive meditation practice. But no sooner did he get settled, than he discovered that the cave was also home to a bunch of little demons—little creatures who enjoyed disturbing his meditations.

So the first thing he did was to try to get rid of them by preaching the Dharma (the Gospel). He preached and did all the customary exorcism rituals and then sat back down to meditate; but they were still there.

After a few more unsuccessful tries at preaching and scolding, he changed his strategy: He would completely ignore them. Maybe this would get rid of them. He tried this for a few days; no matter how loud or obnoxious they got, he sat firm and still, resisting them in his silence. But that didn't work either.

Finally, in total frustration and defeat, he screamed "All right, I give up! I can't force you out of here! But I'm not leaving either; I'll just have to share this cave with you!"

Then he sat down once again, his resistance completely gone. And so were the demons.

How To Sit

WRONG

RIGHT

It's well worth our time to pay attention to the actual physical part of sitting to meditate. Nobody gets spiritual brownie points for looking like a great yogi or enduring unnecessary pain in the knees and back. On the other hand, we won't gain much control over our minds if we slump over into a half-sleep every time we try to meditate.

What's important is a sitting posture which keeps the back, neck, and head in a straight line, yet is so balanced that there's no tension required to hold ourselves in place.

For most of us this takes a lot of practice. Try sitting on pillows or folded blankets, and see what the best height is for you to be able to sit straight with no effort. The knees should be down, not up, when your butt is at the right height. When the knees are down, the back is naturally straight.

Another sitting position is called "seiza" in Japanese. We sit slightly higher, but straddling the pillows like a saddle, and with our feet behind us. This is very comfortable for many people who can't sit the other ways. Just be sure to get up high enough that the feet don't fall asleep and the knees don't ache.

Sitting in a chair is also all right, although a tendency is to lean against the back of the chair, and that usually isn't very straight. If you do sit in a chair, don't lean; also make sure your feet and legs are symmetrical: legs crossed at the ankles or both feet flat on the floor a few inches apart.

In all of these sitting postures, the hands should be placed either on each leg or in the lap in such a way that you don't feel your shoulders being pulled down by the weight of the hands. Hands can be loosely clasped or held separate. Traditionally, they're kept sort of closed, since an open hand is a gesture of going outward, and meditation is a time to go inward.

Just Sitting Still

It's not a bad idea to use the posture itself as a meditation method for a few days or even a few weeks.

For 20-30 minutes at the same time each day, get as straight and balanced as possible, and then simply pay attention to the body sitting perfectly straight. After the first minute or two of minor shifting and scratching, keep the body in one straight position without moving at all. Pay attention to any feelings of muscle tension or imbalance so that you can learn to sit better next time, but for the most part sit through the discomfort without moving. This is the first step in learning how to sit through the tougher mental/emotional stuff you may encounter down the line.

If you do use the body as a meditation method, don't be too concerned about what's going on in the mind. Even if the mind is running around like crazy, you're doing fine so long as you keep sitting perfectly still. For the moment, you're just working on "Silence of body" and "Silence of speech". "Silence of mind" will come later.

Meditation On The Breath

One of the most universal meditation methods is to use your own breath as the one-point of concentration. After getting the body silent, bring all your attention to one of these two points: The tip of your nose, where the breath automatically goes in and out, *or* the lower abdomen, where the diaphragm rises with each in-breath, and falls with each out-breath.

Whether you choose the nose or the diaphragm, keep the mind right there, feeling the whole movement of each breath in and out. Don't follow it in or out; just keep the attention in one spot, observing however it feels as it goes by.

The breath is a very good one-point for concentration, because it's fresh every second; it helps us bring the mind into the present moment. And the present moment is the only place that true meditation ever happens (in fact, it's the only place *anything* ever really happens).

Time and time again—maybe hundreds of times in a half-hour—the mind will wander, and you'll forget all about observing your breath. But the instant you remember that you forgot, simply drop the chain of thoughts in mid-stream, and get right back to the nose or the diaphragm. As in the story of Milarepa, there's no sense being frustrated by distractions, because the frustration is just another distraction. Remember, this isn't really meditation, anyway; it's meditation *practice*. If we were already good at it, we wouldn't *need* to practice.

When using the breath as a meditation method, it's not necessary to breathe any special way, or to try to control the breathing at all. The idea is to *observe* the breath however it is.

Sometimes it may be long and slow, other times short and fast; no matter. Sometimes it's interesting to notice that the breath may change as our thoughts change. This is part of the self-education process. No need to do anything but observe and learn.

It may be helpful to channel the mind into the meditation method by thinking "breathing in..." as you feel the breath go in, and "breathing out..." as you feel the breath go out. But try to make sure that you *feel* the breath the entire time; don't get stuck in the thought.

If the mind seems particularly wild sometimes, it may help to do this focusing exercise until it comes back under control: As you feel the breath come in, think "breathing in" and then *count* the breath as it goes out: "Breathing in...,one; breathing in...,two; breathing in...,three;" and so forth up until ten, then start at one again. The only rule is, if you lose track of what number you're on—even if you're only slightly unsure—start over.

It's really amazing how our minds are sometimes so busy that we can lose count between one and two! It's happened to me many times. This exercise can be a good occasional indicator of how well or poorly our concentration is coming along.

Mantra Meditations

Mantra is a Sanskrit word that means "mind-sound" or "mind protector". Using a mantra meditation simply means that instead of the breath or the posture, we try to concentrate on a particular sound or word (silently). The practice of using mantras goes back many thousands of years. *AMEN* and *ALLAH* are ancient, powerful mantras from the Western religious traditions.

OM, or *AUM*, is probably the most widely used mantra in the world. After getting the body still and straight, you would just think *OM* over and over, either along with each breath, or independent of the breath. Every time you get distracted, you simply come back to *OM* as soon as you remember.

A mantra works on various levels. The obvious one is, like the breath, a mantra provides a single point of attention so we can develop more powerful concentration and non-attachment to our steady stream of thoughts. The mantra becomes like an anchor as our minds toss about in stormy seas.

But at a deeper level, different mantras are said to have different subtle effects. *OM* helps to put us into harmony with the universe, while another—for example, *OM AHH HUMMNN*—may bring more of a feeling of personal power and courage. *SHREE ROMM JAY ROMM JAY JAY ROMM* may bring a more devotional feeling than the other two (it means "Dear God, Hail God, Hail Hail God").

There may be many meanings and powers of mantras which we find through our own experiences, but for general purposes, anyone can use these mantras by trial-and-error and trust their own gut feelings to guide them further. If you do try one, *try the same one daily for at least a month or two to be able to see how it feels.*

The mantra **OM** is also powerful as a *Yantra*, which is the visual version of a mantra. The Sanskrit spelling of **OM** is at the center of this Yantra, and can be used while doing the mantra, or as a "gazing meditation" by itself.

Om was central to one of the most powerful experiences of my life, which happened about 15 years ago: I could see the whole universe being created and dissolving each moment, never stopping, never pausing. It was like a giant fountain, a self-contained system in which *everything* is made of the same substance: Planets, stars, mountains, trees, bodies, wind, fire — all the same stuff, appearing and disappearing with the speed of light.

There was also a *sound* to this never-ending process; an all-encompassing sound which vibrates everything into and out of existence. Vibrate lightly, there's air; vibrate a little more thickly, a body; a little thicker still, a rock may appear. Merely thicker and thinner densities of one Power.

A few years later as I was getting into yoga, I was invited to join a group that got together to chant **OM**. They sat in a circle going *"AAAUUUHHHH HUUUHH HMMMMMMMNN"*, over and over and over. At first I thought they were all a few quarts low, but after awhile, a chilling realization crept up my spine: This was *as close as voices could come* to imitating what I had experienced years earlier.

I looked around and could once again *see* the *AAAUUUHHHMMMMNN* making up our bodies and the walls and the floors and the air between us, vibrating everything into and out of existence.

OM, AMEN, ALLAH, and so many similar sounds passed down through the ages, are clues into the one Spirit which alone creates all form, makes up all the senses, serves as every form of energy. My initiation into mantra was like being on the inside of Einstein's $E=mc^2$.

> *In the beginning was the Word,*
> *And the Word was with God;*
> *And the Word was God.*

Other Meditation Practices

Since the aim of all meditation practices is to bring the mind to one point, anyone should feel perfectly comfortable trying out any methods that feel useful. There are devotional methods like using the word *ALLAH* or *CHRIST*, or an image of Jesus or Mother Mary for the mind to try to hold steady.

There are *non*-devotional methods using imagery too, like holding the vision of a clear sky, through which thoughts keep passing like clouds without stopping. Zen meditators practice meditation with their eyes open, gazing at a spot on the floor about a foot or two in front of them. Many people try to focus their eyes on a candle flame.

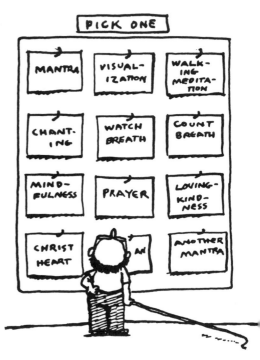

Whatever method you choose, it's a good idea to stick with it for at least a month or more at the same time every day (once or twice a day) before deciding to try a new method. Meditation practice is slow and subtle; it takes a while to know whether the method you choose is working for you.

The busy mind will come up with all sorts of good reasons to drop one method and try another, but that's just more noise. Every method really does the same thing. First we have to develop concentration and control, which just takes time. It's difficult to do no matter what methods we use. The key is not which method, but rather our persistence, patience, and good humor.

AN EXERCISE IN SEEING

This practice requires a partner, and takes about twenty minutes. There are several variations on this exercise, but the point of them all is to learn how to see ourselves more clearly, past the usual fronts. The rules are: No talking, smiling, touching, laughing—nothing but the eyes are involved. There's something that feels embarrassing about this when you first try it, but it's definitely worth getting past that stage!

One variation is simply to sit across from each other like the guys in the photo (taken at SPSM, Jackson, Michigan). Both partners have their eyes open, looking directly into each other's eyes for however long it seems interesting. It usually takes about five minutes before we're able to drop our defenses and mental noise, so give it enough time.

Another variation is for one of you to start with eyes open while the other keeps his eyes closed. Take this rare opportunity to study this person without embarrassment. Look into his (or her) face, look for the clues that reveal more about them than they usually show—traces of sadness, hope, fear, loss; like having loved somebody who died, or who left them. We've all experienced these things, so find it in your partner's face. And then realize it shows in yours, too, and it's all right.

Continue looking for traces or vibes from your partner that help you to realize how similar life has been for both of you. The details may be different, but the feelings and experiences are so much the same! As you see them in your partner, reflect them in yourself too; including the big, invisible question-mark we all have hanging over our heads as we keep guessing our way through life without truly understanding what's going on.

Allow your heart to soften and your compassion to grow as you keep seeing these things in your partner. Allow it to beam out from your eyes so that you're bathing him in love, just as if you were a saint looking at this person in front of you. You don't have to "try" to do anything; just get your ego out of the way and let God's love shine through your eyes.

Now softly say "Okay," and your partner opens his eyes and looks straight into the eyes of God (*your* eyes) to receive all your compassion, understanding, and forgiveness. He can let go of pain, guilt, shame and secrets through his eyes, letting them burn in the purifying fire of your compassion, without a word ever being spoken.

After two or three minutes, you both close your eyes, get centered, and then when he feels ready he opens his and does the whole thing over again with you as the partner. When you're done with both rounds, then just sit and look at each other openly for a minute or so, then slightly bow in appreciation to your partner for helping you to better understand yourself.

This is a *very* powerful practice.

Ending A Meditation Period

The end of each meditation practice, regardless of which method we use, is a good time to deepen our peace and wisdom in several ways.

What deepens our peace is to spend just a few moments offering and receiving blessings of good will, or what the Buddha called lovingkindness.

One way of offering these blessings is to focus your attention on the heart-space, right in the middle of the chest, and imagine the breath going in and out of that place, that seat of love. Then picture the faces of people whom you love the most, *and* the people you hate or fear the most. One by one, offer them all good wishes for their difficult journey through life. Even the people who've hurt us are just stumbling and fumbling through this world like we are; it doesn't help us to hold on to bitterness or anger. So in our mind's eye we see their faces, wish them well, and deepen our own peace and wisdom.

The way to *receive* blessings is to sit in the same heart-space, and begin feeling love from those who love you, anywhere in the world. Your children, parents or lovers, friends, even the great masters and saints whom you can't see—try to feel their love.

Then offer *yourself* the same loving feelings, the same understanding and kindness, that you would offer to others. Forgive your faults, even the ones that you acted on this very day. Picture yourself sitting here in silence, a sincere spiritual seeker just like millions before you since the beginning of time, and try to appreciate just how much you've already changed in order to be doing this.

Try to realize that what you have prayed for is slowly happening—it really is.

> *Though a man be soiled with the sins*
> *of a lifetime, let him but love me,*
> *rightly resolved, in utter devotion;*
> *i see no sinner. That man is holy.*
>
> —*Bhagavad Gita*

These simple practices can be done in a matter of minutes at the end of each meditation. What we're doing is to finally begin taking responsibility for controlling our minds and opening up our compassion—for others, ourselves, and ultimately for God.

After these "lovingkindness" techniques, the end of a meditation period is also a ripe time for reading something and letting it sink all the way in to the depth and openness created by sitting still.

For example, you might just open the Bible, Koran, Ramayana or Bhagavad Gita, or even modern Dharma books like Jonathan Livingston Seagull, Be Here Now, or this very book. Open it wherever your fingers seem to choose, and let your eyes glance anywhere they like. Sit for a minute or two trying to comprehend whatever the message is, and then take that thought out into the day with you.

One of my favorite lines, which I have worked with for years in this way, is from the Ramayana:

> *We look at man's life and we cannot*
> *untangle this song:*
> *Rings and knots of joy and grief,*
> *all interlaced and locking.*

Just walk around the prison or wherever you are and look at all the people—all the pleasures and fears, hopes and sorrows, all the countless complex situations we create for ourselves, and see it as "Rings and knots of joy and grief, all interlaced and locking." Gradually we begin to see our own lives in this way too; and wisdom deepens...

Keeping It Simple

Meditation practice is so simple, time and time again our minds will try to complicate matters just to distract us. But it really is merely a process of sitting down briefly to focus the mind on one point.

So, don't let all these words lead you into further confusion. Each one of us has the ability to sit still and start getting straight with our inner selves. When peace of mind gets to be a high enough priority, that's when we start putting the necessary time into something like meditation practice. Once we put the time in, all the fine points will somehow fall into place with unseen help.

A saint is a very
simple man:
   when he walks,
he walks
when he talks,
he talks
   and that's all.

He doesn't think while
listening,
daydream while walking,
see while touching.

That is very hard.
   That is why
he is a saint.
   Sujata, "Beginning to See"

Meditation and Self-Control

Meditation really is easy, and this chapter has already covered all you need to know to begin your own daily practice.

But the specific issue of self-control is a big one for many of us whose tempers or impulsiveness have gotten us into trouble throughout our lives.

At the end of a meditation workshop I did in Colins Bay Prison in Ontario a few years ago, there were some strong challenges about how meditation relates to self-control and whether self-control is the same as repression. The following discussion was edited from the tape of that workshop. Prisoners' comments come first, followed by my responses.

You talk about "control," but it sounds to me like it's not necessarily healthy. I mean, if you're in a ghetto and a guy messes with you, how can you turn away from him? What I'm saying is, if you have anger and hostility inside you, isn't it better to let it out?

That's one of the traps in psychology: We think if we don't *ex*press a feeling, then we have to *re*press it. It's not really true. For the spiritual warrior, there's a third option: You just let it be whatever it is, but you don't let it control you.

This has nothing to do with whether you defend yourself or not. I'm talking about a state of mind, not a particular course of action. You can walk away, or you can defend yourself without anger or hatred.

That's what the martial arts are all about. Martial arts are meditation-in-action. People learn to focus their minds and let go of fear, anger, and all hostility, and then they can do whatever they need to do without intentionally wishing harm to another human being.

In Aikido, for example, it's considered bad form to injure your opponent—even if that person tried to kill you. The aim is simply to stop him from hurting you, and you do that as gently as you can, because when you see the way things really are, you understand that if he hurts you, he hurts himself as well. So you're doing *him* a service by stopping him. And it wouldn't be much of a service if you killed him in the process, would it?

This question of control versus repression is a big one, I know. But let's face it: a lot of you are in here because of a lack of control. It might be a good idea to look at the whole thing more closely than you ever have. The point is not that anger is "wrong" or sinful; but that it's *a lie*; it's a crock. So why should we express or repress something which isn't what it appears to be in the first place?

*Are you saying that **all** emotions are a lie? I don't understand what you're trying to get across! It sounds like a big head-trip to me.*

Well, yes and no, to both. Emotions are as real or unreal as anything else; but the *object* of emotions is a lie. It's natural to experience anger, lust, greed, joy, fear and so forth; they're all parts of being fully human. They all float around in the air like bacteria, and I may be susceptible to one type while you're susceptible to another. They come into us according to our nature, and then they run through our systems in one way or another, just like a bad cold or a delightful scent.

An emotion like happiness may feel great to express to the people around us. Yet to many monks and yogis, happiness is simply one more passing cloud in the sky of the mind; rather than expressing it outwardly, they sit and watch it pass. How about lust? With the right person at the right time, lust may *also* feel great to express outward toward an "object". Yet lust can really mess up our lives if we express it every time we feel it.

And then there's anger: A terribly destructive, exhausting feeling which can create a lot of new karma and bring more suffering into the world. The only reason modern psychology says "Find a way to express your anger constructively" is that the psychologists don't know what else to do with it in their own lives.

But that whole attitude assumes we're either the "owners" or "victims" of anger, happiness or whatever other emotion washes over us. We're not. We may *allow* the emotions to control us, but it's up to us to someday take responsibility for the consequences.

The control that comes about through meditation isn't intended to repress our feelings. It's the sort of control which allows us the freedom, the self-dignity to determine the best way to live our lives each and every moment. The wisdom for how to handle an emotion is only found in the very instant we feel it; so if we maintain a clear and strong mind, we can express the appropriate ones, and observe the harmful ones *internally* as we let them go. That's not the same as denial or repression.

And yes, this is definitely a head-trip. But that's the way most real change begins. First we look for ideas that make sense, and then we try to take them deeper and deeper into our hearts and guts. If it stays in the head, you're right—it's not worth much.

Yeah, but no matter how much you may want to change yourself now, it all seems different when you're in the middle of your anger. I mean, I don't even know what's happening then; it's like something goes click, and then somebody's laying on the floor before I even know what happened.

Believe me, I know what you mean; I've had fights, I've even *shot* at people, and I thank my lucky stars I never wound up killing anybody before starting to quiet my crazy mind. I surely know what it's like to lose my cool. That's why I say we have to take it deeper, because if it stays in the head, it gets lost as soon as the head gets lost. And as we all painfully know, the head gets lost fairly often.

Through meditation, prayer, martial arts or whatever appeals to you, you *can* gradually gain enough mindfulness so you can see what's happening before you deck somebody. This is why so many of us do this kind of stuff every day. You need to be doing something *every day*—while everything's okay—in order to be ready for those heavy times. It's no different from lifting weights or anything else; it takes some time to get into shape.

I'm saying that all of us eventually have to be able to feel the full range of human emotions without getting blinded from the truth while we're feeling them. Let me describe a typical meditation course to you—15 hours a day, for ten days, of sitting and walking meditation practice; no talking, writing, reading, touching, snacking, tv, radio—you're often not even allowed to exercise or practice yoga.

After a few days in such a limited environment, what starts to happen is that the emotions get starved; there aren't enough objects to stimulate your emotional experiences. So these emotion-bacteria, just floating around wanting to be felt in some way, start invading you for no reason at all. Or they make up reasons like grieving over your father's death, or being angry for how you were punished unfairly twenty years ago.

It's fascinating to watch how the emotions roll in like a tidal wave and then roll out again after awhile, *even if you haven't done anything about them at all.* And believe me, when you're sitting still in silence all day long, there's no way in the world to repress them or hide from them! It's hard to hide when you're spending every moment watching the way your mind works.

So what is it that happens? Why does the emotion go away if it's not acted on? Not only does it go away, but often it leaves so suddenly that it blows your mind how powerful it felt just an instant earlier. It's like a giant soap-bubble that grows bigger and bigger, yet when it pops there's no substance there at all. It *seemed* like it was huge, yet it was all just on the surface; no reality behind it.

And then you sit there for a while feeling pretty clear, and another one rolls in. This could go on for hours. That kind of training helps you to find out for yourself that emotions are just passing "invitations" and nothing more. Then we can begin to handle our lives a lot more skillfully.

It sounds like you turn into a zombie or something; like you have to be so careful every minute. What does that have to do with things you mention like "spiritual freedom?" It doesn't sound very free to me!

That's a logical question, but do I seem like a zombie to you? Remember that the training is just that—training. It's not a formula for everyone to act alike. I've gone to monasteries and zendos where everybody walks around being intensely mindful of every step, every bite of their food, every word they say. It doesn't look free to me, either. But then I might meet the head abbot, or the local saint, and he or she turns out to be like a child—full of joy, very natural and spontaneous, freely expressing all emotions, even what looks like anger.

It's not hard to understand. First we have to gain the freedom to be natural. How spontaneous can we be when our minds are clouded over by habits, traumas, ambitions, fears, bitterness and so much other garbage? So, every tradition has some sort of training period.

First we start watching ourselves more closely than ever before, so that we can *see* all the places we're caught or struggling. When we've seen and let go of all the garbage that holds us back, then we're finally free to live fresh and alive every moment of the day.

At that point, there's no need for meditation practice; we *become* the state of meditation. There's no doubt or struggle, no constant confusion, because we've given up all resistance to our lives. But we can only give it up from a position of strength, a position of complete control. We meditate in order to gain control, so that we can give up control and be free. God has a weird sense of humor.

Can you go through all your garbage and blocks without a teacher or master?

Well first of all, we already *have* teachers and masters who love us dearly and guide us all the time, when we're not too busy struggling against ourselves. That may sound corny or vague, but I assure you it's absolutely real.

But to answer your question with respect to finding a teacher in the "outer" world: Sure, we can do without one. If you just meditated daily and kept opening up to yourself, patiently gained control, self-discipline, self-honesty and so forth; you'd discover the same things that other people may have spent years to find out by going all over the world in search of teachers and masters.

In fact, having teachers often presents as many traps as going it alone. Because someday, each of us has to open into himself; into that seat of intuition and strength inside of us which can guide us perfectly. Even if a master leads us for awhile, still, at some point we either have to find the guidance in ourselves, or call it quits.

Like Jesus said, the Kingdom of Heaven is within you. A holy man or holy woman is just a passing reflection of our own deeper nature. If we get hooked on their personalities or their wondrous powers or beautiful words, or even on how great it feels to serve them and do a bunch of mystical rituals—we've missed the boat. The whole point is to turn us *in*ward, not outward.

A steady teacher, as opposed to a master, poses even more traps. He or she may tell you to do a certain kind of yoga, or to meditate every day. But life goes through a lot of different periods. Diets change; needs change; sometimes after years of daily practice, we may need to *stop* meditating for a while. Who knows? That's why the internal connection is essential.

As the mind gets quieter, intuition becomes stronger. Life moves more smoothly; it's a very subtle thing. Good things happen around you; you may seem to be a focus of good luck for the people who know you. Painful things are a lot easier to bear, and bring wisdom instead of bitterness. You see and hear things that you were too busy to notice before. You become a hell of a lot more perceptive about the people around you.

But these changes all take time. A teacher or master might keep you busy with all sorts of things, but sometimes all that activity can slow down the bigger and deeper changes. The things that may *seem* like tremendous change, "overnight" change, usually don't last, because it's all surface activity—new names, spiritual clothes, strict diets, schedules designed to take up every minute of the day, etc.

Since you're in prison now, it's a perfect opportunity to do it the other way, on your own, and take the time for mature and lasting changes. If it's in your Dharma (destiny) to meet certain teachers, then you'll surely meet them as your intuition develops enough to guide you where you need to be. Look at where it's guided you so far. I must be one of your teachers, because here we are in the same room, talking about all of this stuff. See, the system works!

Everything is going along like clockwork, really. We just need to keep doing the work on ourselves. The whole universe will cooperate.

Do you know my attitude? Books and things like that only point the way to reach God. After finding the way, what more need is there of books and scriptures?

After getting all the information about the path, you must begin to work. Only then can you attain your goal.

—*Sri Ramakrishna*

Dear Bo,

It has now been three years since I have been seeking some meaning in this lost life I have been living. Fifteen of it now in prison with those little spaces outside to create nothing more than a return.

So often have I looked upon my life and said this is not me who causes these ways. And yet I kept waking up to find myself behind bars—a pull that I had no control over. When the time was there, I always knew it was going to take me and I'd just have to do all I could in my ignorance, not to cause anyone harm. And let this force run its course. Have tried stilling its pulls with alcohol and drugs; been committed for psychiatric help. Moved so many times I know not where I came from or where to next.

Yet it seemed to have stilled, and I found such love and peace over the past year. Meditation became life itself. Sharing in love with those that were seeking. So full was life, yet it again became lost when I was transferred to a minimum camp. The period was not complete. All parole preparations with job, seemed to fall away. The strength I had in truth and love was covered with fear and frustration. Not so strong this time. As I walked away it was but hours until I was caught. There was no way I was able to go further and create more karma. The lost is losing its pull, or, karma is being served.

Have been in segregation 8 weeks to dispose of the escape charge. Which is not any burden but a place of peace and self-reflection. Quiet in meditation and in life. As I sat in stillness this past Sunday, the parole board sent me a letter that my sentence had been reduced by one year and they are going to hear my application this month. The Salvation Army has recommended a halfway house I can adjust from.

Just laughing here to myself, how and where I created all this is beyond me. Is it not true that we are all doing what we must? What could I have changed? And now, as the light grows stronger, the rest is lost.

In Love, Arnie/Canada

The body isn't our master,
but it is a Temple.
Keep it loose and strong.

Stretch the mind, stretch the body.
Bring them under control,
firmly but not harshly;
with great patience
and tenderness.

Hatha Yoga is a system of mind/body/spirit development which is thousands of years old. It's not just a system of exercises like calisthenics or aerobics. It's more like the martial arts—a true meditation-in-action. In fact, martial arts have sometimes been called "combat yoga".

The various positions in hatha yoga are called *asanas*,—Sanskrit for "pose," or "posture". The idea is to get better and better at assuming each pose, which will bring a great number of benefits besides toning the body. These include better sleep, circulation, digestion, respiration, less illness, and so forth. Hatha Yoga also works on the *non*-physical "energy body" in many subtle ways.

This chapter isn't intended to make anybody into a super-duper hatha yogi. To make hatha yoga your whole path in life, you would need to live in seclusion somewhere with a qualified master, and follow extremely rigid rules of diet, sleep, activity, and concentration. Like any other intense spiritual regimen, that's a 24-hour-a-day lifestyle.

But we have to pay some attention to the body; it comes with the territory. So instead of blindly pursuing every fitness fad that comes down the pike, it's interesting to try out a system which honors our larger spiritual quest as well.

With just a few basic ground rules, anyone can practice hatha yoga and experience how good it feels to open the body and mind up. Sita and I, like many people, never go beyond simple asanas like the ones given here. I do some basic asanas every morning, and they give me all I need from hatha yoga.

If you ever want to get more advanced (short of moving to the Himalayas), many good books are available with further ideas and instructions.

BASIC GROUND RULES

1) **Pay attention every moment.** Keep your mind focused precisely on what you're doing in each pose. Each day, develop more and more concentration. Otherwise, it's just exercise—not yoga.

2. **Stretch, don't strain.** Yoga is the *opposite* of the "no pain, no gain" idea. Move just up to your own edge—the place where you can feel the stretch, but can still hold the pose calmly for a minute or more. Don't let the competitive ego-mind push you to injure yourself.

3. **Coordinate your breathing with your movements.** Breathe *in* whenever the body expands, opens, or reaches outward; breathe *out* whenever it contracts, closes, or folds. Read chapter 3, **Pranayama**, to get more of an idea of how to work efficiently with the breath. But the bottom line is: *Concentrate.* The breathing is the most important part.

4. **Focus on the spine.** The movements and postures are designed to bring length, flexibility, and strength to your whole back. Especially think of making your spine longer, no matter what position you're in.

5. **Keep up your concentration between poses.** No slouching or sprawling. Notice each movement, each breath, from start to finish.

6. **Hatha yoga shouldn't be practiced on a full stomach.** If not first thing in the morning, then wait at least 2 to 3 hours after a meal.

A SAMPLE ROUTINE

The following is a balance of asanas for strength and flexibility, combining forward bends, backward bends, and twists for the spine. If you were learning directly from a teacher, the teacher would give you a practice especially for *your* body. No book can teach the right things for every type of body. So if anything here seems risky for you because of an injury or weakness, **don't do it!** You must be your own teacher. Be careful not to put stress on your joints (especially shoulders and knees).

Hatha Yoga will prepare your body and mind for sitting for meditation, so it's great to do just before meditation. It's good to do the whole routine, but if you don't have time, do the routine from the beginning through at least two rounds of the "Salute To The Sun."

EASY SITTING POSE (Sukhasana) and
ABDOMINAL BREATH (Raksana Cikitsa)

Sitting on the floor, on a firm cushion or a blanket folded up many times, bend the legs, one foot in front of the other, hands resting on the knees. Sit with your back straight, head straight over the spine, chin slightly down. This may not seem like an "easy sitting pose" at first, but with practice it will become one. (This is also a good way to sit for meditation.) Always begin by sitting quietly, noticing what is going on with body and mind that day. How does your body feel? What state is your mind in (calm, agitated, somewhere in-between)? Next become aware of your breath, flowing in and out from the nostrils (always try to breathe through your nose). Now, as you breathe out, gently draw in the muscles of your abdomen that are around your navel. This will help you exhale longer. As you breathe in, bring the air to your abdomen first, letting go of those muscles you just pulled in, and then let the air fill your rib cage and chest. Take a few breaths this way, trying to make your breath as long and smooth as you can. Now notice what effect the deep breathing has had on you. *Use this way of breathing in all the movements and postures that follow.*

SUNBIRD (Chakravakasana)

Start on your hands and knees, hands directly under your shoulders and knees directly under your hips, knees hip-distance apart. Do one long abdominal breath. On the next inhale, gently arch your back and look forward. As you exhale, sit back on your heels, placing your chest on your thighs and your elbows and forehead on the floor. Inhale and slowly come back up to your hands and knees, gently arching your back, and stopping when your shoulders are right above your hands. Repeat the whole sequence for 6-8 breaths, feeling your back stretch and your spine beginning to loosen. Make your arms and legs do the least work they possibly can, and make your back muscles do most of the work.

THUNDERBOLT (Vajrasana)

Sit on your heels with your forehead on the floor and the backs of your hands resting on your low back. As you inhale, stand up on your knees while sweeping the right arm sideways and overhead. Look forward, chin down toward the chest. On the exhale, fold back down to the heels, sweeping the right hand to the low back and turning your head slowly to the left. On the next inhale stand up on the knees while sweeping the left arm around and overhead, looking forward, chin down. On the exhale fold down, turning the head slowly to the right and sweeping the left hand to the low back. Keep alternating arms, always turning the head away from the arm that is moving downwards. Repeat 4-6 times with each arm. For both the Sunbird and the Thunderbolt you may want to use a blanket under your knees for padding.

TREE POSE (Vrksasana)

Standing straight, gaze at a spot on the floor about 6' in front you. Bring one foot up onto the other thigh, or bring it up so that the bottom of the foot is pressed against the inside of the other thigh (whichever way is easier). Place hands in prayer posture in front of the chest. Inhale deeply while raising the arms out to the sides and then over the head, like the branches of a tree. If it's easy to hold the body steady, let your eyes move around the room, or try focusing the mind at the bottom of your foot and close your eyes. Repeat on the other leg. Hold as long as you feel steady, and come down smoothly.

SALUTE TO THE SUN (Soorya Namaskar)

This is a series of 12 asanas, that when done in a smooth flow, is called a vinyasa. It's actually only 7 different poses, because five of them are repeated. Most of the positions put the spine in either a forward bend or a backward bend, going back and forth between the two, so it's a great way to loosen up the back and spine. The series is traditionally done facing east, to greet the rising sun. Do from 2-12 rounds.

*Notes on the Sun Postures:

1. Positions 1 and 12 are the same. Get centered and balanced with fresh concentration before each new round.
2. Positions 2 and 11 are the same. Raise the arms forward and up, feeling

1) EXHALE

2) INHALE

3) EXHALE

4) INHALE

5) EXHALE

6) HOLD

7) INHALE

8) EXHALE

9) INHALE

10) EXHALE

11) INHALE

12) EXHALE

the rib cage open and lift. Gently arch back, but be careful to keep the upper arms alongside the ears.

3. Positions 3 and 10 are the same. Technically the knees should be straight, but most people need to bend them a little. Just before going from 3 to 4, bend the knees as much as you need to, to get the hands flat on the floor.

4. Positions 4 and 9 are the same (except switch feet). The forward foot is between the hands, fingertips and toes on an imaginary line, knee *right above* the ankle. The back foot reaches as far back as it will comfortably go, with the back knee on the floor. The back is gently arched, chest open, looking forward, chin down toward chest.

5. Positions 5 and 8 are the same. The forward foot moves back to join the back foot, feet hip-distance apart. Arms and legs are straight, heels press gently toward the floor, face towards the knees. Lengthen the legs and the back. Notice the spot between your shoulder blades. This position is called downward-facing dog and has many benefits.

6. If possible, go into position 6 after exhaling all the air out, and do not breathe in until position 7. If this is too uncomfortable, breathe during 6. This pose is called stick position because you try to get your body straight as a stick: Hands under the shoulders, arms bent, head, back, buttocks, and legs on the same level, like the down part of a push up.

7. Move into position 7 on an inhale. Chest lifts and opens, arms straighten, look forward but don't tilt head back. This is called upward-facing dog. Note - hands & feet stay in the same place for positions 5-8.

8. If you have trouble getting the back foot forward from position 8 to 9, scoot the front foot forward with your hand, so it gets all the way up between the hands (don't move hands back to the foot — that's cheating). Whichever foot moved back in 4, move that foot forward in position 9. Next round, switch to the other foot.

9. *Be careful not to strain the low back* moving from 10 to 11. Keep the knees bent and use the upper back and the legs to lift the upper body.

SEATED SPINAL TWIST (Ardha Matsyendrasana)

Sit straight, with legs straight in front of you. Bend the right leg and cross it over to the outside of the left leg, right foot next to the left calf, right foot flat on the floor. Inhale and raise your arms straight in front, to the height of your shoulders. On exhale, lean forward slightly from the hips and then twist to the right. Place the right palm on the floor behind you with the fingers pointing to the wall behind. Bring the left arm around to the outside of the right knee, pressing the right knee gently to the left. Then bend the left arm and let the left hand rest on the upper right thigh. Hold for 6 or more long breaths. Try to lift and lengthen the spine on the inhale, and gently twist more on the exhale. Come out of the pose on an exhale, hug the knees to the chest for a moment (to let the low back stretch), and then do the twist to the left, reversing all the rights and lefts in these directions. Getting twisted up can be confusing, so be patient!

HEAD TO KNEE POSE (Janusirsasana)

Sit straight, with legs straight in front of you. Bend the left leg and place the bottom of the left foot next to the inside of the right thigh. As you inhale, raise the arms overhead. As you exhale, bend forward from the hips and bring the chest toward the right thigh. Keep the back straight for as long as you can on the way down. Hold onto the right leg with both hands, having the elbows bent and the shoulders relaxed. It's good to keep the right knee straight, but if the stretch to the back of the right leg feels too intense, or if the low back hurts, then bend the right knee a little. Hold the position for 10 or more breaths. As you inhale in the pose, gently lift and lengthen the upper back. As you exhale, allow the upper body to move a little closer to the right thigh. To come out of the asana, inhale and lift the arms first. When the upper arms come alongside the ears begin lifting the upper back, and finally use the muscles in the abdomen and low back to bring you the rest of the way up. Repeat the pose on the other side, having the left leg straight and the right leg bent.

BOAT POSE (Salabhasana)

Lie on the stomach, with the head turned to one side. Place the backs of the hands on the low back. If the hands slide off the low back, hold on to one hand with the other. As you inhale, lift the chest and legs as high off the floor as you can, keeping the chin down toward the chest. As you exhale, lower the legs and chest back to the floor. Repeat the movement 6 or more times. When you bring the head back to the floor always turn it to the side so that you are resting on the cheek. Be sure to take turns with the direction you turn your head, so that the neck gets an even stretch. Which way feels better for your head to rest—to the right or the left?

The answer will tell you which side of your neck is tighter. Remember to think of lengthening the entire spine as you lift up into the backward bend.

COBRA POSE (Bhujangasana)

The Boat Pose has prepared you to hold the next backward bend, the Cobra Pose. Lie on the stomach with the legs close together and the head turned to the side, place the hands palms down directly underneath the shoulders, so that the finger tips are right under the tops of the shoulders. The elbows are bent, and the arms should "hug" the sides of the rib cage. Bring the forehead to the floor, and on an inhale lift the chest as high up off the floor as you can without using the arms and hands. Make sure you are using your back muscles, and are not pushing yourself up with the arms. Keep the chin down toward the chest. Hold for as many breaths as is comfortable, come down on an exhale, turn the head to the side and keep the hands in place. Take a short rest and then come up into the pose again, on an inhale. Cobra pose is excellent for making the low back stronger. It also opens the chest and the heart center, so it's good to do lots of it if you're working on opening your heart.

EXTENDED POSE (Urdhva Prasarita Padasana)

Lie on your back with your knees bent in toward your chest and your arms down alongside you. As you inhale, raise your arms all the way overhead so that the backs of your hands reach the floor above your head and straighten the legs up toward the ceiling. As you exhale, lower the arms back to their starting position and bend the knees back in toward the chest. Feel how long your spine gets when the arms are overhead and the legs are straight up. Repeat the movement 6 or more times. This will prepare you for lying flat, and it's also good for stretching out any tightness in the back.

RELAXATION POSE (Savasana)

Lie on the back with the legs several inches apart, the arms alongside you with the palms turned up. Notice how your body feels. What is the state of your mind? How do you feel now as compared to the way you felt at the beginning of the practice? Stay in Savasana for about five minutes, allowing every part of your body to deeply relax.

A Final Word About Hatha Yoga

Be patient in learning these asanas; give yourself time to feel each movement, each pose. The first few times you try hatha yoga, keep going back to read the beginning of this chapter, especially the "Basic Ground Rules", so that right from the beginning you'll be remembering the important parts. Doing even a half-hour a day of hatha yoga can make a tremendous difference in your life. It's a good way to get the body prepared for meditation and higher states of consciousness.

Therefore I say unto you, take no thought for your life,
   what ye shall eat, or what ye shall drink;
      nor yet for your body, what ye shall put on.

Is Life not more than food?
   Is the body not more than clothing?

                                        --Jesus

3. Diet

One day when Josh was just an infant, he and Sita and I were sitting around in Miami under a tall coconut palm. I was born and raised in Miami, so I had done my share of playing around palm trees, climbing them and gathering coconuts all my life. But on this particular day, Sita's mother came out of her motel room and said, "Don't let Josh play there! A coconut could fall on his head and kill him!"

My first response was to reassure her that I had played under coconut palms all my life, and had never even heard of that happening to anyone. A few minutes later though, I couldn't help but notice how many coconuts were lying around on the ground, and how very high were the ones up in the tree, and how ripe and *heavy* they looked....

Diet is a lot like that. A student once asked Hari Dass Baba if he should take vitamins. Hari Dass aswered that he should. The student said "But Baba, you hardly eat anything at all! How is it you think I should take vitamins?" Hari Dass replied, "You *believe* in vitamins, so you need them."

Diet isn't a simple issue, as if we merely have to find out what's good for us and then "eat right". That's often a very uptight way to live. Of course, to eat whatever our crazed minds desire doesn't work too well, either. Neither extreme seems to produce happy, free, or powerful people.

On one hand, a great amount of dietary wisdom has influenced most of us during the past 20 years or so: The move away from junk food, away from fatty and heavy meat diets, the discoveries of the harmful effects of sugar and caffeine; the acceptance of various nutritional principles from other cultures—the effects of yogurt, the benefits of whole grains, balancing yin and yan in a macrobiotic diet, etc.

But on the other hand, food is still just a prop, and so is the body. They both belong solely to the world of appearances. Time brings, time takes away. Good food or junk food, healthy or diseased bodies—all end up in the same pile of bones eventually. Their only real meaning, their only *lasting* value, is to help us in our spiritual work, which involves a lot more than physical health.

In the past ten or fifteen years, our culture has made the healthy body into an object of worship and of obsessive focus. Diet and fitness are multibillion-dollar industries in America. It's been easy to get sidetracked from the view of "honoring the body as a temple" into the view of *worshipping* the body as if it were the God inside the temple. It surely makes sense to stay in shape, but the intensity of our concern is just another youth-oriented, death-denying trap in the world of illusion.

There's got to be a good balance, and though I hate to sound like a broken record, we each must find and honor our own unique balance within ourselves. The laws of nutrition and chemistry would *seem* to treat us all equally, but actually *any* worldly laws are changeable depending on our states of mind and Spirit. A Big Mac can become manna, and brown rice become poison, depending on who's eating which, and how uptight they're feeling while they're doing it.

Life begins to look more like a great thought,
than like a great machine. —Sir James Jeans

I studied Aikido for a short time in Colorado. My *sensei*, or teacher, was a very gentle and powerful master from Japan. When he walked in the room, it was very easy to feel the "Ki" power that the martial arts are about. Everything about him felt natural and perfectly balanced; he seemed always at ease, yet it was obvious he couldn't be caught off-guard. He was certainly a living expression of the path he was teaching.

One day I walked by his office on my way out of the Dojo, and I saw him and his wife (also a black-belt) eating a lunch of all the worst junk food imaginable: Big Mac's, Dunkin' donuts, cokes, fries, etc. After so many years of being careful about my diet, I couldn't help but be shocked that such "high beings" would treat their bodies so recklessly. I said, "Sensei, how can you put this food into your body?" He looked up at me, hardly missing a bite, and said, "Bo, whether food does you good or harm depends on your Ki, on your attitude! Have good attitude, any food good; have bad attitude, any food bad." He smiled respectfully and went on with his meal.

Driving home, thinking it over, it all made perfect sense. And already the visions of Dairy Queen, Taco Bell, and M&M's were floating through my mind—all the stuff I used to love before becoming such a strict yogi. I let go of the dietary controls I'd acquired over the years, and started eating anything and everything I wanted.

The problem was—as I realized while groaning on the toilet one day—I *wanted* to believe as he did, but deep down, I still believed those foods were bad for me. The same food that nourished him was ruining me, because all I was doing was making excuses for a lot of food lust that I had repressed for years. This game is played far deeper than our conscious whims and passing fancies.

I still know he's right about attitudes. Mine have been steadily opening and changing (as well as my diet) since then. But it's a slower, more subtle process than I had realized; and we have to honestly live by whatever stage of it we're in at any given time.

This struggle to find our own best diet is *rich* with teachings about self-honesty, self-discipline, self-righteousness, and wisdom. *Any* diet could benefit one person and harm another, so obviously our needs are unique—as are the lessons we need to learn.

Self-honesty comes up because God always finds a way to force us to look inward for answers rather than to *any* outside source no matter how popular or authoritative. Outside sources supply us with information (one expert usually contradicting another), and then we have to run it through our own minds and hearts to see what rings a bell or doesn't. It's more a process of *recognizing*, rather than "choosing", what we believe our bodies need.

What self-honesty shows us may be at odds with what our taste buds desire, and that's where self-discipline comes in. If my body seemed to be telling me something was wrong, I'd have to pursue it and see where it leads—cutting out cigarettes or sugar or coffee or whatever I believed was behind the problem. If I decided to follow a specific religion, I'd obey the dietary laws of that path in order to give the total system a fair chance. If I got heavily into Hatha Yoga, I'd be a stricter vegetarian and cut way down on spices and stimulants; again, because it's a total system. Self-discipline is what gives us the freedom to alter our diets to suit our needs.

But after gaining enough self-honesty and self-control to experiment with any diets we choose, most of us fall into the trap that what *we* believe about diet is absolute and final Truth. Now come the lessons on self-righteousness. If we allow them to happen, these lessons are more embarrassing than painful. We can laugh at the time we refused to eat turkey with our families on Thanksgiving, etc. But if we try to hold on tight to philosophies about food rather than opening up to higher teachings, we'll miss out on many experiences and a great deal of wisdom.

"*The nature of the food that was served around Maharaj-ji* (Neem Karoli Baba) *is worthy of note, for though it satisfied our souls, our intellects were often appalled. The usual diet at the Temple consisted of white rice, puris and potatoes (both fried), and sweets of almost pure white sugar. The diet was starch, grease, and sugar, and much black tea. All the sensitivity that our Western pre-occupation with diet had awakened in us* **screamed** *at this diet. And yet, this was 'prasad'* (food blessed by a Saint and offered to God). *Did you reject prasad, or did you give up your dietary models? What did you do when the love came in the form of starch, grease, sugar, and tea? Greasy potatoes were one thing; a blessing from the Guru, however, was an entirely different matter.*"

—Ram Dass, from Miracle of Love

Diet takes on an even more confusing role in prison. On the streets, it's mostly a free-choice situation, and the struggle is usually one of self-discipline to clean up our diets without becoming neurotic about it. But in the joint, the struggle is often the opposite: most cons would *love* to get more wholesome foods—whole grains, fresh vegetables and fruit, "holistic" foods like tofu, yogurt, nuts and so forth, but it's nearly impossible to do.

The self-discipline is often the opposite too, because in a no-choice situation, the spiritual warrior's way is to eat, with a happy mind, whatever food is available, and to let go of anxieties about cholesterol, fats, sugar, additives, etc. This is where my sensei's advice about attitude becomes an important key for staying healthy. If you can't change your diet, change your attitude.

Another mystical secret:
*When choices are taken away,
a perfect path remains.*

"Bad" food can be transformed into Spirit-food. Remember, physical laws and "facts" don't always hold true. Reality isn't so unbending. Trust the magic!

This food is my body; this drink is my blood.
—*Jesus*

All food; all drink—depending only on how we see it and deal with it. If there's any degree of choice, it's a good idea to eat fresh fruits and vegetables, less sugar and white flour, less coffee, more water, more whole grains like brown rice and buckwheat, fewer heavy meats like beef and pork, and maybe cut down a little bit on dairy products. But the other stuff is still the body and blood of Christ.

As I learned from my own experience, a head-trip isn't the same as a genuine change of attitude. Genuine changes, deep changes, usually require conscious effort. It's spiritual work, just like yoga or meditation. The best time for this work is *before and during each meal*. Without drawing much attention to yourself, take a minute or so before eating to:
1) Get calm and centered.
2) Look at the food on your plate and realize that all of its energy came ultimately from the Sun; vegetables grow from sun-power, cows and hogs and chickens grow from eating sun-grown grasses and grains—all food-energy ultimately comes from sun energy, which is pure LIGHT.

3) Instruct your body to be receptive to this Light, and not to worry about the rest.
4) Rather than feeling "resigned" about eating this food, give thanks instead, because dealing with this teaching is bound to increase your wisdom and power.
5) Pay attention as you eat, consciously consuming this food for perfect physical and spiritual health. If possible eat alone for awhile so you can concentrate better.

Even if all of this sounds corny to you, trust it just long enough to see how it feels. After all, doesn't it make more sense than to go on cursing the food that you eat?

A Final Word About Diet—

It's not my intention for this chapter to make diet seem unimportant. In fact, I'm extremely glad to see several organizations making progress toward changing the traditional grease-and-starch prison diet into something more wholesome and sane.

Groups like the Kushi Foundation and Gardens For All are actively working to give prisoners a wider range of choices. The Institute for Biosocial Research and a former parole supervisor named Barbara Reed have made great strides in educating corrections officials about a direct relationship between diet and behavior, and between diet and behavior *change*. Many prisons have already allowed a few changes, including salad bars and fewer restrictions on prisoners buying "health foods" from outside catalogs. The big shift has begun. I have no doubts that it'll continue, and I support it all the way.

But like any other political or social issue, we can take part in it with the clear vision of the eagle or the nearsighted scrambling of the mouse. An eagle has the advantage of seeing the way things look from a bigger view, then diving down into the action whenever necessary. In this case, the action is to push for a diet more in tune with the way the human body functions best. It's a good cause.

But we have other important work to attend to as well: To use *every* circumstance and moment of our lives to get a little bit stronger, wiser, and freer. Nothing outside of us—in the food or the air or places or people— can prevent us from doing this spiritual work.

Like a bird, he rises on limitless air
And flies an invisible course.
He wishes for nothing.
His food is knowledge.
He lives upon emptiness.
He has broken free.

—Buddha (Diamond Sutra)

Indrajit laughed. Then he said -- OM! He leaned back and closed his eyes, and speaking no more he began to breathe slowly in and out, slowly and deeply, centering his mind only on his breathing. He made himself one with the breath of Life. The clouds left the sky, and Indrajit shut himself away from the world ---- I breathe. I breathe.

—Ramayana

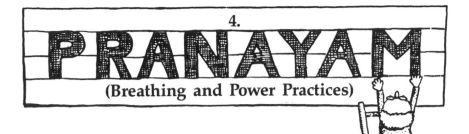

4. PRANAYAM

(Breathing and Power Practices)

PRAN (pronounced "pronn"), or *Prana* ("pron-na"), is the force of all life; the power of all creation. Jesus called it "The Light", Stars Wars called it the "Force". It's the core ingredient of all power; the basic "how and what" of the Living Spirit.

Like an invisible mist throughout the universe, pran comes into our bodies every time we take a breath. It's not the breath itself—not the oxygen, nitrogen and all that stuff—but it *rides in* on the breath. It's the divine energy which sets all the laws of physics, biology, astrology, etc., into motion.

Every time we breathe, we have unlimited pran to draw on—*unlimited power*, if we only knew how to do it right.

The *same* power which Jesus used to heal the sick, raise the dead, and walk on water, is the power which flows into your body at this very moment, as you read these words. Take it personally.

Pran doesn't exist in the past. Pran doesn't exist in the future. Pran *is* the aliveness of the present moment. The props change—forms, colors, sounds—but pran is what remains unchanged, unalterable, eternal. It's the doorway into the Great Mysteries. All *being-ness*, even of rocks and fire and sky, is filled with pran.

Spiritual masters throughout the ages have taught ways we can learn to pay attention while we breathe, so that we can become aware of the pran and of various ways to control it.

As we learn how to open ourselves to more and more of it, we start to shine from the inside like an incredible diamond—like Buddha and Christ and Mary and Moses and Mohammed and Guru Nanak and all those other pran-filled people. No energy existed in those days which is not here right now; it's all over the place, and it's free for the taking.

Pranayam, or *Pranayama*, means "control of power". It means that with practice and discipline (like any other skill), we can learn how to live up to our full capacity. The way most of us are living right now, we're like a 450-horsepower turbo engine which is putting out about two or three horsepower; it's that much difference! We go sputtering along, nearly exhausted all the time, completely ignorant of the *supercharged* force we were designed to feel.

The first step in pranayam—in controlling the power—is to see that *our fears, desires, habits, anger, doubt and judgments severely limit the amount of power we take in.*

There's no heavy morality trip about this; it's simply a matter of natural law—like Karma or gravity. In order to become powerful, we have to start letting go of our attachments and our constant busy-ness. That stuff is like sand in the gas tank.

"ARE YOU SURE THIS STUFF IS LEGAL?"

Along with this first step, it's important for us to realize that with power comes greater responsibility. The powerful person affects other people, affects the world, to a much greater degree than before. The spiritual warrior, in his humility, understands how necessary it is to use one's power in harmony with the very highest natural laws.

Somebody who does all the physical techniques to develop power, without making any spiritual commitment, heads straight for a powerful fall. It's like a couple hundred horsepower suddenly kicking in when our driving skills haven't progressed past the sputtering stage. The *idea* may sound exciting to an immature driver, but there's little hope a crash can be avoided.

In the Eastern spiritual traditions, pranayam has been practiced as a science for thousands of years. Many practical techniques have been developed for working with the breath.

On one level, these exercises are great for the body: They increase our oxygen intake, purify the blood, promote better circulation and so forth.

On another level, they help us to gain the ability to alter our own consciousness without needing to use drugs or booze or hypnosis or loud music or—in the joint—the bootleg hootch you might be able to make from Pinesol or Xerox fluid.

On yet another level, the methods actually increase the size of our "fuel tank". They enlarge our capacity for holding, focusing, and using this all-powerful force. At some point, we finally stop being the limited, complicated people we thought we were, and we become one with the Holy Spirit, the breath of life. That's when we could say, "Mountain move," and the mountain would move.

Of course, at that point we're united with the very force which put the mountain where it is in the first place, so why would we want to move it? Only those who *doubt* their power need to prove it.

One last thing before we get into the techniques: Because pranayam deals with energy, there are many experiences which might happen in the course of doing these exercises. You might feel stoned, dizzy, blank, blissed out, you might see colors or lights, you might even stop breathing for ten minutes or more.

The rule of thumb for handling *any* experience is to allow it to be whatever it may be, and don't get sidetracked by it. Remember, what you're doing is trying to gain *control*, not trying to get a rush. The back should always be kept straight, eyes closed, mind focused on pran.

Fear has *no place* in these practices, so whenever it comes up (like "Uh oh, I'm not breathing; what if I die?"), just watch it come and let it go, and don't get sucked in by it for a moment. There are times when higher forces take over; when physical laws simply don't apply. Trust yourself, and trust your inner guides as you tune into your connection with the power of the Universe.

One simple exercise is called **The Basic Breath**. Sit for just a few minutes with back straight, eyes closed, breathing slowly and deeply. Focus all of your attention on the pran rather than the air. Imagine a fine golden mist coming into your nostrils with each breath, filling your whole body with light.

Don't be bothered by how weak your imagination may be at the start; if you do this every day, before long you'll be amazed that you don't need any imagination at all to "see" and feel the pran as you breathe. You'll tune into it because it's really here.

The second technique is called a **Cleansing Breath**. Breathe out *all* the way, so much that your stomach caves in and there's absolutely no breath left in you. Now *slowly*, from the diaphragm (lower stomach area), begin to breathe in (always breathe *in* through the nose), filling yourself with

calming,
strengthening,
peaceful
power.

Breathe in as far as you possibly can, filling first the diaphragm, then the lower lungs, then the upper lungs, then lift your shoulders up to get in the last tiny little bit. Hold this breath, letting the pran spread all through your body, soaking up all the thoughts, doubts, emotions, nervous energy, and so forth.

Then breathe all that inner litter out, through the mouth, until your stomach caves all the way in again. That's one complete cleansing breath.

It's good to do five to ten cleansing breaths at a time, although it's also very useful to do even *one* here or there throughout the day, as things get too busy or tense. Just breathe in pran, breathe out tension. As time goes by and the mind is able to concentrate better, this method gets much more powerful. After awhile you can dump even the heaviest emotions—anger, jealousy, lust—with a single breath.

Alternate Nostril Breathing is an ancient, natural way to balance mind and body. Our two nostrils are connected to two different nerve paths in our energy bodies as well as our physical bodies. Most of us breathe more from one nostril than the other, which over a period of years causes us to be out of balance in various ways—nervous system, glands, moodiness or depression.

This method helps us to notice and gradually correct that imbalance by stimulating both nerve paths with plenty of pran.

Sitting straight, bring the right hand to the nose so that the thumb can close off the right nostril. The index finger and middle finger rest gently on the forehead, and the ring finger is positioned so that it can close off the left nostril.

With the right nostril closed, breathe *out* through the left nostril. Now breathe *in* through the left nostril. Now close both nostrils and hold the breath for a few seconds. Then keep the *left* nostril closed and breathe *out* through the right. Now breathe *in* through the right nostril. Close both and hold; then open up the *left* and breathe it out. That's one complete "round" of alternate nostril breathing.

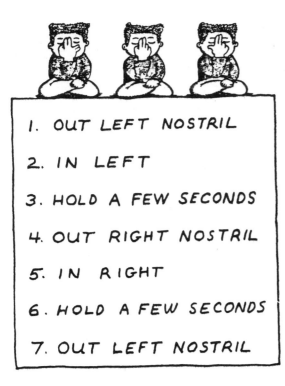

1. OUT LEFT NOSTRIL

2. IN LEFT

3. HOLD A FEW SECONDS

4. OUT RIGHT NOSTRIL

5. IN RIGHT

6. HOLD A FEW SECONDS

7. OUT LEFT NOSTRIL

TIPS:

Notice that you breathe *out and in* through each nostril— *not* in and out. In other words, the pran which goes in one side has to make the connection and go out the other side, which is what helps to bring us balance.

There are different ways to time the in-breath, holding, and the out-breath. You can either do this by your own gut feeling, or try mentally counting to four on the in-breath, eight while you're holding, and four on the out-breath. Another way is to count eight for each part. Many people also count a *fourth* part: holding after the out-breath.

At the same time each day, try ten complete rounds of alternate nostril breathing. Also, at any time you feel a headache, sit down and try it, gently, for a few minutes. It may work a lot quicker than aspirin.

Remember, as with the other techniques, that the mind should be paying attention to the pran, not so much the air. Keep the eyes closed and mind open, and give it some time before deciding whether it's working or not. Pranayam has been around for thousands of years because it really works in a profound way.

A more intense pranayam method is called **Bhastrikha**, which means "Breath of Fire" (it's sometimes called **Kapalabhati**, which means "Bellows Breathing").

Sitting very straight and firm, with fists tightly closed, breathe in and out through your nose, fairly hard and fast. Keep the in-breaths and out-breaths equal; keep the eyes closed so you can concentrate better. Focus your attention on pran, not air.

After 30 seconds to a minute (up to two minutes after you get used to it), take a deep breath in and hold it as long as you can, sitting absolutely still. Then blow it out hard from your mouth, and sit quietly for a few minutes letting the breath come and go easily, feeling whatever you may feel.

Breath of fire is excellent for getting a hit of energy when you're tired or lazy, or clearing the mind for meditation, or even for letting go of heavy anger. Many times you'll feel stoned afterward, because this method breaks up little places you've been holding tight, and lets more of your natural power through.

MEDITATION AND BREATHING PRACTICE

[*The Buddha originally taught this technique, and then Murshid Samuel Lewis, a.k.a. "Sufi Sam" updated it a bit; I respectfully steal it from them and revise it for you.*]

Begin by just becoming aware of the in-breath and out-breath. Then breathe in a heavy breath and be aware that you're breathing in a heavy breath, and breathe out a heavy breath and be aware that you're breathing out a heavy breath. Do this a few times.

Then breathe in a gentle breath, aware you're breathing in a gentle breath, and breathe out a gentle breath, aware you're breathing out a gentle breath. Breathe in a short breath, out a short breath. Breathe in a long breath, out a long breath.

After doing each of these a few times, gradually make your breath long and gentle, long and refined. For the rest of this practice, attentively breathe in and out this long, refined breath. On this breath, breathe in all the joy you're capable of breathing in and breathe out all the joy you're capable of breathing out. Joy in and joy out. Do this for a few minutes.

Then breathe in all the love you're capable of breathing in and all the love you're capable of breathing out. Love in and love out. Finally make the breath even more gentle, even longer and more penetrating and breathe in all the peace you're capable of breathing in, and all the peace

you're capable of breathing out. Peace in and peace out. As you do this, fill the room with peace. Fill your prison or neighborhood with peace. Breathe peace for the whole city, for the whole world in which you live.

Dear Bo,

I have something to offer my brothers and sisters on the path that has been very helpful to me. There is a lot of tension here, as I'm sure must be felt in other institutions too. Also, there are many frightened people. Often when one passes others in the hall or wherever, they're met with a cold stare, a burn, or an under-the-breath remark.

I practice speaking silently to each person I come across, without them knowing it at all. I see them in my mind not as man, woman, black, or white, but as another equal soul; and from the soul within, I greet them with thoughts of love. I might just say in my mind, "I love you," but usually I just become conscious of love and sort of direct it to them.

*It started as an experiment and I was **amazed** at the results. People, all of a sudden, began to respond. They greet me now with, "Good morning, how's it going," or "hi," and almost always they smile.*

Love is God's own energy and it needs no physical touch, no verbal expression, to be felt. It's only when I fall away from the consciousness of love that the faces lose their smiles.

In His Love, Jean/Illinois

Lakshmana sat by the running river. With open eyes he looked around and saw all things as Rama [God], thought of them as Rama. He rinsed his mouth with the clear water and stopped his breathing.

The luminous person within Lakshmana's heart, the soul no bigger than a thumb made ready to leave this world behind. The life-centers stopped spinning and went out, and Lakshmana's energy... rose step by step up along his backbone, seeking flight out the crown of his head where the skull bones join their seams.

—Ramayana

5. The Chakras

After working in a general way with pranayam (breathing/power techniques) for awhile, it's very useful to understand a little more about how this power moves through our bodies, and how we can make even better use of it.

The basic outline of the whole set-up is this: We have an "energy body" which gives life to the physical body. Pran is like the fuel. Our internal sparkplug is called the *kundalini*. The kundalini is our very own individual nuclear-reactor core at the base of the spine. It holds more power than could ever be described.

It could be said that our total "life-force" is a combination of two things: 1)How well we take in pran when we breathe; and 2)how awakened the kundalini is—which depends on the hang-ups, fears, and attachments we hold on to.

Our power moves through seven channels which are called *chakras* ("shockra" or "chockra"). *Chakra* simply means "wheel". These seven main chakras in the human body are like colored filters.

For example, if I put on pink sunglasses, the whole world suddenly becomes pink. Likewise, how we see the world depends on which chakras we're looking through at the time. If we're loose and free, we see things as they really are; a mouse is a mouse. But if we're stuck, say, in loneliness, we may be desperate for the mouse to be companion. If we're starving, the very same mouse begins to look like a pretty good dinner.

It's completely natural for power to flow into one chakra or another. The problem is, our fears and desires push us to *un*naturally manipulate the power-flow so that we don't allow the whole system to work as it should. We develop attachments and bad habits in various chakras, and then all our power keeps flowing through the wrong places, and it gets harder and harder for us to see things as they really are.

THE BASICS

Roughly speaking, these are the areas of body and mind which are associated with the seven chakras:

1st chakra: Survival, self-defense (base of the spine).

2nd chakra: Sensual and sexual feelings—taste, smell, etc. (lower back behind the genitals).

3rd chakra: Power and ego-power (behind the solar plexus).

4th chakra: Love, compassion (center of chest, "Christ-heart").

5th chakra: Devotion and creativity (throat).

6th chakra: Wisdom, self-realization (middle of forehead, "third eye").

7th chakra: Enlightenment—merging into the "All" instead of remaining separate (crown of the head, where a baby's "soft spot" is located).

Everybody has some amount of energy going through all the chakras, but generally we tend to be way out of balance, holding nearly all of our power in the lower three, and subconsciously keeping the upper four chakras closed off. So, a better understanding of what they're about and how to work with them can be a *very* big key for spiritual transformation. With a little training, even some of the heaviest emotional states can be completely changed from a single breath into the heart-chakra.

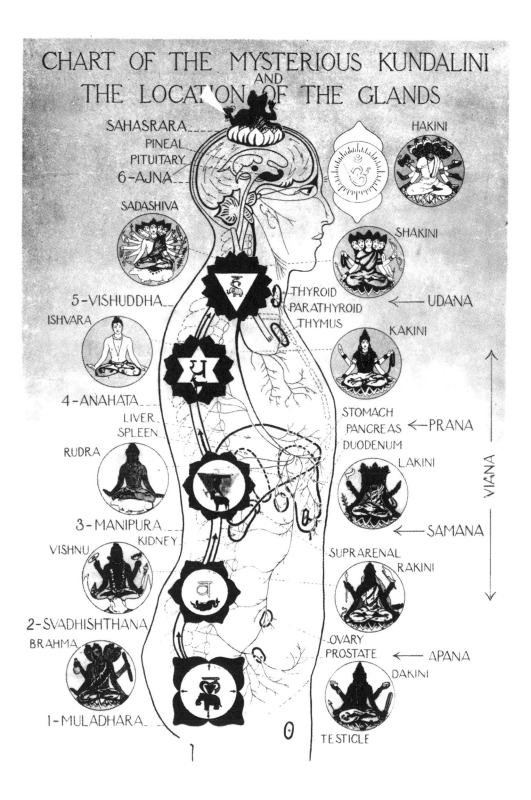

CHART OF THE MYSTERIOUS KUNDALINI
AND
THE LOCATION OF THE GLANDS

SAHASRARA

PINEAL

PITUITARY

6-AJNA

SADASHIVA

5-VISHUDDHA

ISHVARA

4-ANAHATA

LIVER
SPLEEN

RUDRA

3-MANIPURA

KIDNEY

VISHNU

2-SVADHISHTHANA

BRAHMA

1-MULADHARA

HAKINI

SHAKINI

THYROID
PARATHYROID ⟵ UDANA
THYMUS

KAKINI

STOMACH
PANCREAS ⟵ PRANA
DUODENUM

LAKINI

SAMANA

SUPRARENAL
RAKINI

VIANA

OVARY
PROSTATE ⟵ APANA

DAKINI

TESTICLE

In this chapter, we'll take a brief look at each of the seven chakras, and then get into the idea of using the breathing techniques (pranayam) to work on specific chakras & problems. Like the other teachings in this book, these are real, practical, facts & ideas, not merely words or images to collect like a scholar.

1st Chakra—Law Of The Jungle

The first chakra is the densest, thickest, of the seven filters—like wearing dark glasses at night. When life is seen through the first chakra, only one question arises: How to survive? The first chakra isn't concerned with nice colors, pleasant sounds, the needs of others, or anything more sophisticated than primal existence.

A newborn baby is pretty much operating from the first chakra: If it had to press a button to be fed, no matter whether that button blew up half the world, it would push the button anyway. No blame can be laid on the baby; it's just the way its mind deals with reality. Babies are primitive in this way—their minds don't deal with the unseen consequences of their actions.

Most of us get more civilized early in life, but if you look around (especially in prison, but surely also on the streets) you can find many people who seem to be holding a lot of their power in this first chakra.

You may try to reason with them from how **you** see things, but the same world looks very different to them, and they're just acting accordingly—just like people who have phobias about elevators, spiders, public places, etc. Many phobias probably stem from energy caught in the first chakra.

The aim of the spiritual seeker is for this and the other chakras to be wide open, without any set attitudes or habitual responses. If a real threat to our survival comes along, we may feel it in the first chakra because that's what's really happening. But we don't have to live in dread of everyone we meet. That's a terribly lonely way to live.

I had an intense first-chakra experience in the Caribbean in the late '60's, when Sita and I worked on a sailboat. I was underwater with a spear and an armful of bloody fish for our dinner, and I turned to see a huge shark (about a 10-footer) coming toward me, directly between me and the boat.

What a psychedelic trip that was! Every cell in my body, every corner of my mind, was alive with fear. I could *see* fear rippling through the water; I could hear it, smell it, and taste it. My whole world had turned to fear. All my life-force had suddenly rushed down into my first chakra.

It was one of those things that, if you survive it, it was really worth it, just to feel such intensity. That's first chakra.

(Oh yeah, the end of the shark story: Thank God sharks circle their victims! As the shark made his way around me, I got back to the boat and hopped out of the water—arms, legs, butt, all at once—in record time. He was right behind me.)

2nd Chakra—OOOHHH, AAHHHH, OOOHHHH, AAAHHH!

The second chakra, located a little higher up the spine behind the genitals, is the filter which defines reality on the basis of how things feel, look, sound, taste, and smell; the world in which our senses run the whole show.

In a baby's life, this comes right after the first-chakra survival period. Gradually as the mind gets more sophisticated and bare survival isn't such a struggle, the senses open up a whole new world. It's still far from the *whole* world, but it's a lot broader filter than before. Life becomes a never-ending process of sense experiences.

Second-chakra energy gives us the good sense to avoid bitter poisons and remove our hands from a hot stove, as well as giving us the desire for a ripe, juicy apple, or a friendly, warm body.

These can all be perfectly healthy, natural instincts, or they can also be terrible burdens—obsessions which take over our lives and drive us to ruin. Whereas a phobia is an example of first-chakra attachment, lusts and addictions are examples of being stuck in the second chakra.

Again, if we were loose and free, we'd be able to feel fear or desire in tune with the way the world moves around us. But after a lifetime of fiendishly clever sales pitches for everything from candy bars to sports cars to sexual devices, most of us have quite a lot of attachments in the second chakra.

How many thousands of Greeks and Trojans died because some dude wanted to screw Helen of Troy? How many junkies' lives have been wasted in their endless quest just to feel zonked out? How much torment and suffering have fat people brought upon themselves simply because they love the taste of certain foods so much?

3rd Chakra—Make Way, I Exist!

Moving on up the spine, the third chakra is a filter which takes in still a little more of life than the second; it's like a baby's mind proceeding naturally outward. This chakra has to do with power.

Life seen through the third chakra is a world of relationships—relationship to the environment, to other people. A healthy third chakra gives us the cleverness to make trees into lumber so we can build comfortable shelters; it helps us figure out how best to deal with somebody who's angry or crazy.

But as with the second chakra, we grow up surrounded by influences like DALLAS and the hypocrisy of politics; we grow up watching intelligent adults shoot down beautiful animals just for fun, we grow up seeing news reports of wars going on all over the world at any given time. So, by the time we're old enough to think about things, we have a pretty demented sense of what power is all about.

This is attachment in the third chakra. It's like the energy center gets misshapen, and then we think the deformed shape is natural, so we hold it in that position and feed it energy for a lot of wrong ideas. Nazis and klansmen are good examples of people with severely deformed third-chakras. So are all the mega-corporations which are destroying the planet in order to make personal profit. That's crazy! Where will their children spend the money?

To a milder degree, third-chakra stuff is mostly responsible for our hair styles, beards, the way we dress, the kinds of cars we drive, etc. There's a subconscious ratings game going on in our heads, and we try to acquire all the right moves for the high ratings we want. Also, many men have third-chakra sex more so than second-chakra sex; that is, more a power-trip than a pleasure-trip. It's more "Am I the best?" than "Oh wow, that felt so goood!"

One of the heaviest problems we run into because of attachments in the third chakra is in the area of romance. Most of our romances, and even our marriages, are relationships coming from the third chakra.

Third-chakra love is *conditional* love: "I'll love you as long as you love me back and you don't cheat on me and you stay reasonably attractive and you keep treating me the way I want to be treated."

It's a power-trip—a deal negotiated without so many words, but with a great deal of fear and needfulness hiding on the back of the page. Feelings like anger, jealousy, humiliation, betrayal, and paranoia lurk in the shadows of third-chakra love.

4th Chakra—*I Live In Every Heart*

The first, second and third chakras are generally known as the "lower" energy centers, the places we're apt to get stuck if we "lay up our treasures," as Jesus put it, "where moth and rust doth corrupt, and thieves break in and steal." In other words, these are the centers of activity for the world of appearances.

The fourth chakra, the "Christ-heart" right in the middle of the chest, is the first of the higher energy centers. There are still all sorts of attachments we can form in these higher centers—being stuck in bliss or power is still being stuck. But these chakras are the keys to becoming the spiritual warriors we were born to become.

When we look at life through the fourth chakra, we see a lot more than survival, pleasure, and power. The heart chakra is the place where we start to realize our profound connection to all people, to all of existence. True kindness—that is, kindness without any thought of credit or reward—comes from this center of power. True compassion comes from this place too, and so does *un*conditional love, like Jesus, Buddha, Krishna and the others represent.

So, one of the basic goals of yoga and pranayam techniques is to *open* the heart-chakra by focusing power into it as often as possible (see next chapter, "Advanced Pranayam").

Many people *believe* in the love of Christ, but few actually feel it in their hearts. Until we do feel it in our own heart-centers, love is just another head trip.

But we can't feel much power in our heart-chakras at the same time we feel greed, anger, fear, and so forth. For example, look at the nature of greed: It's wanting more for ourselves than we want for somebody else. In order to feel that way, we have to close our hearts a little. An open heart "loves thy neighbor as thyself."

In a way, because of how much our parents loved us, they often wanted better things for us than for other people, and so we innocently learned about greed.

But when we wake up to the real world, we find out that actually, greed doesn't help make our lives work very well; it's the line again about "Lay not up your treasures." Most of us have tried being greedy, and it just never works out well.

So, the emphasis on giving up greed, anger, bitterness and so forth, isn't so much a moral teaching, like "give up these sinful feelings or you'll go to hell," or "these faults make you a bad person" but rather it's a very *practical* teaching, like "If you want to get hip to the way things really are, you've got to let go of your baggage so you can learn how to fly."

5th, 6th, and 7th Chakras—Coming Home

The fifth chakra is the filter which sees life as a journey of creative devotion to God. The first three chakras seem to establish us as individuals, the fourth shows us that we're *all* worthy of lovingkindness, and now the fifth reveals even a little more Truth, a little more of the Grand Design:

This whole life, from birth to death, with all its seeming "accidents" and "meaningless" details, is nothing *else* than a process of opening to our higher nature.

That's the piece of the puzzle which the fifth-chakra reveals.

The sixth chakra, or the third eye (remember when Jesus said, "When thine eye be *single* thy body will be full of Light"?), reveals everything else that can ever be revealed: All past and future, everything that could possibly be realized by a single individual. That's why when the sixth chakra opens it's called "Self-realization"; it's the awareness that we are actually not separate from God in the first place. God-realization and self-realization are one; God, Guru, and Self are one.

The seventh chakra is the gate through which we merge from the One into the All. At that point, there's nobody sitting here knowing *anything*; the self has been liberated, gone beyond words and images.

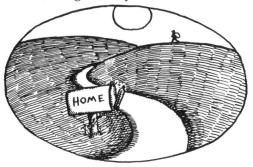

Here We Are...

Where most of us are at, we have a lot of attachments in the first three chakras; a lot of places where we've been holding tight for quite a few years. That's what limits our power, that's what tires us out every day, that's what gets us in trouble time and time again.

But also, most of us have experienced some things in the upper four chakras at one time or another, either when we were young, or through drugs or on top of a mountain, or some other way. We may not even remember, because those experiences may even have been in dreams; but in our deepest minds and memories, we *know* that something inside of us is greater than what we usually relate to.

The exact natures of our chakras—our attachments, strengths, experiences, needs—are probably as unique as our fingerprints. But the reason for knowing a little about the whole system is so that we can take more responsibility for trying to open them up.

Knowing about the chakras helps us to be more objective about some of the things that used to suck us in, like jealousy or anger or greed. If we can just quiet down a minute and *feel* what's going on somewhere in our chakras, we can learn to work with it in a better way than slamming our fists through the wall or biting our nails to the bone. When I get angry, I can feel the hot lump in my solar plexus (the third chakra) for hours. It's just energy caught there. If I have enough control to realize that, I can sit down somewhere and work on moving it up into the heart, where it'll do me and the world a lot more good.

In this way, the system of chakras becomes like a whole system of psychology and power, and each of us becomes our own best therapist, which is as it should be. The next chapter gets into details of some of the ways of doing this work.

Oh Brahma, your life endures
while I exhale one breath!

--Ramayana

6. (Slightly) Advanced Pranayam

The more we begin to relate to our chakras, the idea of practicing *pranayama* techniques takes a new twist: Instead of just paying attention at the nose or the mouth, we can concentrate directly on the chakras themselves.

In other words, a pranayam instructor might say, "Now, breathe in and out of the heart-chakra," or "take five breaths in the throat chakra," etc. Somebody watching you may not be able to notice any difference, but there's a great deal of difference if you're doing it right. By putting *all* of your attention into the area where a chakra is located (see chart on page 79), you're focusing a lot of power into this particular energy-center.

At first it's a bit of guesswork to figure out the exact spot within you where each chakra is located; a chart can only give you a general idea. But after awhile, the seven centers become pretty easy to find, because they're really here, and you're really bringing power to them; it's not just a game.

And when one of the chakras opens fully, or the kundalini power suddenly rises all the way through the seven chakras and out the top of your head, you'll *know* that this isn't a game. There's no more powerful experience in the world.

Locating and Energizing

Even though we have a lot of hang-ups in our lower three chakras (survival, desire, power), that doesn't mean that those three have too much power in them. Actually, *weakness*—not strength—in a chakra causes attachments.

So, one good exercise is to do the *cleansing breath* (page 70) five to ten times in each chakra, starting from the bottom of the spine and ending at the top of the head. As you breathe in, be aware that you're bringing clear, pure energy into that chakra. As you hold the breath, imagine the fresh energy soaking up all your bad habits, hidden fears, all the garbage that keeps the chakra from being free and open. Then breathe it all out.

[notes:
1) for all these advanced pranayam techniques, the breath comes in and out of *the nose only*, unless otherwise noted;
2) In the first six chakras, the breath comes in and out horizontally—straight in and out, from front or back; but at the seventh chakra, at the top of the head, the in-breath comes *down* from above into the head, and the out-breath goes *up* through the top of the head, into the universe.]

PRANA

It may take some patience and persistence for a few weeks or even a few months, but if you hang in there, you'll gradually begin to feel straighter and stronger all day long. Old habits will get easier to break; courage easier to find. This stuff hasn't been around for thousands of years for nothing.

The Heart Of It All

The fourth chakra—the heart-center—can be the key to the whole ball game. Opening this chakra (whether through pranayam or some other way) is absolutely necessary for total spiritual development. It's sometimes called the "Christ Heart", and in that sense, it's what Jesus *really* meant when He said "The only way to the Father is through me."

The heart chakra is like a processing factory: It converts the highest powers of the universe into simple, practical, human love; and it converts all the petty, twisted, or scattered energy of the world back into the highest energy. It's like a giant furnace, where everything gets purified, recycled, and renewed.

There's no such thing as working too long or too much on opening the heart chakra. You can even make it the focus of your whole meditation practice, besides doing pranayam into it. You can focus on it throughout the day, every now and then, just putting the mind there and directing the breath to it. You can pray for help in opening it, in letting you *feel* what "heart-center" really means. Surely, there is no way to God, no way to en-lightenment, which doesn't go straight through our wide-open hearts.

Heart/Head Head/Heart Exercise

One powerful technique is to concentrate on the "processing factory" mentioned above. Imagine the breath moving in an L-shape: In through the heart, hold a few seconds, then out straight up through the top of the head. Then reverse: Bring energy in through the top of the head, all the way down to the heart; hold; then straight out from the heart into the world.

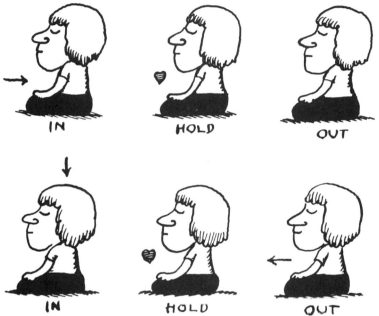

After you get the motions down pat, try to keep the mind concentrated on what you're trying to do:

When you breathe in through the heart, you're taking all the pain and suffering and incompleteness of human life (including your own) into your own heart. You offer this up to God by breathing it up through the top of the head (the seventh chakra) into the universe.

Then you breathe in that pure universal power which is beyond all suffering, and you take it down through the top of your head all the way into the heart, where you give it the touch of your own love and then offer it out into the world as your gift (on the out-breath).

As your concentration gets stronger, this becomes a very powerful way to give blessings and to take personal responsibility for peace on Earth and goodwill toward all.

Christ and other free beings do this with *full* concentration, every moment of the day. How do you think we've survived so long, as crazy as we are??

Mahadevananda Breath

A slightly complicated but powerful method that Sita and I have practiced for years is this one (don't worry about pronouncing the name; it's named after the saint who taught it, and he won't mind what you call it as long as it works for you).

Mahadevananda breath is a type of alternate nostril breathing, so put the right hand up to the face, using the thumb on the right nostril and the ring finger on the left (see page 71).

Closing off the right nostril, take five deep breaths (slow or fast, whatever feels best at the time) in and out of the left nostril. Then five in and out of the right nostril. Then in the left, out the right (1), in the right, out the left (2), in the left, out the right (3), in the right, out the left (4), and in the left, out the right (5). Then in and out five times with both nostrils open. Finally, take one last *deep* breath and hold it for about a half-minute, then let it out your *left* nostril only.

That whole thing is one full Mahadevananda breath. After that, you begin on the other nostril (in this case, closing the left and starting with the right) and do the whole thing again. But the final breath is always out the *left*, never the right.

But that's just the mechanical aspect of the method. The point is, you do the Mahadevananda breath while concentrating on the chakras in one of several ways:

1) Do one full Mahadevananda breath in each chakra starting from number one and going up to number seven (crown chakra, at the top of the head). Sit quietly for five to ten minutes, then do it from number seven down to the heart (fourth chakra), so that your practice ends in the heart. In other words, you'd be doing the full breath 11 times (twice at top of the head).

2) Many people prefer to work only on the four higher chakras with this breath. So you would start at the heart, go up each chakra to the top of the head, then sit for a few minutes and go back down to the heart. This would be a total of eight full breaths.

3) You can also just stay in the heart, doing any number of full breaths in that one chakra.

Depending on your own intuition of what you need the most, you can do the Mahadevanda method so slowly that one full breath takes an hour, or so hard and fast that it's like breath of fire — or any speed and intensity in-between. It can also be specifically to force energy into a higher place.

For example, if you're feeling horny, you can start at the second chakra and go up to the heart (three full breaths), and then from the heart silently ask God to take your lust. If you're caught in anger, start at the third chakra and do one there and then one in the heart, offering the anger up from the heart.

If you can catch these emotions when they first arise, it's not so hard to pull the power up, and it shows you how much control you can develop over your own life. One of my teachers called this technique "The most powerful breath in the universe."

Breath Of Fire

Kaphalabhati, or breath of fire, is also a powerful technique to do while concentrating on the chakras or on one specific chakra, like the heart. It may take a little practice before you can do this technique without getting dizzy or hyperventilated, but once you get used to it, you can push yourself very hard in this exercise and change your state of consciousness quite a bit.

Some years ago, a very fierce spiritual teacher had me and Sita doing this practice three times a day, for two full minutes in each of the seven chakras, holding the breath one full minute in between. In other words, starting at the first chakra do a *hard* breath of fire for two minutes without stopping; then hold the breath for 1 minute, sitting perfectly still and straight; then focus the mind on the second chakra and do it again... then again... all the way up. Then after meditating awhile, breathe the head-heart breath (page 91) to end the session in the heart chakra.

This was very intense and exhausting, but it took us into altered states of consciousness time after time. It also broke up a lot of blocks and let our power move more freely.

These methods can be practiced in any way you want to experiment with them. One general guideline that most teachers agree on, though, is to end these practices by bringing your attention and your power into the heart—because the heart is where we need to live from.

Someone who does intense work on their third eye (sixth chakra) or other higher centers may experience a lot of interesting things, but without coming back to the heart, their lives get a little weird; they may start feeling spaced out all the time, or uncaring about the people around them. The heart is always the key to living in the world.

Each moment of every day, all the power we need is right here available to us. Pranayam is simply an ancient, detailed version of the folk wisdom "When you get angry, take ten deep breaths." We hear stuff like that all our lives without realizing that much of it goes deeply into the science of existence.

Prayer & Love are learned in the hour when

prayer becomes impossible and your heart

has turned to stone.

-- Thomas Merton

7. Prayer

Through the languages of every spiritual tradition the world has ever known, God has said, "If you ask for my help, you'll get it."

Prayer is our safety-net from free will. Adam and Eve didn't *need* prayer before they tasted of the apple of knowledge—in other words, before we human beings got free will. Up to that point, it was all God's will; life unfolded in perfect harmony.

But from the moment we felt naked, or separated from God (this is all "Original Sin" really means)—*prayer* was built into the system as one way we could maintain at least a thread of our connection. Our Great Mission—as individuals and as a species—is to learn how to use our free will wisely enough to go full-circle into oneness with God.

A thumbnail sketch looks something like this: First there's God's will, and no suffering; then there's man's will *versus* God's will, with plenty of suffering; and finally, after a long search for relief from our pain, man's will becomes the same as God's will (enlightenment).

We go through the whole cycle on many different levels—over a period of centuries, in the stages of each lifetime, and even in the course of a normal day's struggles. It's an exquisite design.

Prayer is the way we can remind ourselves of the whole thing, and also ask for any divine help which is allowed under the rules of the game. And since we don't know what all the rules are, we have to use our best guesses about how to pray (or what to pray for), and we must accept on faith that every prayer is heard and answered in the best way, for our own good—even when it doesn't look like it to our limited vision.

Just like true meditation, prayer itself is not really a "method"; it's more a *relationship* to God (or to Self, life, the universe, however we want to say it). Praying as a spiritual practice is just that: it's practice. After enough practice, and as we get more mature, prayer just starts happening all day long—again, just like meditation.

Most of us tend to use prayer like a secret rabbit's foot or something—we whip it out when we need help with the "big" things. But every moment of our lives is truly the same size as every other. The spiritual warrior *lives* in prayer, rather than praying "for" this or that. The wise rely on God for their very next breath. The truly strong realize their utter helplessness without this next moment of God's Grace. The holy don't even brush their teeth without getting into harmony with the rest of the universe.

After about twenty years of using many forms of prayer, I notice that I'm finally beginning to be in a conversation with God most of the day. I notice that the immediate effect of my prayers—the help that seems to come—is simply that I'm able *to pay closer attention* to whatever is going on. By paying attention, every situation seems to furnish all its own answers. They may not be fun; they may not be what I wanted to hear, but at least they're obvious.

And then sometimes there seems to be no help at all. Prayer feels lifeless, empty—a stupid game, or a superstitious head-trip I've fallen into that's no more meaningful than biting my nails or cracking my knuckles.

Yet, I find that deep in my heart I really do believe what all the holy books say: Help comes when we ask for it. So at those empty times, I know that something's happening in some way that I just don't yet understand.

How To Start Praying

Who is it that we pray to? And is it necessary to figure that out? Many people have no problem at all with their inner feelings about God, Christ, Holy Spirit, Great Spirit, Allah, Jehovah, Krishna, Rama, or any other form to whom they address their prayers. But many of us are confused. After all, it's *true* that we're not really separate from God anyway—we're just under the *illusion* of separateness—so who or what is there to pray to other than our deepest selves? And if God is handling the universe perfectly, what is there to pray about?

But even a savage knows in his gut that he has some kind of mysterious connection to the world around him. Prayer is simply a way of probing that connection. Maybe we pray to our deepest selves; maybe we pray to the intelligence behind nature; maybe prayer is just a way of discovering some of our own hopes and fears. The answer doesn't really matter, because the bottom line is,

as a spiritual practice, prayer works.

It may work in an entirely different way than what we thought we wanted, it may not even be recognizable in the way our answers come—but it works; you can bank on it. God said that.

When we really get it right, praying is about the most intimate thing we could ever do. Besides calling on God, we're also revealing our innermost selves *to* ourselves—we discover our deepest hopes and fears, our basic innocence, and we prepare our subconscious minds for the major changes that are bound to come about during the spiritual journey.

Eventually, the words for most prayers will come freely out of the depths of our own hearts. The following prayers are offered merely as practice; as an inspirational guide to point the way. They can be repeated, imitated, changed, used or discarded. Every genuine prayer ever uttered, belongs to us all. Blessings to you.

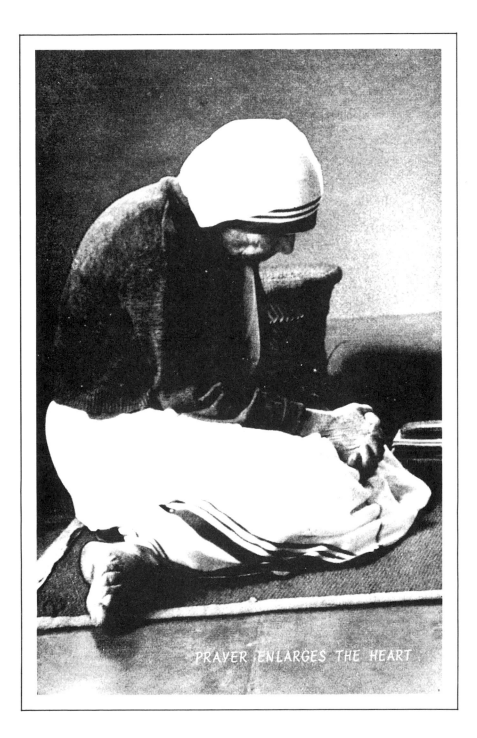

PRAYER ENLARGES THE HEART

God, help me to open to your power.
Help me to open to my power.
Help me even to pray to you.
Please, come into my life,
and fulfill the Sacred Promises
you have made through the ages.

Oh Great Spirit,
Whose voice I hear in the winds,
Life to all the world, hear me.
I come before you, one of your many children.
I am small and weak.
I need your strength and wisdom.
Let me walk in beauty and make my eyes
ever behold the red and purple sunset.
Make my hands respect the things you have made,
my ears sharp to hear your voice.
Make me wise, so that I may know the things
You have taught my People,
the lesson you have hidden in every leaf & rock.
I seek strength not to be superior to my brothers,
but to be able to fight my greatest enemy--
Myself.
Make me ever ready to come to you
with clean hands and straight eyes,
So when life fades as a fading sunset,
my Spirit may come to you without shame.

-- Yellow Lark

Lord, help me to keep my thoughts pure,
my words true,
and my deeds kind;
That alone or with others,
I shall be at one with thee.

God, be in my mouth
and in my speaking.

God, be in my heart
and in my thinking.

--Sarum Primer, 1558

I sit inside my jail, Jesus.
I constructed it with my own hands,
stone upon stone, lock inside lock.
Here I am a model prisoner of my own will.
Here I am the slave of self.

Freedom is what I long for, Lord.
My weary body and tired mind
cry out for new life.
My soul is parched and life is in decay,
with dreams crumbled and energy stifled.
Depression is heavy upon me. I feel hopeless
in this moment, Jesus. I am only sorry for myself.
I ask if there is any use to struggle with life.

But still I want a voice to cut through
my silence, Jesus. Let me hear laughter.
Let me see a burst of Light.

I want to care again, Lord,

-- Malcolm Boyd

O Thou, who are the perfection of
Love, Harmony and Beauty,
The Lord of Heaven and Earth,
Open our hearts that we may hear thy voice,
which constantly comes from within.
Disclose to us Thy Divine Light
which is hidden in our souls,
that we may know and understand life better.

Most merciful and compassionate God,
give us Thy goodness.
Teach us Thy loving forgiveness.
Raise us above the distinctions and differences
which divide us.
Send us the peace of Thy Divine Spirit,
and unite us in Thy Perfect Being.
So be it.

--Hazrat Inayat Khan

Oh perfect friend, Father, Mother;
May we know Thee more clearly,
Love Thee more dearly,
Follow Thee more nearly,
For ever and ever. Amen.

God, grant me the serenity
to accept the things I cannot change,
the courage
to change the things I can,
and the wisdom
to know the difference.

Brahmapanam ~ Brahma havire
Brahmagni ~ Brahmana hota
Brahmai-tan ~ Gantabyam
Brahma-Karma ~ Samadhinah

This ritual is God
The food is God
We who are offering the food are God
The fire of hunger is also God
All karma is God
We who know this may find God

— Hindu blessing before meals

Lord, feed me the blood and body of the Christ
through the food on this table.
Feed me, Lord, for my genuine transformation.
Amen.

— Christian blessing before meals

Lord, make me an instrument of Thy peace.

Where there is hatred -- let me sow Love;

Where there is injury -- Pardon;

Where there is doubt -- Faith;

Where there is despair -- Hope;

Where there is darkness -- Light;

Where there is sadness -- Joy.

O Divine Master, grant that I may not so much

seek to be consoled, as to console;

To be understood, as to understand;

To be loved, as to Love.

For it is in giving that we receive;

In pardoning that we are pardoned;

In dying that we are born to Eternal Life.

--St. Francis

From the point of Light within the Mind of God,
Let Light stream forth into the minds of men.
Let Light descend on Earth.
From the point of Love within the Heart of God,
Let Love stream forth into the hearts of men.
May Christ return to Earth.
From the center where the Will of God is known,
Let purpose guide the little wills of men --
The purpose which the Masters know and serve.
From the center which we call the race of men,
Let the Plan of Love and Light work out;
And may it seal the door where evil dwells.
Let Light and Love and Power
Restore the Plan on Earth.

--The Great Invocation, for world peace

Grandfather Great Spirit,
All over the world the faces of living ones
are alike.
With tenderness they have come up
out of the ground.
Look upon your children that they may
face the winds and walk the good road
to the day of Quiet.
Grandfather Great Spirit,
Fill us with the Light.
Give us the strength to understand,
and the eyes to see.
Teach us to walk the soft Earth as relatives
to all that live.
Help us, for without you we are nothing.

--Sioux prayer

My Lord Creator of all,
Master of all worlds,
Supreme, compassionate and forgiving,
Thank You for Your Torah,
Thank You for allowing me to learn from it
And to move toward serving You.
Thank You for revealing some of the
Mysteries of Your Way.
I'm amazed this is truly happening to me.

Please forgive my foolishness and unkindness,
The sins of my past.
Sincerely I pledge to live more uprightly
That I may be ever closer to You.
Fill me with that awe of You that
opens my capacity
For loving.
And open my heart to the mysteries
of Your Holy Way.
Reveal Your Torah, I pray.

From the Unreal lead me to the Real,
From Darkness lead me to Light,
From Death lead me to Immortality.

--Brhadaranyaka Upanishad

All religions are the same. They all lead to God.
God is everybody.... The same blood flows through us all,
the arms, the legs, the heart,
All are the same.
See no difference; see all the same.

-- Neem Karoli Baba

I bow to God, who lives in this world within us.
Whoever calls Him by any name,
by that name does He come.
--Mahabharata, by Wm. Buck

8. Religion As A Method

*[This chapter is reprinted from the Prison-Ashram Project Newsletter, Christmas 1983; it was originally titled WILL THE REAL CHRIST PLEASE STAND UP? Although it uses Christianity as a focus, the main point applies to all religions equally: that religions can be useful as methods just like any other discipline, but people tend to make them something much more sacred. And **no** method is sacred in and of itself.]*

The most wondrous mystery, the most sacred event, is the appearance in human form of the one Holy Spirit. It's almost beyond imagining: The awesome powers of all Creation, the Unlimited and Eternal, in a limited, mortal body; a living and breathing human being, yet one whom by a touch or a glance may turn water into wine or bring the dead back to life.

Such a being has walked the Earth not once, but many times. And although each appearance has been very special, the message has always been the same:

CALM DOWN; BE STILL, TURN INWARD TO THE ONE GOD,
WHO DWELLS DEEP INSIDE YOU;
DON'T GET CARRIED AWAY BY THINGS THAT GLITTER,
JUST LOVE EVERYBODY AND TAKE COURAGE,
FOR I AM ALWAYS WITH YOU.

However it's been phrased, that's always been the gist of it. Jesus told us to pray in the closet, alone; Buddha said the "Big Mind" is within each of us; Native Americans taught that Waken-Tonka, the Great Spirit, speaks to us from within; Jews were to listen for the "still small voice"; the Muslims are taught "La Illaha Illa Llah," ("There is no God but God"); The Hindus know that "Atman", or the Godhead, lives in every heart. Who cares how it's worded?

It's all the same because, as every religion is quick to point out, there **is** only one God, one Holy Spirit. And that Spirit has always tried to convince us to catch the real message, but each time, we've gotten hooked on the messenger instead.

Many of us are religious, but far too few are spiritual. Spirituality is the core of all reality; it's a mysterious but certain essence at the center of everything we see or do. As C.S. Lewis said, "There seems no center because it's **all** center." But religion, on the other hand, isn't such a natural part of Creation; it's man-made, and a quick look around suggests that maybe it's not made so well.

Even when religious followers aren't out on the battlefields slaughtering each other, religions seem to compete like college fraternities. Priests, ministers, rabbis, & imams function mostly as lay psychologists or community organizers—which is very helpful, but has little to do with the eternal mystical truth which every religion is based on. Most of the clergy have forgotten about that level of it themselves. A Catholic priest once told me that neither he nor any of his fellow priests or nuns ever talk to each other about the possibility of a mystical experience of the Christ, because it's "much too far out" an idea. Yet all of Christianity is based on that single far-out idea! Clearly something's been lost in the shuffle.

There's nothing wrong with religion being a method; a path to the One. Each genuine religion through the ages has begun from the Divine inspiration & authority of a being who **knows** God, and who tells us various ways to live right & turn inward so that we can become as free as they are. But within a few generations, time and time again we've come to worship the religion itself instead of the One; the body of the messenger instead of the Soul.

Christians, for example, have no problem at all accepting that there is only one Son of God, one Light, one Way. The trouble is, the vast majority also insist that Jesus of Nazareth was the only genuine appearance of this Holy One. It's considered blasphemy to suggest that Jesus was just a passing form for the one true Christ; a body & identity He used briefly, like we put on & take off a coat.

This inflexibility and closed-mindedness of the Christian tradition chokes & twists the very Spirit it tries to honor. When Jesus said *BEFORE ABRAHAM WAS, I AM,* was He referring to the 33-year-old carpenter who had been born from Mary's womb thousands of years after Abraham's time?

Jesus said *GOD IS A SPIRIT, AND THEY THAT WORSHIP HIM MUST WORSHIP HIM IN SPIRIT AND IN TRUTH.* Even **during** His days on Earth, Jesus sometimes took other faces & forms, almost playfully, as if trying to say, "Hey, don't get caught by appearances! Tune in to my Spirit, not my face!" Isn't that what happened with Mary Magadalene outside His tomb, when Christ spoke to her and she saw Him as a gardener? Or when He appeared to His disciples that same day as a traveller on the road, and He walked all the way into town with them unrecognized? Preaching the whole way, he sat down to dinner with them before He dropped the disguise and said something like "Hey guys, it's me! You gotta stay sharp!"

In several other passages in the Bible, Jesus seems to appear & reappear or change forms at will, like leaving an angry crowd who was going to stone Him, *GOING THROUGH THE MIDST OF THEM* without being seen at all. He moved in & out of the physical body with ease, because that's no big deal to the power which created all forms.

But have we stayed sharp? How keenly have we tried to recognize the Holy Spirit moving in and out of form? From what we know of His powers, why is it blasphemy to imagine that he has **also** appeared as

Buddha, Rama, Krishna, and other men & women of all lands & races? Jesus told us *I WILL NOT LEAVE YOU COMFORTLESS; I WILL COME TO YOU.* He also said *BY THIS SHALL ALL MEN KNOW YOU ARE MY DISCIPLES: IF YOU HAVE LOVE FOR ONE ANOTHER.*

D. Netto, Fla. State Prison

Has Love been our guide as we've met people of other religions? Did we love the Native Americans before we massacred them as "heathens" and then tried to save their souls with the gospel of Christ? Did we sit with them to feel whether their Great Spirit and our Holy Ghost were simply two different terms for the same all-powerful force? Jesus said *JUDGE NOT ACCORDING TO THE APPEARANCE*, yet for centuries we've assumed that anyone who calls himself a Christian is closer to Christ than someone who calls himself a Buddhist, Muslim, Sikh, Hindu or Jew—or one who gives no name at all to his spiritual heart.

Since man first drew breath on this planet, the one Holy Spirit has been taking and changing forms so that all God's children in every age and land could have the opportunity to turn inward to the One Way, the "narrow

115

gate" which leaves no room for anything but our souls. There is only one final religion, and it can't be limited by any single name.

Certainly Jesus said *I AM THE LIGHT AND THE WAY* and *YOU CANNOT COME TO THE FATHER BUT THROUGH ME*. But He also said *FEED MY SHEEP*. Did the apostles run out to buy sheep food? And He said *HE THAT EATETH MY FLESH, AND DRINKETH MY BLOOD, DWELLETH IN ME, AND I IN HIM*. Did Simon Peter start chewing on His leg?

Why then treat the "Only Way" statements in the narrowest, most hostile sense, and thereby declare war or pity on three-fifths of the world's population, who relate to the Spirit in other forms? Blunt as it sounds, it's nothing but bigotry—no matter how compassionately we phrase it, or how politely Christians mingle with Jews and Buddhists at spiritual garden parties. For Christians to think they've got an exclusive handle on God is *wrong*, pure and simple.

Jesus tried to warn us about this during His ministry. In fact, He came to tear down such distorted views, not add to them. He told us Spirit is a personal thing, that it has nothing to do with public opinion or respectability. In fact, He said *BEWARE OF THE SCRIBES, WHO DESIRE TO WALK IN FANCY CLOTHES, AND LOVE GREETINGS IN THE MARKETS, AND THE HIGHEST SEATS IN THE CHURCHES, AND THE CHIEF ROOMS AT FEASTS; WHO DEVOUR WIDOWS' HOUSES* (take their money), *AND FOR A SHOW MAKE LONG PRAYERS.*

It's hard to imagine a more precise description of multi-millionaire evangelists like Jerry Falwell, Jim Bakker, Jimmy Swaggart and many others who spread their fear-and-hatred gospels throughout the world. Yet millions of sincere Christians support these self-righteous emperors simply because they *claim* to be speaking on behalf of Jesus. How could Jesus have tried to caution us any more clearly?

Nearly 2,000 years after Jesus of Nazareth tried to show us how to love one another and live in the richness of the Holy Spirit, we find our poor beautiful planet closer than ever to being blown out of the skies—not from any inevitable disaster like the sun leaving its position or the stars falling from the heavens, but simply from our own continuing poverty of Spirit; our fear, greed and insanity.

Spiritual sanity isn't as flashy as religious cheerleading, but it's the One Way which has been preached since the beginning of time. Not one way for Christians and another for Jews and yet another for Buddhists, etc.; and certainly not one Christian Way for all, or one Islamic way for all, etc.

The true One Way goes straight through each of our hearts, far beyond words and images. That's the meaning of the saying, "If you meet the Buddha on the road, kill Him." So long as we still see the "Way" outside of ourselves, in limited and separate forms, then we're missing the point.

116

It is all an open secret.

—Ramana Maharshi

The world is the embodiment of Divine Love. All created things are its material expression. If you can once rouse yourself to that Divine Love, you will see everywhere in this Universe only the play of the One. Isolating himself from the Divine Love, man fumbles about and misses the real import of life.

—Ananda Mayee Ma

117

The Christ Spirit is truly indestructible and eternal, just like the Bible says. When we dig in deeply, in our own "closets", we find that Christ, Narayana, Buddha, Allah, Yahweh, Waken-Tonka and all the other names of God dissolve into a single boundless power and joy right at the very center of our own selves. It's all one; all-one; al-one. We have to do it alone. *THE KINGDOM OF HEAVEN IS NOT OUT THERE, OR OVER THERE, OR UP THERE; BUT LO, IT IS WITHIN YOU.*

Religions can help, but only if we use them rather than following them blindly. The perfect success of any religion is to bring us to the same level of God-consciousness as its founder. That's all any religion was ever intended to be—a method for spiritual development in the particular flavor of a God-conscious being.

Even before enlightenment, we may reach a point where we no longer need religion at all; when we become so deeply connected to God within ourselves, that we become universal holy people—fearing no one, feeling separate from no one—like all the masters were. It should be a profound joy for a minister or rabbi to "lose" such a person from the congregation. That's like graduation day from that particular method.

Jesus said *IS IT NOT WRITTEN IN YOUR LAW, I SAID, YOU ARE GODS?* He never intended for Christians to hide behind Christianity for all time to come. He's much more powerful than that. The Gospel (which means "good news") is actually much better news than most of us realize!!

Born-Again Blues
(a song written in 12-bar blues; c Bo Lozoff, 1983)

I had a dream about a convict, a crown of thorns was on his head;
He came gliding down the highway, looked up at me and he said:
"Hey don't you know me? Don't you remember my name or my crime?
I was busted and convicted, strung up in my prime,
   when I came to help everyone do their time."

I tried to be cool but I was shaking,
   I couldn't walk, I couldn't see;
I said "But I'm not one of the faithful Lord, So why have you come to me?"
"I mean, maybe I'm not doing great, But I figured at least I was doin' fine!"
"And I'm a free man, a do-as-I-please man,
   So what's all this talk about doin' my time?"

He said "You can climb the highest mountain;
　　swim the deep blue sea;
Roll around naked in money,
　　But you'll never, no never be free;
So I've come to assist you, If you're willin' to learn how to let your light shine."
"And I've had dozens of faces and names,
　　So don't you get stuck in competitive games;
You just have to love everybody all of the time."

I said "But Lord, my brother's in prison, and you know my back hurts all the time;
My daddy died a cripple,
　　and baby sister can't stop drinking her wine;
Politicians cheat me and steal, and look what you're askin'me to feel—I'm sorry, I respectfully decline!"
Then without a word He touched my heart,
　　And I felt something crack apart,
Like a door that hadn't opened in some time.

I saw the Earth and everyone on it,
　　I saw the Light all over me;
The good in everybody,
　　I saw it the way that He must see;
and I felt His love for it all, and how He marks every sparrow's fall, and how sorrow always has its reason and rhyme;
He let His hand fall to His side,
　　and I cried and cried and cried,
And He said "Now let's take it from the top about doin' your time."

"If you've got a cross, then I can bear it,
　　But you have to seek if you want to find;
Got a song, then try to share it,
　　But try to be simple, and try to be kind;
And don't get too carried away
　　By the things that pass every day,
Try to keep My Peace in your heart and mind.
　　That's all My Gospel and it's true, and all you really need to do,
　　Is be loving everybody all of the time."

Love everyone, serve everyone,
and remember God.
                --Neem Karoli Baba

9. The Path of Service

When we live in harmony with the **Dharma**, or the Great Natural Law, everything we do is an act of *service*. Wherever we are, whatever we do with our time, we're lightening the load of the whole planet just by finding and following our own perfect roles in the movie; our own paths to a simple, happy life.

But service is also a specific spiritual practice; one which is widely overlooked and terribly misunderstood. There's a secret, a great spiritual treasure, hidden within our ability to relieve suffering—feeding the poor, tending the sick, loving whom Jesus called "the least of these." It's a practical discipline as much as meditation, yoga, and prayer, yet it's *also* a whole lifestyle, just like medicine, business or sports (good job security too; there's an endless supply of people to serve!).

Keys To The Kingdom

What do we learn in school on "career day"? Representatives always come from the business world, the professional community, colleges and so forth.

But is anyone invited from Salvation Army, or Oxfam, or Save The Children? Does anyone mention Covenant House, which takes in runaways and bums and bag ladies from the streets? Or Plenty, an agency that sails ships full of food and supplies to Central American refugees? Or Habitat, which helps people all over the world build their own homes so they can live indoors, often for the first time?

Such service is very powerful; literally a key to the Kingdom of Heaven, yet few of us choose it as our main work in life, because we hardly get the opportunity. By the time we're grown, *we* avoid such ideas with our kids. Yet we often feel so empty and unfulfilled! Could there be a connection?

When Mother Theresa was interviewed about her work with the dying and destitute in the streets of Calcutta, she said **When I look into their eyes, I see the Christ.** Instead of passing her comment off as a noble shrug of modesty, think about it:

> *I see the Christ.*

Consider the possibility that she's telling the actual truth. Imagine how *stoned* she must be all day long if she's looking into the eyes of Christ!! Has she stumbled onto a secret about human service that most of us haven't yet awakened to?

Of course, we can't get to that same point by imitating Mother Theresa's life. We have to begin guessing our *own* way, with as wide-open a heart and mind as possible. The point here is simply that service is an exciting lifestyle which we've been trained to ignore in favor of competition, profit motive, recreation, and status—none of which have a very good track record for bringing lasting happiness.

One alternative lifestyle is to work for a non-profit organization whose sole aim is to help people in need. There are thousands of such agencies all over the world and many of them welcome good new workers. If human service is right for you, a tremendous degree of awakening will come into your life as you explore the possibilities.

As we wake up to the magic of serving others, the distinction between selfish and selfless becomes non-existent. The best thing I can do for me is to help you. The best thing you can do for you is to help me. Follow our

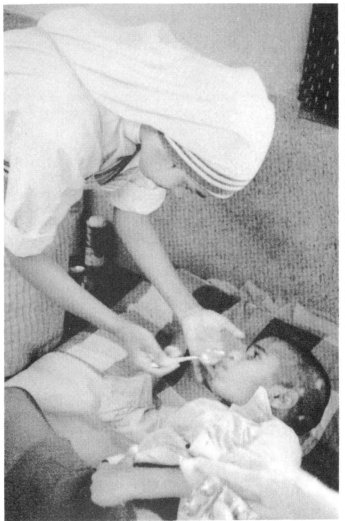

own best interests, and everyone benefits. What a different concept of life than the idea of "survival of the fittest" or "grab what you can!" And it really works, even for old hippies like Sita and me with no degrees, no formal job training, no respectable credentials of any kind.

The fact is, just about every part of life on Earth needs fixing; so this particular strategy— the path of service- —is about latching on to whatever grabs our hearts the most, and start helping out. Everything else we need will be provided.

The Razor's Edge

The slippery trap of self-righteousness is the razor's edge in the path of service: throwing around phrases like "selfless servants of humanity"; or giving to charity or doing volunteer work because we feel guilty—like the old "guilt-ridden liberal". Or we think it's more spiritual to do service even if we have a natural passion for something else. Or we may "sacrifice" ourselves for a cause because it seems easier to struggle endlessly "for the people" than to get our own lives happy and balanced.

But in truth, we're all connected; we can't be sacrificed for each other's good. That's what so many people don't understand about a person like Mother Theresa. She feels no sense of sacrifice; she's doing what gets her stoned! What is she sacrificing—Star Wars and Sugar Frosted Flakes, to look into the eyes of Christ? Is it any sacrifice to give up petty fun in order to be bathed in joy?

Our lives here are a process of development, plain and simple. We're all at different places on the wheel, and that's why we each need to find and follow our own destinies. Service with guilt or righteousness is not the path, but service from the Heart—even for a short period of time—has a remarkable ability to help us get straight with ourselves, open our hearts, heal old wounds, defeat lifelong fears, and see the noblest side of human dignity.

Many times in our lives we're unsure of what to do next. Maybe we've just gotten out of prison, or are recently divorced, fired, unhappy, or confused. Instead of making a feeble gesture of change—swapping one situation for another almost exactly like it—we have the opportunity to sit down, decide on what form of suffering touches us most, and go out and help fix it. Real change! Real Magic!

> *Bees gather nectar, trees grow, garbage trucks collect garbage, and servants serve others. No big deal; no credit due; just everything doing what's best for itself; everything following its own nature.*

The Buck Starts Here

Of course, if we waited until we could serve egolessly before we serve at all, there would be very few servants or activists in the world (this book wouldn't be here, that's for sure!). As in any other spiritual discipline, we have to start from where we are, do the best we can, fall flat on our faces a million times, get up a million-and-one times, and keep going.

A good place to start is in quiet reflection about what kind of service seems both satisfying and realistic for our own abilities. Does it have to do with prisoners or children or the elderly or street people or any other special population? Hunger or housing or peace or wildlife or the environment? What sort of contribution would we like to make toward the happiness of the world?

A logical next step is to check out what's already being done in that field. A librarian can help locate the right organizations. A clergyman or a social worker can describe various volunteer projects. Take time to check things out, to write to the agencies that might be most helpful. As we get closer to the work that's right for us, our needs and opportunities start falling into place.

Maybe at first there'll be a tremendous amount of ego and self-righteousness about helping others. But if we can just endure this stage honestly, the power of service itself will purify and mature us. It's a very joyful path, and as usual, there's much more happening *behind* the scenes than up front.

PRISONERS IN COMMUNITY SERVICE

Many prisoners have told me that one of the worst things about prison life was to be unable to lend a helping hand. But here are just a few of the ways prisoners have been able to serve in the larger world:

* In Ft. Worth, Texas, the local United Fund sponsored a program for prisoners to go into the community as volunteers in a variety of areas, such as coaching at the local YMCA. In New Mexico, maximum-security inmates used the prison shop to build playground equipment for a low-income day-care center, using materials donated by local businesses. Such projects help people to realize that the prison is still a part of the community.

* In Tennessee, Maryland, and Colorado, prisoners have worked as volunteers in translating books into braille for the blind. Other such projects include reading books onto cassettes for the blind.

* A prisoner-tended garden in Connecticut has raised food not only for the prison, but also for local nursing homes and needy people in the community.

* Massachusetts prisoners coordinated—by writing to friends and family outside—a winter clothing drive for Sioux people in South Dakota. An outside volunteer drove a truckload to the reservation in a donated Hertz truck.

* In Vienna, Ill., a group of EMT-trained prisoners now operate the only local ambulance service for a three-county area—a service which was desperately needed. In Connecticut, prisoners developed "Cabbage Patch", a radio show for children, from inside the prison. Many other prison groups have sponsored meetings and programs aimed at steering kids away from lives of crime.

Only our imaginations limit the ways we can work for the good of others, no matter where we find ourselves. This poor, struggling world needs all the help it can get from *all* of us.

I was hungry, and you fed me; I was a stranger, and you took me in; naked, and you clothed me; I was sick, and you visited me; I was in prison, and you came unto me.
If you have done these things for the least of my brothers and sisters, you have done them for me, and you shall inherit the Kingdom of God.

—Jesus

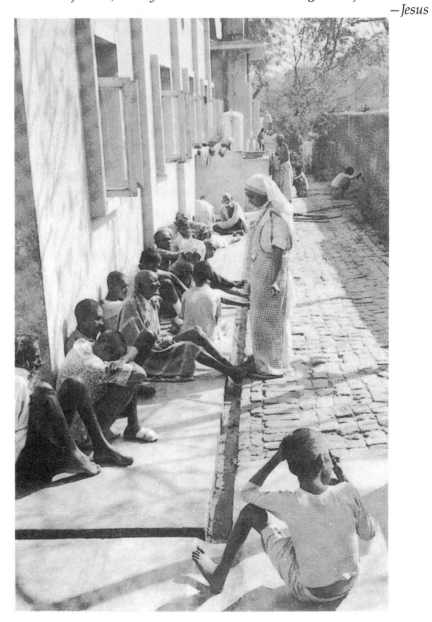

To know and yet not to do
Is in fact not to know.

—*Wang Yang Ming*

A dog is not considered a good dog
because he is a good barker.
A man is not considered a good man
because he is a good talker.

—*Chang Tzu*

10. Turning Information Into Wisdom

There's a tremendous amount of information in this book, drawn from all the ages and cultures of our planet. But whether information ripens into wisdom is the choice each of us makes in the way we apply it to our lives. When all is said and done, it's not what we *know* that counts; it's what we *do* about it in a daily, practical way.

Spiritual work takes place every moment of our lives, but for at least the first sixty years or so, it's almost impossible to keep pace with it unless we have some sort of regular practice; a period set aside from each busy day when we take time to get centered and charge our inner batteries for another day's challenges.

In the East, this part of the day is called *sadhana* (pronounced *sodd*-na); it's like a regular exercise regimen for the Spirit. Our Western tradition of the Sabbath started out along the same lines, but the way it's generally been presented to us as we were growing up is more like an obligation to honor God rather than what it truly is—a precious and powerful time to stoke our innermost fires and gather all our strength into focus.

Different Stages

My own sadhana has gone through many changes over the years. These days (1985), each morning I do some hatha yoga and pranayam, a little singing or chanting, and a period of meditation. I usually meditate again at night.

There have been times when spiritual practices have taken up most of my time every day for years at a stretch, and other times when I've done none at all. And there are so many times when sadhana takes tremendous discipline—just to stop all the busy stuff and get down to it, you know?—yet then there are those wonderful times when it takes discipline to *stop*; to get *up* from meditation to face the "ordinary" world again. These stages keep moving like phases of the moon. Part of our task is to keep pace with them, so whatever we're doing on any given day is fresh and alive, not a canned concept of what we think we should do.

I used to feel fear and guilt when I didn't do practices, as if I were blowing all my chances for enlightenment. That's pretty much gone now, and I can do my daily practices for the very best reasons of all: They make a noticeable difference in the way I feel, in the way I can concentrate and do whatever I do throughout the day.

This is essentially the same advice The Buddha gave His students:

Don't do something just because other people say it's great, or because you read it in a book, or because teachers promise you various benefits; do it only if, after you try it, in your own experience, you see that it enriches your life.

Copping Out

The problem is, doing spiritual practices isn't usually like dropping acid or smoking a joint. There may not be such an immediate rush that makes it obvious something's going on. We may try meditation once or twice, then laziness pops up and we start using the Buddha's advice as a way out. "Hey, I just don't feel anything, you know?"

But a good rule-of-thumb is this:

If you decide to try a certain spiritual practice, take a vow to do it every day for at least a month before you decide whether it suits you or not. A month is not a very long time for these ancient techniques. Most of the change in our lives has been on the surface; if we want to try for deeper change, we have to be willing to put some patience into it.

The mind will come up with every cop-out known to man to screw up the regularity or intensity of daily spiritual practices. It's just a problem that comes with the territory; it's no different for you or me than it was for Abraham or Moses or Bilal. So if you *want* a cop-out, don't worry, a good one will come up with no conscious effort on your part.

A friend of mine who has a lot of problems with hypertension and hyperactivity took a course in meditation and was blown away with how calm it made him feel. Then after just a week or two, he developed a terrible pain in his left shoulder every time he sat down to meditate. That was the only time he felt that pain. So, he stopped meditating. The pain went away (along with his new calmness). Unfortunately, most of us go through the same sequence in any of a million ways: Ego threatened, ego responds, ego wins, threat gone, back in a rut, business as usual.

But somebody else I know, a yoga teacher, tried handling it another way. He had been attempting to do a certain advanced asana (yoga pose) for years, and one day he finally made it. But he knew that the only way he would be able to master it would be to do it every day, a little longer and more comfortably, until it became part of his routine.

However, the day after he accomplished the pose for the first time, he came down with a terrible flu. His body ached; he felt too stiff to do yoga. He stayed in bed that day, and then the next day he felt no better. He began to realize that this flu could set him back *months* of the practice he had invested in this asana; so he crawled out of bed, head aching, feeling terrible, and did his whole yoga routine.

It took him another two or three days to accomplish the full pose again, and he was sick the whole time. But then a funny thing happened: As soon as he got into the pose and stayed there, the "flu" suddenly disappeared and didn't come back. The whole thing had just been one more example of ego working against his success. Like Hari Dass Baba wrote, *Mind makes, mind takes.*

Keeping Up

The fascinating thing about the journey of a spiritual warrior is, ego can take any form and so can Spirit. The above examples could be presented in the opposite way, and make just as much sense: The guy with shoulder pain may have done the right thing by "yielding to his inner guidance", and the yoga teacher may have been full of attachment, stubbornly forcing his body through such pain. Who knows?—only they do, and even *they* may only know in the quietest part of their minds. This is why so many of us keep meditating each day—to get better at "listening".

Truth isn't told in books; that's just information. This becomes obvious when we realize how many contradictory ways people can interpret passages from the Bible and other holy books. Truth, like beauty, is in the eye of the beholder, so we need to keep our eyes as clear as possible *every single moment of our lives*. Here's a moment of Truth right now, as you're reading this. Here's another.
And another.
And another...
and another...

And so our lives pass, never pausing or stopping for even a fraction of a second. Part of us—what I'm calling ego—thrives on a security and stability which Truth never offers. Truth requires openness; what Suzuki Roshi called *Beginner's Mind*. Ego likes habits, plans, backup plans, categories, labels, tidy explanations—none of which is found in Truth. And yet we need ego to function in this world of appearances. Our lives often seem to be a moment-by-moment battle for control between these mysterious parts of ourselves.

But this isn't unfortunate; it's *wonderful*. It means that every moment of your life, of mine, is a unique, creative situation. We can use all the teachings of the ages as guidelines, but the *wisdom* for what to do in each moment, is to be found only in that moment. What a brilliant design!!

The warrior's task is to maintain such a clear, strong, open mind and heart that he or she can spot the Truth behind the appearances every time. This is the only valid reason to do spiritual practices (but it's a good one!).

With so much noise, hype, fears and desires bombarding us all day long, it might take a lot of daily practices to help us spot the Truth within and around us. But what else is there to do—live like suckers, shucking and jiving and lying to ourselves all our lives, feeling secretly weak and disconnected from this incredibly beautiful world we could have held in our immense hearts?

EXAMPLES OF DAILY SADHANA

One Hour—
> Hatha Yoga (ch. 2)- 20 minutes
> Pranayam (ch. 3) - 10 minutes
> Meditation (ch. 1)- 20 minutes
> Prayer or reading—10 minutes

Hour-and-a-half—
> Hatha Yoga—30 minutes
> Pranayam—15 minutes
> Meditation—30 minutes
> Prayer or reading—15 minutes

Two Hours—
> Hatha Yoga—45 minutes
> Pranayam—15 minutes
> Meditation—45 minutes
> Prayer or reading—15 minutes

Sample Day-Long Retreat (in silence)

6 AM:	Wake up, wash, bathroom
6:15:	Hatha Yoga
7:00:	Pranayam
7:30:	Meditation (usually ending with prayer)
8:30:	Breakfast (or, if fasting—just rest)
10:00:	Reading
11:00:	Pranayam
11:30:	Meditation
12:30:	Hatha Yoga
1:00:	Deep rest (or nap, whichever comes first)
2:30:	Pranayam
3:15:	Meditation
4:00:	Supper, rest
5:00:	Reading
5:30:	Meditation
6:30:	Standing or walking meditation
7:00:	Pranayam
7:45:	Hatha Yoga
8:30:	Meditation
9:30:	Go to sleep

Some Tips

These practices and retreat schedule are ones I've used and taught enough times to be able to recommend them personally. There are many other methods or routines that would be just as good, depending on your individual needs. But whatever you may choose to do, here are some general rules of thumb to prevent the ego-mind from running the show:

1) **Commit yourself in advance to a particular set of practices for a certain time period.** Don't change in mid-stream. It may seem a lot easier to dig twenty ten-foot wells than one 200-hundred-foot well, but the deeper one is what we're after.

2) **Don't be unrealistic in making a commitment.** It's better to start slow and move gently than to think you can "conquer" enlightenment by how hard you're going to be on yourself. That's still ego talking.

3) **Keep your practices fairly private.** This is between you and the ancient One, so you don't want to talk and analyze all the power out of it.

4) **Observe, but don't get swept away by, your range of experiences and emotions.** I wish I had a dollar for every time I thought I could never again feel _____ (fill in the blank—anger, lust, jealousy, depression, etc.), only to be overwhelmed by it the next moment, day, week, month, or year. Experiences of enlightenment or insight are great; it's only in the busy mind's interpretation that the troubles begin.

5) **Honor yourself and honor the practices.** This is not a silly game; it's an ageless, unbroken path which you're being initiated into. Be open to the realization that your own efforts are just the tiniest spark for a process far more profound than we could possibly understand. Yet that tiny spark sets the whole thing in motion.

A Final Word

That's really the whole thing in a nutshell: we have so little power, really, that it's ridiculous. And yet, the way the Universe is designed, it's all just waiting for that insignificant little spark from our hearts to set all the beauty and truth in motion, spinning like a top. It's so unimaginably perfect! Powerlessness forces us to be humble, yet when we recognize who we really are in the big scheme of things, we become enlightened and suddenly we have access to all the power in the universe.

And herein lies the difference between the age-old spiritual warrior's way and all the modern psychologies and growth-movement disciplines which sound so much the same, yet miss it by a mile.

The ancient Way isn't ultimately concerned with living a happy, enjoyable human life in the world of props. These practices aren't "coping techniques" for dealing with stress or being successful and so forth. There's absolutely nothing wrong with those goals, but they're very different from what the spiritual warrior has always been after. Even the most significant human joys or tragedies of all time don't mean a thing to the mysterious heart of the Universe. No matter how seriously we take it, the world of appearances, accomplishments and failures is just a game we play.

There's much more *here*. And there comes a time in our lives when we have ears to hear and eyes to see the "more" that I'm talking about. It's natural to try to have as good a time as we can in this beautiful world of appearances, but we can also devote some of each day toward something deeper. Is there any better way to spend our time?

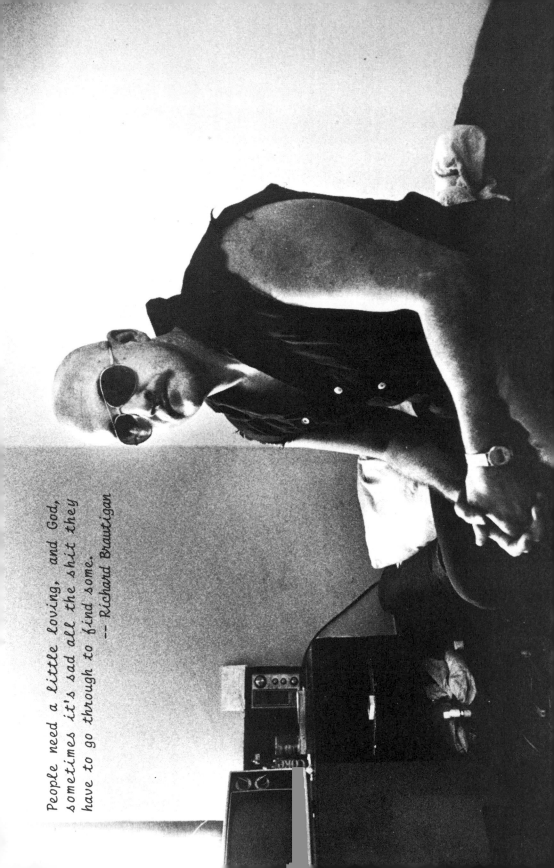

People need a little loving, and God,
sometimes it's sad all the shit they
have to go through to find some.
-- Richard Brautigan

Book Three:

DEAR BO

Letters of Prison, Letters of Freedom

Some of the names in these letters have been changed to protect the guilty.

People asking questions, lost in confusion;
  I tell them there's no problems, only solutions.

They shake their heads and look at me as if I've lost my mind;
I tell them there's no hurry, I'm just sittin' here doing time.

—*"Watching the Wheels", by John Lennon*

The road to wisdom? Well, it's plain and simple
to express: Err,
  and err
  and err
  and err again,
  but less
  and less
  and less.

—*Piet Hein*

Introduction

In a sense, letters have always been the heart and guts of the Prison-Ashram Project. From the very beginning, when we thought we would be sending yoga/meditation instruction to mostly middle-class, educated inmates, the letters we received taught us how wrong we were on both counts. What was needed was (and always is) much more personal and demanding than mere instruction, and the people who reached out to us were a cross-section of the entire prison population—not just acid-heads in for their first bust.

Now I get to share with you a small fraction of this mail from the past 11 years. Reading and responding to these letters has been a great spiritual practice for me, and I've begun to understand that I read only about myself; and write only *to* myself. It's my hope that you, too, will take these letters personally; not so much to understand the writer, but to see more of yourself, of your own journey through life; your own struggles. It all applies.

I also hope that you allow the letters to serve you over a period of many years rather than getting through them quickly like a novel. Trust your own fingers to open the book to the right spot to read something you need to see at the time. It's amazing how the same letters can appear to be so different at different stages in our own lives.

Each chapter begins with a brief quotation that sets a "theme" for the letters in that section. Take your time with these quoted passages, because they speak deeply to all of us. I find one or another of them echoing in my bones in the course of every day.

Tremendous power and insight await us as we open to the mysteries of how we're all connected. We're all so different, yet so much the same. I hope these letters help to unlock some of the riddles for you as they have for me.

May the Great Mystery make sunrise in your heart.

—*Native Sioux Blessing*

My heart is not to my heart's liking.
How I wish I knew
How to unite the two!
                    --Sufi Poem

1. Not To My Heart's Liking

Tommy

Dear Friends,

I'm searching for my spiritual awakening that so far I've not been able to find, but my life has come to a point where I need to find myself before I'm lost in the terrible maze of unknowing.

Let me take a few minutes to tell you a little about myself and my present situation. Hopefully it will help you to know what it is I'm trying to find. I'm 27 years old, born Sept. 9, 1950. I'm presently in the Idaho State Prison for first-degree murder, two counts. I was sentenced to death in March 1976, but the Idaho Supreme Court vacated my death penalty. (Tommy's death penalty has been reinstated, and at this time (1985) he's back on death row.) *These two charges in Idaho aren't the only ones I have. There are seven more in other states. Please let me explain why I did these cold-blooded, without any mercy, killings.*

In April of 1974, eleven men entered my home in Portland, Oregon, raped my 17-year-old wife, who was three months pregnant at the time, then threw her four stories out our apartment window.

You see, I had been running drugs and guns for some people out of Nevada. My wife had asked me to stop so I tried to get out but they said no. On my next run I kept the goods I was to deliver and told them I'd turn it over to the feds if they tried causing me any trouble. I never would have, but they thought I was serious. Well, they set me up on a phony bust to get me out of the way thinking I had told my wife where I had stashed the stuff. I never did!

So, when they went to our house, after beating her and realizing she really didn't know where I put the stuff, they gang-raped her and threw her out the window. By some freak accident she lived for several months after that, long enough to tell me who most of the eleven were. She committed suicide while in a state mental institution, as her body was so crippled up from the fall, she had lost all hope and just wanted to die. In August of 1974, I went after the eleven guys who did it and caught nine of them in several different states. I was unable to complete my death mission and get the last two because I got caught here in Idaho.

Since all of this happened, I've had no inner peace at all. All I can think of is my wife, the only person who ever loved me and all I had in this world. I can see the men I killed and the look of pure fear and disbelief that I'd found them, as I took their lives. I'm not saying I was right for what I did, and I can't really say I'm sorry. I only know that I have no peace, happiness, or love, but at times I feel that I can have, but I just don't know where to look. I need help but I have nobody to turn to. My family has turned from me and I have nobody to write to or to visit me. I can't carry my burden alone anymore, so I ask you from the deepest of my heart, please send me any material that you think might help me. I am in maximum-

security, solitary confinement and have been for almost four years.

Really, all I want to do is find that something that I know for a fact exists that will free me from all my burdens. I would appreciate any correspondence that can help me find my way to a new and better life. Thank you for your time. Please reply!

Sincerely yours, Tommy/Idaho

Dear Tommy,

Your letter has touched me and Sita deeply. You're a beautiful brother and we're happy to know you. In one sense, you've got an unusual story; yet in another sense, you're in exactly the same place we all are: Simply a person who's waking up to the journey, and wondering what you can do to get on with it. As heavy and fierce as your own life has been, it's not the details so much that matter once we start this process of awakening.

It's true that every thought, word and deed counts. But it's also true that the journey is a much bigger one than most people imagine, spanning maybe millions of years rather than sixty or seventy. And in the course of all that time, it's possible that each one of us has to pass through the very gates of hell and madness like you, your wife, and her attackers did during the past few years.

I don't mean to imply that you should look back and feel good about it, but just to try to understand that no accidents happen in this universe. Even the most horrible experiences are still steps along the way. And the pain which may still lie before you from the karma of killing nine people – just more of the same: difficult, necessary steps on your path.

This understanding is the beginning of true faith. My faith first woke up when I was eighteen and I drove head on into a tractor-trailer at close to 100 mph. I was a bodybuilder at the time. My whole life was based on body-stuff, and suddenly I'd never be able to do any of that again. I had permanent injuries; I could bitch about them, but they were what they were regardless.

The same thing happened to me as is happening to you: I knew there had to be something, some way of looking at my life, that could open the door back up to the possibility of happiness. In your case, the "permanent injuries" are the fact that you'll probably never see the streets again in this lifetime. That's a fact you need to face in order to plan a strategy for your life.

A good first step is to begin quieting the mind, and this is what all our meditation materials are about. All the answers, all the guidance you ever need, is already within you, but the noisy mind can't figure out how to tune into it. What I mean by noise is stuff like desire, fear, guilt, self-pity, anger, hatred, pride, pettiness and so forth. The way most of us grow up, our lives are pretty much a confusing combination of such noise from the time we get up in the morning until we fall asleep exhausted each night. No wonder we're so tired!

But meditation practices, especially with the kind of time you're doing, can be your gateway into the deeper realities of life, the deeper parts of yourself which can help you go *through* your pain rather than trying in vain to go around it.

It's not going to be fun or easy. Meditation is always pretty hard, and when you may be opening into intense guilt or grief, it's harder still. The only thing harder would be to try to ignore it all, and live an empty life, feeling alone and isolated.

Besides meditation, I suggest you study a little about karma. *[Most of the section on karma in Book One was written as part of this letter to Tommy.]* Nothing too analytical, but just enough to understand that there is no such thing as "good" karma or "bad" karma. It's more a matter of facing whatever your karma is, and using it to become free.

Of course, all of this is much easier said than done, I know. I know you've been through terrible pain. I'm just trying to help, and I figure if I throw about a million words at you, maybe three or four will hit home. At least you can count on having a family again, bro. Much Light for your day,

Love, Bo

Dear Bo,

I just received your most beautiful and encouraging letter and I was so happy to hear from you. Thank you so very much!

I'm not always an emotional person as far as letting my feelings show, as my past lifestyle required that I never let nobody get close or at no time let anyone know what I was feeling at any time. But in these past few weeks since I first read **INSIDE-OUT**, *I've been becoming aware of myself and of other people more each day, and I've been experiencing feelings that I had all but forgotten. Then today when I got your letter and the books, something happened to me that I never would have dreamed possible.*

Since that first day I picked up a half-torn copy of INSIDE-OUT and began to read it, I felt that at last I had found what it was I had been looking for all my life. And something told me to write and find out more of what this had to offer me in my search for spiritual awakening. At first I was pretty skeptical because I had been through so many other trips, and had been let down so many times. But something kept telling me not to just read this to help pass the hours away but to read it and keep it in my heart and mind. So, each day I've been applying some of the things that I've read to my daily life, and I've been like a new person.

When I got your letter today, I noticed my hands were shaking as I was taking it out of the envelope. Well, as I started to read I felt a warmth come over me as I have never felt before, and a voice within stilled my fears and seemed to say that

at last you're coming home and you have no need to fear ever again. As I read on I noticed that I kept having trouble seeing and my face felt like it was on fire. So I reached up and started to rub my eyes and it was only then that I realized that I had tears in my eyes and running down my face. Then they came freely as I knelt to thank God for that little book and for you and all the others that are trying to bring the world together to live in harmony with each other and with God.

It has been a long time since I was able to let my heart open up and let myself really be free and feel again. What can I say except, I thank you and you have my undying gratitude and friendship. Not only because you have come into my life and touched me, for the many others that I know you have touched and helped to find that wonderful road to a new and better life, the only life! Thanks, Bo, for the letter and for sharing part of your life with me. May God give me the strength, faith and courage to continue on this journey that I have been fortunate enough to find. Now I'm happy again and it's been a long time, but it sure feels good....

I enclose a couple of poems for you and hope you enjoy them.
Please feel free to use my letters or poems in any way that you feel might help others. I'm not ashamed to tell the whole world that I have found a new life. I see a lot of changes in my life already from my daily meditation practice; it's working wonders, and I seem to be getting closer to people already.

With Love and respect, your friend and brother, Tommy

DEATH ON THE WIND

People kill things everyday,
  from love to idle time,
And some things die anyway,
  from life to idle minds.

It couldn't really hurt to die,
  no more than it hurts to live,
The people left always cry,
  when there's nothing left to give.

Death is just the final sleep,
  as dust to dirt we go,
In little piles, that dirt we sweep,
  and the wind outside still blows.

And the wind kills time itself,
  it eats away this earth,
And everything once known as wealth,
  the wind will turn to dirt.

To know death is to know the wind,
  That whispers through the trees,
And death is just another friend,
  Blowin' on the breeze.

Scum/Mike

Dear Bo,

I've been in such a state of confusion lately, looking for answers and continually drawing blanks. The administration here plays so many mind-games with us! They keep trying to provoke me into reverting back to my old ways, my violent ways, and it's really hard for me sometimes. I chose the path of meditation and yoga to overcome my violent nature, for I realized (somewhat late) that violence doesn't solve anything.

Before I was busted in 1976, I was a member of an outlaw motorcycle gang on the East Coast. I also served four years in the U.S. Marine Corps before that. I fought in Vietnam, Cambodia, and as a biker I fought in many gang wars on the streets of New Jersey. I am serving fifty-five years in prison for killing a man in a bar fight. When I arrived here I started studying my life, and realized that I never gained or proved a thing through violence.

I'm sure you know how rough life can be for someone who tries to be gentle and wise in prison. So many people mistake gentleness for weakness; and I am by no means weak, but I don't want to have to hurt someone to prove it. Every time someone in here tries to provoke me, I do my best to return their animosity with love, but man, IT'S REALLY HARD, you know? I try, I really try. But this place is so full of blind ignorance and prejudice, and it shouldn't be that way. Prejudice and ignorance make me angrier than anything else. I meditate and pray twice each day.... to erase prejudice and ignorance from the universe, to bring all of us closer together, that we may live in peace and harmony with each other.

Believe me, receiving letters from people who really care helps a lot. May you always walk in sunshine and peace.

Love, Scum/Colorado

Dear Scum,

Hang in there, bro; you're fighting in the biggest gang war of all, and you're on the right side and you're doing fine.

You said you've asked God for help in overcoming your violent nature. What you have to try to understand is that the whole environment you're complaining about *is* the help that God has sent you. Just think, if you can learn to rise above the anger and violence in the middle of where you are, is there any place on Earth you'd ever get back into it?

Every bit of prejudice and ignorance, every bit of harassment, is just part of your training. You asked for it, so *use* it to become a warrior of peace and true strength. How could you overcome your violent nature if you were in a place where everyone was cool and everything all right? Hell, anyone can be non-violent in a place like that.

I know it's tough, bro, I really do. But I believe in you and I know you can handle it. Maybe it's time you let go of the nickname "Scum" and began to see that you're really not the same person who earned that name. And you don't have to "act" gentle and wise; just *be yourself*—a person who is strong, who ain't gonna take shit, and is gentle and wise too. No conflicts. Being gentle doesn't mean letting people step all over you. Being wise doesn't mean you always know what to do or that you never make mistakes.

There's an old story about a cobra who goes to a saint and says "Please give me teachings so that I can be more spiritual." The saint says, "Well, first of all, don't bite people anymore." So the cobra goes back down the mountain, happy that the saint has accepted him as a student, and he sits by the village path all day long, thinking over the saint's advice. But after a couple of days, people begin to notice him, and since he's sitting so still and looks so happy, the people get curious. After a few more days, unafraid of the cobra by now, some of the children have started poking him with sticks and teasing him, throwing pebbles at him, kicking dirt on his head; and a few cruel adults, too, toss garbage on him and kick him when they walk by.

After about a week, the saint walks down the village path and sees the poor cobra sitting there all bruised and bloody and full of mud. The saint says, "My God, what's happened to you?" The cobra replies, "I was just following your instructions, master; I don't bite people anymore." Realizing all that had happened, the saint looks down lovingly at the cobra and says, "But I didn't tell you not to *hiss!*"

Prison's rough, so hiss if you have to; just keep love and prayer in your heart the whole time. You're right on the yellow line in the center of the road. You're doing fine, really.

I love you, Bo

Dear Bo,

I sincerely hope you don't mind me writing so often, but you're the only real friends I have.

I've made some progress since I last wrote you about my anger and violence; also you may notice how I signed this letter—"Mike", instead of Scum. I guess it's time to let a lot of the old stuff fall away. I've completely quit smoking marijuana, and I've cut my cigarette habit down from three packs a day to one.

Well, I've just about made up my mind as to where I'm going once I'm released from prison. I'm sure you know where the Yukon Territory is. I want to get as far away from "civilization" as possible. Away from cities, crowds, pollution, atomic reactors, and all other forms of manmade garbage. I've been doing a lot of research on organic farming, solar energy, wind power, water power, cabin building, etc. I want to grow my own food, raise a few horses, and live the way I believe God meant for us all to live; in harmony with nature. The only time I'm really happy and relaxed in the free world, is when I'm alone, or with someone who truly understands and cares for me, walking along deep in the forest, not saying anything, just listening and feeling nature. I miss being able to do that more than I miss anything else in the world.

I've always been a loner, I guess. Is it wrong to want to be alone, Bo?

I sure appreciate all your help and love. It's hard to explain, and I'm lousy with words, but it's like I feel something for you and Sita that I've never felt for anyone before. It's not just love, for it goes beyond mere love. It's like we're three different people, yet we're one. Whenever I think of you, I get this fantastic, warm feeling all over. It starts in my spiritual heart, and spreads to cover my entire body. Whenever I meditate, I try to absorb as much of God's love as I can, and at the same time I try to send that love, and mine, to the two of you. I wonder sometimes if my vibrations are strong enough to reach you out there in North Carolina.

May your days be filled with sunshine, and may you always walk in peace and love.

Baraka Bashad, Mike

Dear Mike (boy, that's a lot easier than "Dear Scum"!),

Yeah, your loving vibes come through loud and clear; we return the same. It's a nice feeling to know we've helped you to tap into that place of love in yourself that will now keep getting stronger forever, no matter what happens to us.

I'm pretty much a loner, too. I don't see anything wrong in it, but it sounds like there's a little more to your letter than that. If you're heading for the frozen tundra just because you haven't figured out how to be happy in the civilized world, then the Yukon is just a big, frozen prison, not the paradise you want it to be.

I can definitely feel what you're saying about not wanting to hit the streets and get back into all the old crap, but there's a whole other side of life than that, so don't assume your options are so limited. You've seen the worst sides of the human spirit, so it's made you want to run away from humanity.

But go back and re-read your own letter to me, about how Sita and I have helped you feel the "fantastic, warm feeling" of love in your heart. Imagine how good we feel when we read something like that! It reminds us of the very *best* sides of the human spirit, and inspires us to keep on truckin' along. Maybe instead of making tracks for the frozen tundra, you might consider some sort of service work so you too can tap into the higher end of the range of how we humans relate to each other.

Listen bro, you've still got a lot of time left before you need to decide where you're going to live. It's just natural that when you're in a place with bars, walls, and lots of noise, you find yourself dreaming about the wide open, quiet, empty tundra. But keep it light. Life is a lot more fun and interesting when you make your decisions based on what you want to find rather than what you want to hide from.

All my Love, Bo

"Come with me", said Hawk, and he walked to the edge of the camp with the boy. "Now look at the camp," Hawk instructed the boy. But Hawk had thrust his face almost within an inch of the boy's, and every time the boy moved his head to see around him, Hawk moved his own head to block him.

"Now lie down in that grass on your stomach," Hawk said, pointing to the ground. "Now look again at the camp." When the boy had done so, Hawk said, "Now get up and follow me," and he led the young man back to the center of the camp. "Look at the camp now," Hawk said, but as the boy began to turn around Hawk slapped him hard. The young man's face turned livid with rage.

"You are making a fool of me," the young man said through clenched teeth. Hawk swiftly drew his knife and held it to the boy's throat. "Turn around and look at the camp again," Hawk said, his face empty of expression. The boy turned slowly, looking everywhere for help.

"I was making no fool of you, little brother," Hawk said as the boy finished turning. "I love you deeply. I needed you angry, and I needed you afraid to make you understand. Here, you can have the knife."

Hawk sat down on the ground, and the boy sat limply beside him. "I do not understand," the boy said after recovering his balance. "What were you doing?"

"How did you feel when I kept you from seeing around my face?" asked Hawk. "Foolish!" answered the boy.

"And what did you see when I made you lie in the grass?" Hawk asked. "I could see little of the camp, because of the tall grass and because your feet were in my way," answered the boy.

"And when you were slapped?" asked Hawk. "I could not see the camp again because of my anger and fear," the boy answered.

"These are the problems that face men all the time, in everything they do. These are the difficulties they must overcome in trying to see both themselves and others," said Hawk.

"And the stories that are told to us by you and the other Teachers are meant to show us these things?" the boy asked. "Exactly", Hawk answered.

—edited from SEVEN ARROWS, by Hyemeyohsts Storm

David

Dear Mr. Lozoff,

I'm presently doing time in South Carolina. I found one of my friends reading your issue. He let me read some of it and I liked it. I'm very much into meditation right now, but I don't get off too good. I feel something is missing. I don't talk to too many people. I'm sort of locked in myself and I can't find a way out. I don't fight people, I'm sort of scared to and my mind won't let me. I'm really confused and need some help. If you are ever down this way please look me up.

Yours truly, David/S.C.

Dear David,

Nice to know you. You know, if you think about it for a minute, you weren't so "locked in yourself" when you wrote me this open, honest letter. You were upfront, not at all afraid, reaching out in friendship to somebody you've never even met. So maybe you're not so bad off as you think.

Don't push yourself too hard about talking with more people or anything like that; try to keep in mind that you're already in the process of some powerful changes, and it's going to take some time. Since you write about your feelings so well, it might be a good idea to keep a diary, or write to me or other friends—just to keep your head as open as it was when you wrote me. A lot of people keep a spiritual "journal" for years and years; it's a good idea.

About not "getting off" on meditation—It's not so important to get a rush or feel high. Just keep sitting still. Even though it feels like nothing's happening, I promise you it is. It's so gradual and natural that it's hard to notice; especially for those of us who are used to getting blasted on drugs or booze. Be patient. We're all really in the same boat, and doing the same thing.

Love, Bo

Charles

Dear Bo,

My sentence is 5-15 years for manslaughter. I received this sentence while on parole for second-degree murder for which I received a sentence of 3-20 years. In both cases, the victim was my common-law wife. The cause of death in each case was strangulation. I was under the impression that my love for these lovely persons was genuine, absolute, or sure thing. After stepping onto the path in myself, I discovered that this love was conditional, superficial—not even love at all. I am now in touch with my wrong thinking that led to their deaths.

However, there is not total peace within me. There is this burning urge to communicate with their families. Even if their families do not receive me with open arms and even if they want to kill me, I am willing to confront death just to communicate what I feel deep within me. It has taken me until now to free myself from guilt, sorrow, and other sufferings, but I am not totally free. Though I am aware that my freedom should not be dependent on something on the outside, I do feel that I must make this communication. None of these persons has heard from me in five years. This brings me to my first question: Should I contact these persons or leave the past alone?

I have three other questions: First, how do I know when I am seeing the world clearly? By this I mean without coloring it with my beliefs, prejudices, and opinions. Second, is there a time when I should separate myself from another being? I mean this in the physical sense. For example, if one of my brothers attacked another brother, should I see this as a predicament to facilitate my growth, or should I attempt to bring harmony into their midst? I could also choose not to see the circumstance at all. How can I view this without separation?

The third and final question is, how is it that the universe is unfolding as it should, and simultaneously, I am the creator of everything in my world? How can I be responsible for various incidents if the world is unfolding as it should? The fact that two people are dead because of me can be viewed as having created this for myself, but it can also be viewed as the world unfolding as it should. How do I see this clearly?

Peace and Love, Charles/Mass.

Dear Charles,

You ask some tough questions! The thing is, you're asking for answers when what you're really aching for is wisdom, which is really very different. Wisdom develops over a long period of time between you and God. There isn't just one answer to each of your questions, as if the spiritual life could be lived perfectly if you just think of all the right questions. The *true* spiritual life is a lot tougher and more creative than that. It requires opening up to our hearts and guts instead of just taking a bunch of philosophies into our minds. It's a lot more demanding, but it's the only way to real freedom.

For example, your letter makes it pretty clear that you haven't really gotten "free... from guilt, sorrow, and other sufferings" at all; quite the contrary. Notice the way you chose to describe what you've done: "I received this sentence"; "The victim was...my wife"; "cause of death...was strangulation"; and so forth. You're not yet able to put it all in the first-person and say "I killed two people!" What you're doing is a head-trip, yet what's aching is your heart.

The things we've done to hurt other people are powerful teachings for us. A feeling of shame might open up our deepest humility. Guilt might show us the need for self-control and taking responsibility for our actions. Feeling bad about someone else's pain—especially pain we've caused—might be what we need in order to feel how deeply connected we are to all other human beings. This is all very tricky, I know, and most psychologists and spiritual teachers seem to say that guilt and shame are uncool. But to me, the spiritual life runs the whole range of human feelings, not just the pleasant ones. Feeling and learning from these feelings doesn't mean we have to get lost in them or let them destroy us.

When I was sixteen I seriously injured a 12-year-old boy who was walking across a field where I was throwing a discus. It hit him right in the head, and as soon as they took him away to the hospital, I split and put it as far out of my mind as I could. But over fifteen years later, it started coming up every time I sat down to meditate. I tried to say, "Well, be here now" and all that, and let it go, but God wouldn't allow me to do that without opening up further.

When I finally did open up, I went straight through the middle of fifteen years worth of repressed guilt, shame, and fear in a few months' time. I really needed that; I really needed to grow up in that way.

It doesn't haunt me anymore, but it will certainly be in my memory all my life; no reason for it not to be. I did enough checking into old hospital records to find out that the boy didn't die, but I never could get his name (privacy act) or contact him directly. I guess he's doing all right without hearing from me; I have faith that these things happen as they need to.

Even when we deny it, we feel pain for pain we cause, and it's going to have to come out sometime. I learned that lesson the hard way, but that's over now. I think I was secretly afraid to feel just how bad that pain might feel, but now I see how much more compassion and tenderness I have as a result of finally letting my heart get torn apart. I don't think you've done that yet, bro. I really don't.

Yeah, the world is unfolding exactly as it should, *and* you are personally responsible for the terrible things you've done. Your mind tries to choose between the two as if they can't both be true at the same time. But the heart understands. Keep praying for guidance.

I love you, Bo

ps: About contacting the families, I'd wait awhile before thinking about that; it's going to take some time to sort this all out, and you wouldn't want to contact them unless you could help ease their pain in some way.

pps: Another prison friend, Salik, wanted to respond to your letter too. His letter follows:

Dear Bo,

If I could add a word to brother Charles about guilt, sorrow and suffering over murder from the same space he occupies: I too suffer for like reasons. I pray that my guilt and pain not harden my heart, but lead me on the path. I feel the pain will never leave, but I know it is a clear connection of love to the person whose life I took.

I choose to feel the pain and guilt straight rather than hide from it, for when I hide I become irritable and judgemental.

When I feel the guilt and pain, it subsides when I open to it long enough. At first it was weeks of deep pain, then a few hours a day, and now an hour or two every few days.

This guilt and pain has also made me more sensitive to my brothers—their pains, forgiving their slights, seeing without judgement. I wish that I had learned these things another way, but—after the fact—without justifying what I did, I learned them this way.

I believe you can only understand your capacity for tenderness when you understand your capacity for violence.

In my situation, I chose not to contact the ones close to my victim, for it would only hurt them more. But every situation is different.

Flow like the river and be clean, Salik/Ca.

To be really sorry for one's errors
is like opening the door of Heaven.

—Hazrat Inayat Khan

Larry

Dear Bo,

Sorry I have not written you sooner, but things have been pretty hectic here at the prison. We had a massive shakedown and threw away some of my religious books, such as, BHAGAVAD GITA, TEACHINGS OF BUDDHA, and THE TEACHINGS OF LORD CHAITANYA. I told the guards they were religious books, but was told that I still couldn't have them.

I realize that I should love everyone, no matter who it is; but I can't find it in my heart to love the guards here, or even like them. Would you please give me some advice, because I really would like to love everyone.

Much Love, Larry/Indiana

Dear Larry,

Don't feel like the Lone Ranger, bro. Learning how to love everybody is the ultimate spiritual struggle for all of us. Don't be hard on yourself, but don't give up the effort either, because you're heading in the right direction. In fact, isn't your desire to love them actually a kind of love already? There's something you feel inside that's making all your anger and bitterness unsatisfactory to you. That's love. Just let it keep growing. Maybe you're looking far and wide for an idea of love or what love is supposed to feel like when in truth, Love is already beginning to seep into your bones. Love may not feel as mushy or emotional as your mind has made you expect. Sometimes it's low-key—simply wishing people well on their journeys, or just knowing that everyone's going through what they need to go through. Don't look too hard for what it "should" be; just try to have faith that it's happening. It really is, I swear.

Remember that the guards took sheets of paper from you; nothing else. The holy books are no more than scraps of paper. Maybe it's God's way of helping you to realize that the books aren't as important as loving the guards.

Much Love, Bo

Do not let the ways of the world dismay your heart, being a warrior.

—Ramayana

Mark

Dear Bo,

I've been wanting to write this letter for a long time. I've been in prison for going on six years, of which four years has been spent becoming aware of myself. I feel as tho I can grasp a position in life. I feel as if I really don't belong here. Sometimes I have a lot of energy—and I want to get this energy into something positive, like telling a stranger that I love them. But I never do and the energy comes out in frustration.

I've studied many different paths, and have gained from all of them. But still I can't place myself in one securely! It's almost like having something wrong with me. I find myself with very little motivation and entrapment in laziness. I work with a lot of the inmates on the compound, helping them with their own problems, when really I can't solve my own. I find letting go of personal desires very difficult. I find little things in life are the most things that upset me! Maybe it is lack of self-control? Maybe it is lack of the Light? Maybe it's that I don't want to get in-volved in the egotistical world around me? I feel sometimes I should close off the world around!

What I really need is some firm basis to start going positive from. Do you have any ideals that would help? I realize you have a lot of people writing to you, but I appreciate it if you could answer me. Give Sita and all, my love and light.

Thank you, Mark/Florida

Dear Mark,

There's nothing "wrong" with you. Everything you describe sounds like the standard spiritual problems we all have to go through: Studying a lot of paths but not taking one all the way; helping others more easily than we help ourselves; lack of motivation, etc. It's always been easier to talk and think about the journey than travel it. So welcome to the club.

I do see a problem that you may not be recognizing: you say you "really don't belong here". I surely agree that you're not a wicked person, if that's what you mean, but don't we all *belong* exactly where we find ourselves? It may change tomorrow, or even the very next minute, but right now, you and I are acting our parts in exactly the right scene, setting, line and cue. Where else is there to be? If you feel like you're in the wrong place, then what good are all your practices going to do? They all get down to starting right where you are.

Patience is also important. You know how patient you try to be with other people? Well, you have to be that way with yourself as well. It's good that you're getting fed up with laziness and being scattered, but you want to make sure that you don't get so heavy that you lose the sense of humor you'll need to take you through the hard times. There's nothing more boring or dangerous than a humorless fanatic, of *any* persuasion.

152

There's already a process of awakening happening in your life, and it's really beautiful; try to appreciate it. Look at how you were ten years ago; hasn't a lot of wisdom begun to sink in since then?

Of course, your dissatisfaction is part of that process too; that's what pushes you further, pushes you to work harder. So appreciate the griping and grumbling, but don't beat yourself up too much over it. Let your discontent turn you toward some spiritual disciplines like meditation, breathing, prayer, etc. Then it'll have a good purpose.

Everything I'm saying could fall under what the Buddha called "Right Effort". You might want to chew on that phrase every now and then to keep yourself balanced between laziness and guilt. The journey does indeed take effort, but it's never like we've "fallen behind" or anything like that.

Love, Bo

Dear Bo,

Thank you so much for being you, and for being a part of me! I wish I could express the oneness I felt after reading your letter—if only the entire planet could have the same awareness.

The night when my last letter was written I was feeling a complete impact of change. Since then it's been a little hilly and I guess it will be for awhile longer—so I'm just more or less flowing and growing.

I have been in prison for six years and this place has had a big hand in my direction, now though I am thinking about getting out and how much change will be opened up into me.

My room partner and brother on the pathway has only been in for almost two years, and him and I sit and talk of the past and the streets. I don't let such talks get me down, but it does bring about desire.

I was sixteen when I was incarcerated, at 17 I was sent to the Rock, so you can probably see the changes I went through. Anyway, all my attention was solely in and on prison, and the streets was left somewhere out in left field.

Now though, I am beginning to feel and see them, it's joyfull, because of the new sense it brings about. Well anyway, I know I have a few blocks inside and a few more changes to go through, and I really want to say that it's wonderful to realize that God has set before me others who have already passed the changes (like mine) and are there to help.

Thank you and God bless everyone,

Light and Love, Mark
Love to all!

Terry

Hi Bo and Sita,

I hope this letter finds you both doing well. I don't know if you remember me or not from when you were here around Christmas, at Metro Prison. I'm the blonde-headed dude who told you I used to hang around your head shop in Atlanta in the '60's. Anyway, I didn't write you to discuss that, but my present position as far as my head goes.

I have a problem of dealing with the everyday crap of these pigs here, if you want to call them that or not. I try to ignore it, but these situations arise and sometimes it's hard to deal with it.

Anyway, I still think a bunch of you both and want your advice as to how to shut out or deal with the people and situations you don't like. I discharge from here next year and really want to get back with nature and the good karma of brotherhood with all.

I thank you both for bearing with me. Keep in the Spirit and keep me in mind when you are meditating.

Keeping the Spirit, Terry/Ga.

Dear Terry,

Sure we remember you, even when you were fourteen and hung around our shop. Wild days, weren't they?

I understand your problem about dealing with the guards and all the hassle of prison life. The thing is, you have to try to *see* the whole thing clearly: When you "hate the pigs", you lose your real power; it's as simple as that.

The more power you lose, the worse you feel. The worse you feel, the more you hate yourself. But since you don't like to admit you hate yourself, it's easier to look around and spend your hatred on the guards. So then you hate them even more, which takes away *more* power, which makes you feel even worse, which makes you hate yourself even more and it could go on 'til you're six feet under, bro. That's not the way of the "free Spirit" that you want to be. It's more like a puppet on a string.

Well, you asked for my advice, so that's about it. You and I go back a long way, and you know that I understand everything you're saying about where you really want to be. Try to trust me when I tell you that the shortest way there is to begin right where you are, letting go of anger, bitterness, and hatred every time they begin to take over your brain. You don't have to wait a year before you begin to feel free, I promise.

Love, Bo

PJ

Dear Bo,

I have a question: I know that total love is a part of the path. But being in prison and being small and white—I've become prejudiced against blacks. It takes a lot just to tolerate them, and being in such close quarters with 'em, not all, but a large percentage act like animals, and trying to feel total love is considered feminine and weak—ya hafta wear a hard steel armor and hard act—I've been locked up 30 months now and still find it hard to be around these blacks. In feeling this racial hatred, will it interfere with my path? I'm also afraid that this total mistrust will carry over into the streets. Have you any advice?

In Divine Love, PJ/Ohio

Dear PJ,

Real Love is neither weak nor feminine; it's the strongest power there is. But you don't necessarily have to be walking around the joint hugging blacks and saying "hello brother" in order to be feeling love. If you stay open in each situation, in each *moment*, then other people who are open will gradually drift your way—people of any color. And you'll also be able to sense when others *aren't* open; in other words, your own honest clarity will guide you to stay clear of blacks and whites alike who are so stuck that they're dangerous.

Your observation that "a large percentage act like animals" could just as well be said about white inmates, couldn't it? If you think about how temporary these bodies are, it feels pretty ridiculous to separate people by their color. Don't give in to what you know is wrong. Bigotry robs you of your human dignity and wisdom. Keep resisting, bro.

Rainbow Love, Bo

Leonard

Dear Ashram,

I want to thank you very much for all the literature you have sent me. It has opened my soul to the truth. But I am having a very difficult time coping with it. Let me clarify this: I'm in the prison section labeled "D Quad", which is for mentally ill convicts.

The reason I was put here was because I have psychological problems. And these are depressive moods and hyper-active behavior. These, I'm sure, are caused by a disease called hypoglycemia. Which is in turn generated by a lack of proper vitamins and a poor diet. The reason I say that, is because on the outside I had the same problems years ago and cured them with a mega-vitamin intake program and a proper, low-carbohydrate/high protein diet.

I have seeked help from the prison's medical authorities, but they failed to recognize the problem, due to the fact that it is a fairly new disease and not much is presently known about it. For me, it's no picnic. It's a lot of daily suffering. Your literature has help me some, but I'm still having problems. And these make it hard for me to concentrate, in turn making it hard for meditation and true prayer. Therefore slowing me down, to a point of near idle, on the spiritual path towards God.

I'm also having a hard time understanding some spiritual truths. I read a book entitled THE MYSTERY OF DEATH, by Kirpal Singh. It talked about different planes that we pass through after our departure from the physical realm. Then lately I read a book entitled SEARCH FOR THE TRUTH, by Ruth Montgomery. That talked about communication with disembodied spirits, and I noticed a striking resemblance between Singh's description of these planes and the description of the same planes by souls who were already there, talking through Mrs. Montgomery, using automatic writing. I knew then and still know now beyond a shadow of a doubt, that those planes are real.

Here comes the problem. Singh's book talked about different spiritual realities (some of them very unpleasant) for people who had different realities in the physical realm. And reading Mrs. Montgomery's book confirmed it. Here we are, the scum of the earth, killers, thieves, and psychomaniacs. Are we doomed to eternal punishment and suffering? Because according to the passed-away souls, we have blasphemed to God and deserve eternal retribution.

This makes me feel very guilty. And I don't think this is fair at all. Because I see here in prison poor souls that can't even situate themselves in this physical reality because, let me explain it in another way, their minds are ill in various degrees. So how can they be accounted for their actions? And I believe very strongly in today's psychologists saying that what you become in later years in life depends very much on how you were brought up and the experiences you had at an early stage of life. Plus nutrition, I know for a fact, has something to do with your behavior. I'm a living proof.

So how can we be blamed totally for our actions, hardly being responsible for them? If God is love, then how can he judge us when he tells us to love others and not judge them? If only God could heal me physically, I wouldn't have this depressive and hyperactive behavior. I could do so much more for him by loving others at a much higher level.

*Now let me talk to you about the subject of suicide, which is something I have contemplated from time to time and still do. From what I read—and I'd like you to clarify it for me—let me quote, from Mrs. Montgomery's book, SEARCH FOR TRUTH, "Now, as to those who take their own lives without destroying others; through God's infinite sympathy they **may sometimes** purge their souls of this horrible blasphemy against God, but the way is dark and long." Now why should I go through this (if I take my own life, that is) not having been equipped with the same tools as others to face this earthly life, therefore not having the same chance, as some of us unfortunate souls don't as everybody else?*

I would appreciate very much if you could pray for me. As I'm in desperate need of prayers or any other help I could get. Thank you from all of my soul for whatever help you might give me. I hope to hear from you soon.

In God's Love, Leonard

Dear Leonard,

You ask a lot of deep questions. I'm not sure how much good I can do with words, because I think a lot of what's messing you up is that you read too many words. The line of your letter that stopped me cold, though, was when you said "in turn making it very hard for...true prayer." Leonard, "true prayer" happens from *exactly* the state of mind you've described—the worst, the lowest, the most desperate you could possibly feel.

I think the first time I discovered true prayer was a few years ago when I found myself lying face down on the floor with absolutely no faith left in all the yoga, all the methods, I had ever learned. It all seemed empty, just a bunch of bullshit. I was lying there and I couldn't even move, because I just didn't have any power left at all. I found myself *begging* God for help; I didn't even realize I was "praying". I wasn't praying like I had always thought prayer was supposed to be—I was flat out on my face, begging God to have mercy on me and help me in some way. And then it dawned on me that I had finally discovered *true* prayer. And that was the answer to my prayer.

It sounds to me like maybe your very best time is at hand, because you're getting right down to the bottom. Try to have more faith in the whole process, instead of feeling like your situation is the product of so many "accidents" of nature or the way you were raised or the illnesses you have, etc. All those things count, sure, but none of them are accidental. Nobody has it easier by virtue of "luck", which is what your letter implies. We all deal with the things we really need to deal with, and God knows about every problem we face—*and* their causes. Remember the line in the Bible—*He marks the sparrow's fall.* God hasn't forgotten about you while everyone else is on the high road to enlightenment; you're right in the thick of it, as much as me and Sita.

About the practical things—I would say to talk with your caseworker about hypoglycemia, and tell him that you either want to sue the state for proper treatment, or you want another diagnosis. But meanwhile, on your own you can do whatever you can to cut out the sugary and starchy foods and cigarettes, coffee, etc. Do some stretching and breathing exercises too. Our newsletters are full of practical techniques that'll help you settle down as well as possible.

Neither Kirpal Singh nor Ruth Montgomery knows exactly what would happen if you were to commit suicide, murder, or anything else; that's between you and God. Lighten up on your head trips and remember that Jesus talked about the peace "which *surpasses* understanding."

I think your desire for suicide is really your desire for freedom. And in that desire, you're joined by me and everyone else in the world. I know that you hurt a lot right now and you'd just like it all to end, but try to hold on for the right kind of relief, which suicide probably isn't. All suicide does is get rid of the body. What happens to all the pain in your mind? You're still going to have to deal with it in some form or other. Believe me, true relief is no farther away than your own heart; you don't have to wait for a thing. All my love, Bo

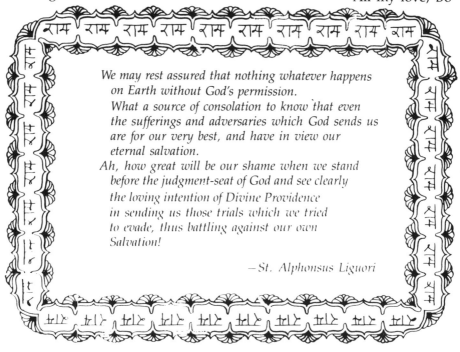

We may rest assured that nothing whatever happens
on Earth without God's permission.
What a source of consolation to know that even
the sufferings and adversaries which God sends us
are for our very best, and have in view our
eternal salvation.
Ah, how great will be our shame when we stand
before the judgment-seat of God and see clearly
the loving intention of Divine Providence
in sending us those trials which we tried
to evade, thus battling against our own
Salvation!

—St. Alphonsus Liguori

Billy

Dear Bo,

Hi. May God bless all of you lovely human beings at Prison-Ashram. I was transferred from Avon Park here to "The Rock" at Raiford for possession of a .22-caliber bullet and a matchbox of reefer. Needless to say, I was aware of reefer in my cell—but the bullet was not mine or my cell-partner's and I didn't know it was in my cell or I would've flushed it where things like that belong.

So, I am dead-locked in a cell 24 hours a day and come out only for a 3-minute shower 3 times a week. Every time they open the door they handcuff you behind your back and escort you to wherever you are going, blah blah blah; you know the drill, I'm sure! At any rate— how beautiful a monastery this is. I have a cell partner if I feel like talking, and 24 hours a day to read, meditate, yoga, or jerk off!

*The book on Gandhi the Man had the tears just rolling down my face as he was such a beautiful human being— so much what most of us would like to be. I only wish I had that kind of **real** courage and heart and love. But like most violent people I am a coward and my fear causes me to act like an animal—if someone frightens me I get so angry I would kill them. I'm a real mess of a human being and I have stabbed people and set people on fire—and God, do I feel like a piece of shit!*

I did not know what or why I was doing all those things for so many years, and that is my only excuse—I was blind and deathly afraid. After over 20 years of bars and walls I am becoming aware of what real freedom is. I feel more free right now than I ever did in society, and I do have a measure of peace for the first time in my life. I thank God and the AA and NA programs for that.

I do hope you have time to write, as I really love hearing from you. "May you be in heaven a half-hour before the devil knows you're dead."

Love, Billy Bananas/Fla.

Dear Billy,

Nice to hear from you. You know, you said that you were a coward and a real piece of shit, but if that's so, then who was the sensitive, intelligent human being who was moved to tears by the story of Gandhi's courage? That takes a lot of courage and openness, too, you know.

I can see feeling bad about a lot of things you've done, but watch out you don't limit yourself *now* by a bunch of harsh self-definitions that don't really fit anymore. The most inspiring thing about Gandhi was his total humility, which means that he would see you (as I do) as somebody who has the very highest *and* the very lowest within him, just like the rest of us.

Many "nice" people on the streets might think they could never stab anyone or set anybody on fire, but you know better than that, don't you? You know about that terrible side of us all, the part of us that can do unspeakably cruel, perverted things. *So did Gandhi*, Bill. And so did Christ and every other saint. That's why we can feel such incredible love from them—because they know it all, and they still love us.

You obviously have no problem in accepting the down-side of your own human nature. But what about the up-side? The fact that the very *highest* in Gandhi or Christ is also in Billy Bananas, sitting on a cot in Raiford?

A lot of convicts think that people like me and Sita are somehow more in the "center" of the spiritual journey than they are. But nothing could be further from the truth. Your past, your struggle against your demons, are the real battles along your path. The way you work with your life is very important for people like me and Sita to learn from. So don't feel like you're on the outer edges or that you're not really in the club; you're sitting square in the middle of your journey, and you can go all the way even in 24-hour lockup. All the best, bro,

Love, Bo

Dear Bo,

Received your thoughtful and kind letter, and all I can say is WOW! It really feels good to have a letter like that from really beautiful people. I think I can learn a lot from you and perhaps help you on your journey.

*At any rate, I am no longer in confinement, but in the N.P. annex which is the "bug ward", and they have me on heavy doses of medication, so if this letter is sloppy or incoherent, you know why. I'm not in a position to refuse the medication as I have been on anti-psychotic, anti-depressant meds **every day** since 1973 and I've developed a complete dependance on these drugs; can't sleep or relax without them; or at least that's my excuse.*

After over 20 years of confinement, I have read quite a few books, to put it mildly! The books that have done the most for my head so far are Alan Watts, Kahlil Gibran, Steinbeck, Hemingway, John O'Hara, Albert Camus, Hermann Hesse (especially SIDDHARTHA), Jean Genet, Franz Fanon, Voltaire, Plato, Socrates, Shakespeare, and I could go on and on for at least six or seven pages. I'm sure you realize mine has been a shotgun approach rather than a disciplined, guided journey. I'd appreciate any guidance you can give me along these lines to progress.

Needless to say, although I read, enjoyed, and intellectually agreed with the ideas expressed in these books, they did very little to "reform my character" so to speak. By the way, my nickname "Billy Bananas" I got from the mobsters in Atlanta Federal Pen, and I have the reputation of being very dangerous and very crazy. I'd like to get away from that type of thinking and action, as it only feeds the irresponsible part of my nature and ego. I also am known by my friends as a loyal and trustworthy person. I stand by my word and try to always mean what I say and say what I mean.

Of course, being a criminal by choice and inclination, I am very fragmented in my personality and can do two completely contradicting actions within the space

160

of a few minutes, and be sincere in both of them 100%. This is why most people regard people like me as "phonies" when in reality we can be quite sincere but totally inconsistent. I am sure you're aware by now that the average person in prison thinks he owns the world (and owns you too if you write to them) etc. etc., ad nauseum. I don't play those games, as I'm aware of a manipulation part of my own personality. So what it boils down to is, that I will attempt to be honest with you down the line and will try not to impose on you. This is new for me, but I am trying, and that is better than the barrage of bullshit I used for dealing with the world for 36 years.

I must admit I am high right now on the stimulation your letter gave me, as I have only spent 12 months in society in the past 11 years, and my mind has stagnated because it is hard to find a decent conversation in places like this—and I really try not to get off into "war stories", as the blend of fact and fiction in them is very evident and rather boring, and I am just as much of a liar as the rest of the people here.

You think I'm hard on myself, but that isn't true at all; I'm a very self-serving person and am sick of the games I have played my whole life. I have to maintain a constant vigilance and do a moral inventory every day, as if I open the door even a crack, the whole smear comes jumping out in a short time.

Well, I'll close for now and say with all my heart, "God bless you and yours."

Peace, love, light, Bill

Dear Bill,

I think you're doing great. I'm not trying to say you should let yourself run wild or apply for saint-of-the-year yet; just don't get too solid about how bad you are, how quickly you'd "jump out" if you opened the door, and so forth. People really do change, you know, all the way down to the bones. All I'm saying is to be open for that kind of change, instead of defining a world in which you're only all right so long as you keep a tight leash on your evil self. That's my only complaint about groups like AA and NA; they seem to reinforce an attitude that you'll always be weak in certain ways. I don't buy it.

You've read about fifty times as many books as I have, so I'm not sure of what "guidance" you're asking me for. I think it might be a good idea not to keep reading so much, though.
What good does it do to read calculus if you haven't mastered arithmetic? You've already read thousands of years' worth of wisdom from all over the world, and if you think about it for a minute, you'll realize that the bottom line is always the same: *Do* it, don't just read about it.

For example, maybe it's time you gave serious thought to a practical plan for getting off drugs—all drugs, legal or not. Talk to your caseworker or psychologist about cutting down and maybe using yoga or meditation to help keep you stay cool while you're doing it. I'd be glad to write a letter or talk to them if that would help.

You get an "A" for self-honesty, which is very important; you're good at looking at your thoughts and motivations. But you're not looking deep enough or high enough. You're not taking *personally* all the stuff you've read. SIDDHARTHA is about *you*, Bill. All the books are. You can do it; you don't just have to read, talk, and write about it. You can change. You just have to get out of your head a little; start paying more attention to each moment as it comes and goes. Look at the sky for awhile, and don't daydream while you do it. Watch a roach crawl across the floor, notice in tiny detail everything he does, the way he moves. Listen to the sounds of the joint as you sit in your cell. Pay attention. Use more of your senses than the mind. It'll take self-discipline at first, but the rewards will be obvious as time goes by.

The journey is a great adventure, and I think you're at a big crossroads right now, if you want to take it. I started to write "Think about it", and then realized that's exactly what you shouldn't do. You already do quite enough thinking. Just dive in.

Much Love, Bo

Dear Bo,

Will attempt to get a psychologist interested in a program of what you suggested to replace the drugs; will let you know.

*For grow I must, as change is the one constant in the universe and I feel like I'm on a journey that has its rewards; and it may very well be that those rewards are the journey itself! For I believe that happiness cannot be obtained by seeking but is a by-product of living the right kind of life. And my definition of the "right kind" of life is doing what **you** believe God would have you do.*

The humorous and wonderful thing I am discovering is that all the disciplines I am studying—AA and NA, the Bible, psychology, yoga, philosophy—are all saying the same thing in different ways. I am recognizing the same signposts and key principles in so many things I read or meditate upon and I find that very exciting and gratifying. Truly, this quest for truth is the most satisfying and rewarding action I have ever undertaken, and I get so much higher than I did with 20 years of drug usage. I get better rushes chanting and doing yoga and meditating than I ever did injecting drugs.

I don't regret any of my past life except for the people I hurt and the needless pain I caused; but it was all necessary for me to reach this point. It has helped me understand my proper relationship to other human beings and my creator. I think you know what I'm trying to say.

I want you to know that you and Sita are in my heart and mind a lot more than just when I write, and my prayers are going forth for you and all who are on the path.

Peace and Love, Bill

Terry

Dear Bo,

I am incarcerated at this moment. I am a white male, 22 and single. I've been reading your book, INSIDE-OUT.

Well, I have a problem that really gets out of hand at times and I think of killing someone. And I would if I could get to them. But if I could overpower this problem, then I'm sure I wouldn't think of harming anyone.

I'd like to be rid of this problem before I get out, 'cause if I'm not, I may hurt people, even my own family. I really would appreciate your help and advice very much. I hope to hear from you soon!

Thank you, Terry/Ga.

Dear Terry,

I'm sure it must be scary to feel such an overpowering urge to kill someone when you really don't want to hurt people at all. Try to remember: **no matter what feelings pass through you, you can control your actions**. An urge may be heavy, fierce, powerful—but it's still just an urge. Take courage and start psyching yourself up to beat this thing with your own spiritual power, which is far greater than whatever force the urge is made up of. You can develop the kind of self-control which would allow you to be standing an inch away from a person you want to kill, and not lift a finger.

These feelings don't "belong" to you anymore than a sneeze or a cough. For a bunch of complicated psychological reasons, the urge to kill comes through your mind now and then. With it comes a big, ugly *fear* which is even worse than the urge itself. Fear says "Look at this, look at this! You're going to lose control and kill somebody and fuck up the rest of your life!!" The fear screams "You're a bad person! You're a pervert!" and all sorts of things. And you listen to the fear, and you feel this terrible urge, and you think, "Well, I guess it's true; "I *am* a bad person; I *am* crazy."

But these feelings are a part of *all* human nature, just like kindness and courage. Remember that Jesus said *"Resist not evil"*? This is what he was talking about. By "resist not", He meant not to give those forces such power and importance by freaking out over them. Instead, learn how to sit still (meditation), stand strong (self-control), and face everything squarely. Let the urge to kill come up in your mind, screech and howl and threaten, and don't even blink your eyes; don't lose a night's sleep.

It would help a lot to begin daily meditation practice—just sitting for a half-hour or so, perfectly still, focusing all your attention on the breath going in and out. While you're doing that, what will happen is that you'll begin to notice a lot of the thoughts that go through your mind. Some of those thoughts might help you to understand why you get the urge to kill.

Sometimes the most perverted, ugly, or evil thoughts imaginable might come up while you're meditating. Resist not evil; just sit perfectly still and watch them come and go, even if you feel terrified or like you're losing your mind. Meditation can get very heavy or weird, and you need to develop the self-control to stick it out.

It may help to think, "This too shall pass; this too shall pass; this too shall pass..." when things get really scary.

But don't move or get up!

Keep in touch, Terry, and trust yourself. Remember that fear is a demon; it's never really the wise voice of caution it pretends to be. And when you've tackled all this garbage and come through it, then you'll be able to help somebody else who's in trouble. Life is a difficult school with powerful lessons, but try to remember that these are indeed lessons, and you're in the middle of a wonderful education, not a meaningless nightmare.

Love, Bo

When God's Divine Love rises as a wave, it washes away the sins of a whole life in a moment, for law has no power to stand before Love; the stream of Life sweeps it away.

—Hazrat Inayat Khan

Lloyd

Dear Bo,

I hope this letter finds you exceptionally fine. A lot has happened in my life since I last wrote you. I decided to cut my own foot to get into the hospital. When I cut it I went in at the bottom of my foot in which now I'll never be able to run again.

Also I got hooked up on a "battery on another inmate" charge. This dude who was involved in the death of my partner came here, and I couldn't back off from trying to take him out after I heard him bragging about it. I took an iron leg off of a chair and walked up behind him while he was playing cards and tried to knock his brains out, but it only knocked him out and put him in a coma. I was locked up and now am on maximum-security lockdown.

I don't have any regrets at trying to kill him and even if he died and I received a life sentence, I still would not regret it. I know you feel I'm wrong, but I respected my partner and I's friendship to the extent that I felt what I did had to be done. I'm old-fashioned when it comes to values and morals and living by the convict code, but that's me, and I've never claimed to be anyone but.

In eternal friendship, Lloyd/La.

Dear Lloyd,

I hope you meant it about "eternal friendship", because I'm going to be straight with you. Sounds like you're snowing yourself, my friend. You're picking an argument with me over what you did, when I haven't judged you in the first place. I think you're arguing with yourself, and laying it off on me.

I'll play along; I'll answer as that part of yourself that wants to argue about what you did. You talk about the convict code, but that's bullshit. There's a higher code that we all answer to, and it says that when we purposely bring more suffering into the world, our own lives will suffer as well. The guy you offed brought suffering to your partner. Now you've brought suffering to him. Next maybe a friend of his will hear about it and come looking for you. And then a friend of yours.... You know, with good "old-fashioned" convicts like you around, the state hardly needs the death penalty!

You knew what this letter would be like before I wrote it, because it's coming from the part of you that has been hip to the stuff we've been sending you through the years. I appreciate how much it hurts to feel the death of a friend, and especially to hear someone bragging about it. And I'm not even saying you shouldn't have done what you did. All I'm saying is cut the shit, and face up to exactly what it was: A self-destructive, spiritually uncool act that came out of attachment and anger. It had nothing to do with living up to codes or moral values.

In view of what you did to your own foot, too, it's got to be getting obvious that you're way out of tune with your own happiness right now. So stop making excuses and inventing philosophies, and start thinking about whatever you need to do to come back into the center of the picture. Since you're in the hole now, maybe you can use some of this time to pray for help, and get back into meditation and that sort of thing.

You can't undo anything you've done; none of us can. But you *can* start taking honest control of your life again and open yourself up to the deeper, higher realities which can help you get your head straight. Life is really much bigger than you've been allowing yourself to experience. Did you think all this spiritual stuff is just a bunch of poetic words and high-sounding nonsense? It's a lot more real and powerful than the convict code!

Come on back, bro, Bo

A young Samurai warrior stood respectfully before the aged Zen master and said, "Master, teach me about Heaven and Hell." The master snapped his head up in disgust and said, "Teach *you* about Heaven and Hell?! Why, I doubt that you could even learn to keep your own sword from rusting! You ignorant fool! How dare you suppose that you could understand anything *I* might have to say?"

The old man went on and on, becoming even more insulting, while the young swordsman's surprise turned first to confusion and then to hot anger, rising by the moment. Master or no master, who can insult a Samurai and live?

At last, with teeth clenched and blood nearly boiling in fury, the warrior blindly drew his sword and prepared to end the old man's sharp tongue and life all in one furious stroke. But at that very moment the master looked straight into his eyes and said gently, "That's Hell."

Even at the peak of his rage, the Samurai realized that the master had indeed given him the teaching he had asked for. He had hounded him into a living Hell, driven by uncontrolled anger and ego.

The young man, deeply humbled, sheathed his sword and bowed low in awe to this great spiritual teacher. Looking up into the master's ancient, smiling face, he felt more love and compassion than he had ever felt in all his life—and at that point the master raised his index finger and said kindly, "And *that's* Heaven."

—an old story

Dear Bo and Sita,

I hope that this letter finds you both well! Your philosophy has touched me deeply, thus this letter to you. Since my first writing to you a good while back, I have been going over all of the newsletters that you have sent me. I have found that there are some truly good and kind people in this world, who care about others.

Prior to reading the newsletter, I was under the opinion, "that it is everyone for themself," and I was one who was going to get mine, no matter what the cost to me or others, I just did not care. But I now see that my opinion was a dead-end street, and I just about travelled the length of it! I thank you for opening my eyes, and I hope to hear from you again.

In friendship, John

Dear Bo,

Two days ago (Sunday) I found myself in a situation that has become increasingly present in this penitentiary: Racial prejudice. Except in here it is reversed, as whites are in the minority, about a 70/30% ratio.

To make a long story short, the drama finally evolved to the only credible answer in here — violence. Picture this drama, I'm standing in a large crowd, ready to do battle, when the flashing thought went through my mind, "Why am I getting ready to fight?" "I'm not going to fight just to feed these people's egos!" So I just turned around and walked off.

But, in the realm of things, people who are non-violent are looked upon with suspicion. So I am now sitting in a cell for administrative protective custody. But my here and now is content. God, in His infinite wisdom, knew I needed this space to get back to the journey. I have all my books, and am starting the inward search through meditation once again.

What is so beautiful, and a new experience for me, is that I'm not plagued with needless fears and worries. What will be will be, and I can only deal with the now. The journey continues, ceaselessly.

I love you, George/Virginia

He rejoices more over finding

that one lost sheep,

Than of the ninety-and-nine

that went not astray.

2. The One and Ninety-Nine

Ray Neal is one of my very favorite people. At one time one of the most feared cons in the American prison system, Ray was one of the few remaining cons at Alcatraz when it was finally shut down. He had also done time at Leavenworth, Atlanta, Huntsville, and other tough places. By his estimate, he had robbed more than thirty banks in his day, and had been caught for only a few of them.

But now it seems Ray has passed through the eye of that needle; he's let go of the bitter, self-destructive convict within him, and taken responsibility for a whole new life. In the best sense, Ray has allowed himself to be "born again" in mid-life, and he's enjoying himself like a kid at Christmas.

Sita and I first met Ray in 1976, at the Federal Prison in Butner, N.C. He was 40 and had been on the streets only a few months during the past eighteen years. The first day I showed up to teach a twice-weekly meditation class, the associate warden pulled me into his office and said "Listen Bo, I don't usually talk to teachers about the men in their classes, but there's one inmate who signed up for your class that I think you should know about. His name is Ray Neal, and he's the kind of convict who could put out the word on somebody in a prison across the country, and that man would be killed just as a favor. He's in close-custody, which is tighter than maximum. I'm not sure why he signed up for your class, but I think you'd probably be better off if I pulled him out. The decision's up to you."

I declined the offer. In fact, since I had no idea what Ray looked like, I was curious to see whether I could spot this vicious desperado in the class. I found my way to the basement of the education building and sat quietly for a few minutes to center myself. When I opened my eyes, about twenty men were sitting in front of me.

It wasn't hard to spot Ray: He was the only one who looked like he had just stepped out of a George Raft/Jimmy Cagney prison movie; the kind where convicts talk out of the sides of their mouths. He looked hard and gray—a prison look that would seem very much out of place on the streets.

The first class was a pretty straightforward introduction to how we would be using our time together. One thing I mentioned was that during the last 15 minutes of each class period, I would go out into the hall for a private meeting with one guy per day. Since we had two classes a week, I'd be able to have met everyone individually within a couple of months. Sita led the rest of the group in a meditation.

I explained the system and then asked for a show of hands as to who would like to go first. Seven or eight hands went up, and then went down very quickly the instant Ray raised his hand. He definitely had influence.

Sitting across from Ray in the tiny hallway, I told him there was only one rule-of-the-game for this private interview: That we maintain eye contact the whole 15 minutes. Other than that, we could talk or just sit, I didn't care. Ray agreed, but he had obvious difficulty looking into my eyes. And I noticed that as he began talking, he could meet my eyes until he said things about how tough or vicious he was; then he'd look away, and I would have to remind him. He must have looked away a dozen times in 15 minutes, but he finally blurted out: "Look: I've hurt a lot of people and have done a lot of bad things in my life, and I guess what I'm wondering is, what's my karma going to be for it?'

That was quite a moment of opening for Ray; quite a rare expression of trust and honesty. We instantly became close friends, and in fact, Ray was the support-post for that whole group, which lasted about a year.

He never missed a class, never copped out in a discussion or took the easy way out of a practice or discipline. And largely because of his rep, the meditation class wasn't seen as a collection of wimps or weirdos. We attracted the strongest, most independent cons at Butner—blacks, whites, young, old, gun-runners, bank robbers, the "Nashville Bomber," drug dealers, the Black Muslims—they all came together in that little basement room every Tuesday and Thursday.

As the months passed and the group became a family, Ray's appearance went through an amazing change. He looked years younger than before, and all the grayness from his face was replaced by a sparkle in his eye. He kept his clothes neater, started jogging every day, trimmed down on his weight.

The officials didn't know what to make of his changes, so they weren't about to cut him any slack. In fact, Ray got into serious trouble around that time for "possibly planning an escape". The truth was (really!) that Ray and a friend got up to meditate every day at 5:30 AM, and sat facing a window that overlooked the perimeter road around the prison. The guards were *sure* that they were timing the patrol car, so they wrote him up for disciplinary action. After all, this was the infamous Ray Neal!

In late '77 Sita and I moved to Colorado. On our last day of class at Butner, Ray didn't show. No one had seen him all day. Although it was illegal as hell, I walked right through the prison compound into the living units to find him. He was sitting on his bunk, very surprised to see me there. He explained that he wasn't up for heavy goodbyes, and that frankly, he was afraid that he might get all choked up if he came to the class.

I said "tough shit. These guys have been through a lot with you and they love you. What's the worst thing that could happen—you show your true feelings? They'd respect you even more!"

We walked back to the class together. Toward the end, I opened my eyes during the meditation and saw Ray sitting there, eyes closed, with tears just streaming down his cheeks. He looked like an angel, he really did.

Even after we ended the meditation and started talking, Ray continued to sit silently and let the tears flow. Looking around the group, I could feel the immense power his purity was creating for everyone in the room. Ray may have changed many lives forever that day. And it had been 30 years or more since he had allowed himself to cry. What a meeting-in-the-Spirit he provided for all of us!!

Ray has been out now since 1979. At first we lost touch with him for about a year, during which he went through the "growing pains" of several jobs, women, a brief marriage (to a female bank robber!), money troubles, and bouts with alcoholism. After all, it had been a very long time since he had been on the street.

But in the fall of '80 he called us and said he had finally "touched down" and was going to be okay. He spent Christmas week here with us in North Carolina. As he and I walked through the forest cutting firewood, I realized that although we had been close friends for years, this was the first time we had ever been together as free men.

One evening that week, I taped a conversation with Ray which turned out to be a fascinating con's-eye-view of his own life, struggle and spiritual renewal. A transcript of that tape is what follows:

Ray, where were you at in 1976, that somehow found you in the basement room at Butner for our class?

Well, we could talk about it as karma, or dharma, or destiny or fate; that's the reason I ended up in that room. But how I got there took a whole lot of suffering and stupidity and ignorance; just a whole lot of ass. I was a slow learner. I was like everyone else, you know: wanted everything going my way, took a whole lot of shortcuts; followed a rainbow looking for a pot of gold, and I found a pot all right, but it wasn't full of gold!

So you were fed up with the bullshit?

Well, you have to put it all into proper perspective. You see, I was 40 years old, I had become very comfortable in prison; I mean, I knew more about prison than the free world. And I was a big man on campus and I could have lived happily ever after, short of being killed in prison. It was a way of life. But there were so many unnecessary killings, people who had known each other for years killing each other over a hundred dollars worth of dope; made me realize that I couldn't live in prison no longer.

So before then, you weren't really *ready* to get out?

No; and if I had got out I wouldn't have stayed out. I probably functioned on about ten percent of my mental, just slide by. I had paid my dues, right? I had a place in that world.

In prison most people aren't in touch with reality. They're living either in the past or some fantasy future. Life on the streets is never the same as the fantasy. The people you left behind, they're not sitting around waiting for you to come out. If you think they are, you're a damn fool.

Most cons are like me, they've dedicated their lives to self-destruction, you know, bring ass to get ass. Then there's the paranoia: There's three killings in a row, always, and everybody gets on a paranoia kick. People like me, the closest we ever came to reality was through the barred prison bus windows as we were getting transferred from one prison to another. The rest of it was through the tv set, which is all just fast cars and beautiful women—that's not really what's out there, but that's all we got.

*The **real** reality of the whole damn thing is that there are very few people who care what happens to you, be it administration, family or loved ones. I mean, even the ones who do care, they don't have their shit together any more than you do; you can't lean on them. The bottom line is **you**; you've got to have your heart open to be able to hear what's being said to yourself.*

I don't think it's true that nobody cares. All the social workers and Jaycees and volunteers who come into the prisons...

No, no. I mean, even though you have kids and a wife and people who care about *you, you still can't live your life for them alone. You've got to know that how you decide to support yourself, or what you do with your time, that it's not just your parole officer's decision or your wife's or other people's. I mean, everyone has their own **journey**, you know, and you ain't going to be any good for anybody nohow unless yours is on a good footing. You just have to take the time to listen to your own heart, still your mind, and do it with the greatest amount of sincerity you can, and above all, start living for your own highest self. See, I had never done that in my whole life, and that's true for most people in the joint.*

You mean assume responsibility for yourself?

Yeah, for your own actions; for your own ideas and dreams, and to not be destructive.

I've noticed something for years having to do with the way a lot of prisoners talk about their lives. For example, I can be sitting with a guy who just blew three people away with a .38, and he'll describe it like "I was convicted of three counts of murder." It's always in the passive tense of what was done *to* him, rather than the active tense of what he did. "They convicted me, they sentenced me, they violated my parole, etc."

*Yeah, and the thing is, prison life just reinforces that whole thing. You become where you're anticipating a bell, or a door clanging, or some sound to give you the signal to do something; you're never on your own in prison. The cracking of a door tells you you can walk out in ten seconds, or the lights go out and you know you can go to sleep now. And the atmosphere creates a tension, I mean it's a hassle just to go eat. You get four or five hundred men trying to get through one doorway just to get something to eat or to get into a movie. You're **never** alone in prison. You can have a single cell and be sitting there meditating, and all of a sudden have a flashlight in your face. So it's easy to get used to laying everything off on others, especially if you've been doing it all your life.*

And I guess when you're treated badly in the joint, that just reinforces it; it's easy to blame everything on other people when you get treated unfairly.

Yeah, for example, when I got to Butner, the word on me was that I'd pick up both fences and run under them before they hit the ground, so the staff there went out of their way to road-test me. Remember when they got me, Tom and Jim for planning an escape? We were getting up at 5 in the morning to meditate, and they made a report that said we were looking out the window timing the perimeter patrol cars. They actually charged us with planning an escape; everybody was so paranoid. So it just makes you feel "hell's bells," why try to play by the rules if they throw you in the hole anyway?

Of course, the answer to that question is, at some point or another you have to find out you're doing it for you in the first place, and that's good

173

enough; or you're doing it all for you and God.

Well, you're doing it all for you and God; but not the God you grew up with being rammed down your throat. I mean, you've just gotten busted and you're facing fifteen years and the pastor comes up to you, hands you a Bible and says, "Son, this is the answer to all your problems." And over on one end of the cell there's a crap game going on, and over in another cell they're ripping off a young kid for his ass, and you're just supposed to take that Bible and solve all your problems with it. Before I met you and Sita, I just never knew I had any real options; I think people need to have options.

Well, what options did we give you that were different from the pastors with the Bibles?

*I don't know; not so much that it was **different**; it was **how** you said it. I mean, it was like the **sincerity** or something. If you remember when I first came into your group, I told you I could never swallow Christianity. But back then, you see, I had been in trouble all my life, rejected by society, rejected by everything **big**, and for me to have considered going into a church, well, that was out of the question. That would have been like joining my opposition. And of course, I'd been raised a Christian—a Baptist—which never seemed to do me much good, or be very real.*

*Of course, the **inner** feelings—looking up at the moon and seeing there's something greater than me—hell, a **savage** has that; you don't need no intellect or be educated or anything to realize that.*

*I remember your first class, I was sitting there and I wasn't listening; I mean, I didn't know **how** to listen. I was just casing everybody out. But my first impression was, well, like take Sita: Here's a young woman in a room full of men who hadn't saw a woman for some time, and well, the two of you were just so damn **sincere** or something, who could look at Sita with lust? Y'all were just compatible or harmonious or something, I don't know how to say it.*

*Of course, it's easy to read about Christianity or Hinduism or Buddhism in books and say "Yeah, I believe in that," or whatever. But here you two are sitting there like you're in your own living room, and Sita is a young attractive woman who has on one black sock and one blue sock; I mean, neither of you was afraid or trying to impress anybody or anything, and you're surrounded by all these convicts from all over hell, and you're just as comfortable with us, with yourself, as anyone I'd ever met. I knew there was **something** there I wanted.*

*I was giving myself one last shot at something. I had known about yoga and meditation for years; I'd take candles and shut my eyes and do all sorts of stuff in my cell; but I knew I didn't have the discipline to give me more control over my mind. I didn't know how to shut it down. When I came to your class and you started talking about a quiet mind, and you **had** one; and breathing techniques and the seven energy centers, the chakras; well, I knew there was really a way to begin doing it all down the line.*

I don't know if you remember, but I had so much energy pouring out of me—so

174

*much "Shakti"—I was **embarrassed!** I mean, the things my body used to do in class when I was first cleaning up my system, remember? I used to have sweat pouring off of me during meditation!*

Why do you think that stuff happens so often in classes?

Because they're all holding on so tight. I mean, you take your average Joe Shmoe off the streets, and his lifestyle is so predictable and slow, like he don't get caught up in all the drug killings and knife-fights and all this; so he's not holding on like the average guy in prison. The guy in prison doesn't have a hundred little ways to blow it all off; he can't go have a few beers and forget about it, you know?

That sounds funny in a way; most people would think it's the other way around: That prisoners' lives are predictable and dull.

Well, in a way it's repetitious, boring, dull; I mean, you've got a whole lot of people reminding you of your past—your caseworkers, your counselors, your mother in the visiting room saying "how could you do this?," okay? And there's nothing big happening in your life today except what's going on inside you.

But you can't walk up to people on the yard and say, "Hey, I'm really fucked up today. I mean, my head, I don't know what's going on and what I'm going to do." And you can't walk up to somebody and say "Gee, I had the most beautiful experience in my cell," or "You know, I've been really thinking deeply about things."

You can't just talk about these things, so you never really get to dump your feelings because you have your image to keep up. So you talk about football games or handball, you talk about anything except what's really happening inside you. The future is something that may never happen, so you live in the past and you deal with a phony present; it's all bullshit.

Welcome to the world. I think you just described life on the streets as much as in the joint.

I think people in and out basically have the same things—they're all scared, searching for love. But people escape through valiums, they escape through books; hell, America today is stuck together with valiums. A man in prison has a golden opportunity that he can take that the average American can't, because the average American is working all the time just to stay even. You get caught up in money games outside. I mean, hell, you got bills, bills, bills. People get credit too easily. Hell, you can be all kinds of ex-con and still get all the credit you want. So you come out of prison with a sack in your hand, and a year later it takes 2 Mayflower trucks to move you.

That's part of the recidivism thing. You can be in a year or ten years, it don't matter. You get out and you don't really know anybody, you don't know where to go, so you just start getting as many things as you can. And you start drinking and you get on the phone and call Joe Blow who's in the same predicament, and pretty soon you're sitting together somewhere half-drunk, and deciding that the only way to get ahead is if you just burglarize this place or rob that place, and neither one of you really wants to do it. Most people in prison just wanted to pull that one big score and then live like everybody else.

And you're thinking, "The worst that could happen is I'll be sent back inside where everything's all figured out for me."?

*Hell, the **worst** that could happen is when you succeed. You don't know what to do with the money anyway. The **easiest** thing is you'll be back in the joint, listening for the door to crack, hanging out on the handball court. It's a slow suffocation, that's what it amounts to; you suffocate. The great majority of people who get out of prison, **break** back in.*

Well, you haven't had an easy time since you got out almost two years ago. You've had a few jobs, a lot of one-night stands, you got married and divorced, your wife stabbed you in the heart, you became an alcoholic, and now you're a member of A.A. When you talk now of the part our classes played in your life, it makes me wonder where it all was during the past two years?

*Well, I couldn't have done all that without you! (laughs). I mean, there were many times when I would just be alone in my bedroom and pick up your news-letters or turn on the tapes; no matter how caught up I was in the everyday situa-tion, the **real** reality for me was my inner peace, which I kept going back to with that stuff.*

But how does the inner peace mesh with the fights you've been in, or the times you'd sit drunk in a bar; where does that fit in? Was it all just karma you had to work out?

*I think I brought 99.9% of it on myself. I mean, they were drinking and fighting and killing each other in bars while I was in prison, and they'll be doing it long after I'm dead. I believe it's just part of our society. I guess I had to bottom out on that. It wasn't a drinking problem, or a dope problem, it's more a **thinking** problem really, you know? I mean, I reached a point in prison where I just **knew** that I didn't belong anymore, but at that point you can't just say, "You can let me out now, it was all a big misunderstanding."*

And the same thing on the streets; you still hang out in the places where you're allowing yourself to be around all that shit, so you can't ask for anything else other than what you get. I mean, it's not that you're always wrong in a fight; you may be perfectly right, because there's a lot of crazy people in this world. But if you put yourself into the same places all the time, you're going to wind up in fights. Most of us go through life setting ourselves up, and then we want to shift the weight and say "Well, I wasn't really wrong."

So now you just stay away from bars, away from the rough places?

Yeah, I really doubt if I'll ever find myself in that setting again. You know what helped show me that? I got robbed! I'd been working all day and then drinking whiskey, and I went into a club and I'm drunk, I mean really drunk. This guy says, "Hey, let me help you to the car," and I say sure. When we get outside this one person turns into three people, and all of a sudden there were six legs kicking me. They got me on the ground and they beat the hell out of me, took $240; they didn't just beat me up, they really stomped me.

But what they really did was to give me three days in bed thinking about my life. You can imagine how I felt being robbed! That was a new experience, boy! But I appreciated the punch line, I really did. The joke is always on us, on people who live their lives like I did. We get caught up in the belief that you can go from A to Z by taking a whole bunch of shortcuts. By the time you get to Z you're all messed up, your head's not on straight. You get the pot at the end of the rainbow, but it's shit instead of gold, and then you spend the rest of your life trying to convince yourself that shit is actually gold.

But is it because you took so many shortcuts, or is the pot of gold bullshit in the first place? If you're after sex, money, and power, which is mostly what people in our culture learn through shows like DALLAS, then does it really matter whether you take shortcuts or pay the dues to get it? The entire goal is fucked up right from the beginning.

Yeah, but I think the average American is doing a job he don't like, is mismatched with his wife, and is so caught up in the mortgage and the bills and the babies and the braces and just trying to get by, that he can no more step out of it than take a stake and drive it through his heart.

But it doesn't matter what you do for a living or how many bills and braces and babies you have; it only matters how you see it all. Are you living to get the pot of gold and try to escape from all pain and suffering, or are you living to learn whatever God has in mind for you?

I'll go along with that. I mean, it's not like I'm living 24 hours a day for God, but I do know that God is alive and living 24 hours a day for me. I know that all the major events in my life—be that a car wreck or making a fortune or getting a heart attack—are coming from God; I know this. When I first met you, you said, "Think about the most painful times in your life, and then think about the times you grew the most; weren't they the same times?" And I do know that one. So now when hard times come, I deal with them, and I'm not all freaked out wishing it wasn't happening or thinking I don't deserve it. I don't go off on a two-week drunk and rob a bank; I deal with it.

How does that affect your life in general?

I truly believe that life on Earth comes down to the interactions between people. Once you reach a point where you see that people aren't your enemies, and there is love in people, love in giving, there is so much to be gained when you see people as they are; not as potential tricks or potential scores or potential lays. You see people as they truly are and come to love them through those eyes; and the only way you can do this is when you find that love, that inner serenity, in yourself. You can't love nobody else until you love yourself, and you can't love yourself until you're comfortable with yourself. And the only way you can get that is between you and God.

[We keep in touch with Ray every few months, mostly by phone. His new-found life on the streets has kept evolving in interesting ways. Mostly he just enjoys being alive, and this second chance he's gotten to mix and mingle with all the crazy people on this planet.]

(1981:)
Dear Bo and Sita,

Wow! So much has happened in my life. What you see behind me (in the photo) are carpet samples. This is what the stores junk about four times a year. I turn this junk into about $500/wk (half profit).

It's early in the morning as I write this— I'll go run 5 miles and then maybe paint a few hours. And Marleen will be over this afternoon. My life is so great—the more I let go, the more things seem to happen to me.

My spiritual growth is perfect—my heart is so light and filled with love—I'm working through so much. I haven't drank in three years, smoked in two or dipped in one (sex is still great though!).

I love you all, Ray

(1985:)
Hi you guys—

Y'all are always with me and help me through some rough spots. My life is great. Marleen is fine, Mark [stepson] is 15 now, and DeDe [stepdaughter] runs one of my places.

My greatest teaching lately came from a cat (pure love). It taught me about love. I failed to teach him about freeways, and he was killed....

Somehow, someway, I'll see y'all....

Much Love, Ray

The Crossing

While roaming the shoreline of life,
Be aware that the tide
Will soon erase every sign of yr passing.
Look to the horizon
And ask yr heart
Why you dally at the water's edge,
When there is no longer any doubt
As to the inevitable crossing.

Go lightly, be as free as you can,

P.J. Johnson / Lompoc, Ca.

Come, come, whoever you are,
wanderer, worshipper, lover of leaving;
Come, ours is not a caravan of despair.
Though you've broken your vow a thousand times,
Come, come again.
—*Rumi*

3. Come, Come Again

Gary

Dear Bo,

Having served twenty years and being nearly forty, Ray Neal's story [ch. 2] was easy to identify with. I'm now back for violating my parole after being outside a little over a year. During the last eighteen months I discovered many painful things about myself, among which is that although wanting to be outside, I wasn't equipped to be free yet.

Your answers to Tom [Ch.5] started me thinking about a need in my life: A need to get out of the shell of penitentiary role-playing and self-centeredness and to get involved with people in a genuine, caring way.

My past, if it makes any difference, is not like Tom's. Instead of being on the receiving end of aggression and violence, I've been a taker — aggressive, belligerent, taking what I wanted instead of earning or deserving it. Even my giving had an odor of taking about it: Using people and circumstances to achieve my own ends, self-concern at the expense of others (although true self-concern can't be at someone else's expense). After so many years of being tough and cold, it's difficult to change all the old patterns, even with some insight of what's behind them. Playing the penitentiary game cost me a lot of self-esteem and personal dignity, a fact which I didn't discover until I took an honest look at myself and the things I've done.

Having several trades and being willing to work has made employment no major problem for me. I didn't violate my parole by stealing; I violated it by getting drunk and tearing up my ex-wife's clothes.

My problem on parole has been trying to discover a lifestyle that's fulfilling for me. The old days of being a gangster and playing at cops and robbers are gone. That's a dead-end street, always was, and the consequences are now more immediate and long-lasting. Besides being sick of living that way, that lifestyle is no longer compatible with my personal standards and goals. For me, that eliminates association with nearly everyone I know.

My parole in 1975 lasted 22 months, and the one in 1982 lasted 13 months. Both times I failed to establish any enduring personal relationships. In addition to being frustrating, that hurts; especially when I know I'm a reasonably decent person. I'm also aware that people don't have to like me, don't have to accept me, and that there's nothing I can do to make them like me.

I think that 20 years of prison life has developed some behavior and attitudes that offend — and even frighten — others. I want to be accepted, to be liked, and ultimately to be loved.

Can you give me any suggestions about what I might do to call a halt to this "prison experience"? What can I do to find a place where I fit in society on the outside? I don't steal anymore, and I want a fulfilling life, but I just don't fit anywhere at this point. What are my options?

May the Grace of God be with you and may He hold you in the Heart of His hand.

Yours in peace, Gary/Kansas

Dear Gary,

After doing as much time as you have, you may need to be patient while some fine-tuning goes on in your adjustments to street life. You might want to start with a job that's not too demanding, so you can spend time as a volunteer at a crisis center or rehab program. The sooner you begin filling the need you described to give rather than take, the more relaxed and confident you'll feel about your own life. Also, you'll start to make new friends whose outlook on life is more like your new "personal standards and goals".

You've got tremendous insight and self-honesty; it'll just take some time to get it all into practice. I think you're doing great. One thing is, you might want to swear off booze forever. It seems to have caused you enough problems in your life, and it certainly doesn't help with self-control or changing chronic behavior patterns.

You mentioned not making any "enduring personal relationships". But most of the people on the street don't either, Gary; look at the divorce rate. Lasting relationships take more time and energy than most people are willing to spend. And I don't mean just for a lover; I'm talking about the people at the grocery store, the mailman, the lady at the bank, your parole officer—*everybody*. If you just take the extra few seconds to *notice*, to care about the "bit players" in your life, you'll be amazed how people change toward you, and how the "right" people will come along to fill all your needs.

You may well have some mannerisms from prison life that turn people off, but if you keep seeing your life as honestly as you see it now, those mannerisms will be easy to spot and gradually change. The people who count will be willing to bear with you in the meantime. Another concrete suggestion is to keep meditating daily. Meditation is especially good for seeing yourself and the way you appear to others. But again, if you can just be as straight and open with others as you are with me, I think you'll have as many good friends as you want.

You've already got one lasting friend, bro.

Much Love, Bo

Gloria

Bo,

*I really understand what you're always saying about being simple and open, not playing games with people, and I know that's the right way to live. My problem is, I've never done anything else **but** play games and manipulate people. How can someone like me possibly change, when the change you're talking about is like my whole personality? Where do I start?*

I hate to sound pessimistic, but at this point in my life I don't see how I can turn it all around. Conning and hustling and even lying, are lifelong habits that just keep coming up without me even trying.

Sincerely, Gloria/N.C.

Dear Gloria,

Yeah, I hear you; I really do. The thing is, first of all, who is it who wrote me such a beautiful, open letter and signed it "sincerely?" Don't overlook what's right in front of your nose: You *are* a good person who really wants to change in a big way. So, you're already off to a good start.

The second thing is, the ONLY way any of us ever change our old behavior patterns, is *one moment at a time.* When you think of changing all the millions of tiny ways you lie and hustle, you get overwhelmed and feel like you'll never make it. But the true spiritual warrior (which you really are, you know) doesn't get sucked in by that kind of future-tripping. The only lie you need to stop telling is the one that starts forming in your throat right now. The only scam you need to let go of is the one your mind is beginning to think about.

Do you see what I mean? Thinking of how big the task is, is just *another* cruel mind-game, just another hype to keep you from taking control of your life. Try to realize that you're at least as good in fooling yourself as you are at fooling others; so be on guard, and don't let your mind get ahead of you. Be suspicious of despair and pessimism. Find various ways to remind yourself (meditation, keeping a diary, using a mantra, etc.) of what you're trying to do, and of the fact that *the real work is just one moment at a time.* If we had to make huge changes up front, none of us would ever see the Light. Big change is just a bunch of little ones.

Much love and encouragement, Bo

183

David ("Son of Sam")

Dear Prison-Ashram Project,

I am an inmate who has a long time left to spend in prison and I would like to make the best of it. Several other prisoners are into meditation and yoga and I can see amazing results in their lives.

Could you please send me the book INSIDE-OUT. I too, would like to learn and apply myself to the art of spiritual meditation.

Sincerely, David/NY

Dear David,

Hope you enjoy the stuff we're sending along. I don't usually ask people personal questions based on their past, but yours is so famous that I'd be phony to ignore it. In fact, the same day I got your first letter, I was reading NEWSWEEK and saw the copies of your letters about "Sam" which you sent to the media. Your handwriting hasn't changed at all.

I'm very interested in how you're doing, and the changes you're going through. How do you deal with your crimes, your "fame", and how do you see these things in reference to meditation and your spiritual work? I'm very interested in how our project helps or fails to help somebody in your situation.

What do you think? Would you like to pitch in to help us all understand ourselves a little better? I'm working on the new book now, so maybe we could include something you write in that.

If you don't feel like it, that's cool too. You're still on our mailing list, so we'll always be in touch that way.

Love, Bo

Dear Bo,

I want to thank you for your concern about me, and yes, I have found your materials very helpful.

As you know, the prison community is filled with tension, mistrust, and hatred. My notoriety, of course, has made things difficult at times. There are many things around me which fill me with sadness: The treacherous tactics of the authorities; the poverty and illiteracy of many inmates; the hopelessness and lack of positive outlook for the future; the separation and breakup of families; and in my particular case, the financial exploitation of my crimes by book publishers, Hollywood moguls, etc. However I have pulled through nonetheless.

My hobbies are reading, exercising and walking in the outside yard regardless of the weather, and my own form of meditation.

I have never been instructed in the art of mental and spiritual meditation by any master. However, on my own I have done well, I believe. My technique is to find a quiet, isolated spot in the yard after my exercise period and sit down. Then I let my mind drift off to various places, places associated with the happy experiences of my past. Of course I think about the "crimes" from time to time, but it's too difficult for me to forgive myself.

Yes Bo, I am doing a lot of time, yet I have gained a great deal of inner strength. I know now that I will never succumb to the environment and let myself languish in a prison cell. From this cell I have spiritually escaped. However, I'm still a long way off from finding true inner peace. I look forward to your next book, and may God brighten your path.

Very truly yours, David

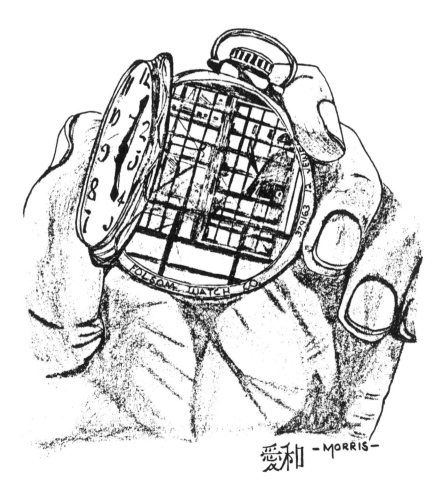

John Morris, Folsom Prison

Mary-Jo

To Bo Lozoff:

My name is Mary-Jo. I spoke to you when you came to Prison for Women. I am 18 years of age. I enjoyed the peaceful feeling after I meditate; but someone told me all this stuff about spirits drowning my spirit, my spirit could get lines crossed and I could go into a coma for the rest of my life. Is this true?

Let me tell you about myself first before you answer. Age-wise I am 18, but mentally I am 13-14 years of age. I am very naive about a lot of things.

I was taken out of my natural home when I was three. I was moved from foster home to foster home until I was 7. Between the ages of 7-12 I can't remember. Most of my memory has returned after a year of who I was. When I was charged the cops told me something that was very upsetting which I was in shock for quite awhile. But I lived a year in total darkness of who I was, why I was in jail, etc.

I hope I am not boring you but I felt I should tell someone what is going on in my head because the shrink or psychologist doesn't understand the real me. They want a false person. I try to act normal for me but then I get dirty looks or sworn at.

They want a more mature person with no problems at all.

I can hold everything in me until I finally explode. What I mean is either I hurt myself or set a fire. When I told the shrink all he asked was "when were all the other explosions?" So I told him and he asked if I was ever on medication for my problem. I say no and he puts me on nerve medication.

You only talk to shrink for fifteen minutes, then he kicks you out.

I hope you understand what I am saying, if you don't please ask. I have to close now. So bye for now.

Sincerely, Mary-Jo/Canada

PS: I need an understanding friend.

Dear Mary-Jo,

I'm already your friend, so you don't even need to ask. Please feel free to write me anytime. I do remember you; you're the beautiful young Native-American girl who talked to me during the break about the fires you set while you were babysitting. *[Mary-Jo is in prison for several counts of murder by arson.]

It's good that you enjoyed meditation, and don't worry even slightly about crossing lines or going into a coma or being influenced by other spirits or anything like that. Meditation gives you more control, not less. It's simply a process of gradually quieting your mind, and it's very safe and has been around for thousands of years. If anything frightening ever happens while you meditate just write me about it and we'll discuss it.

You have to remember that it's fear itself that is the problem, not fear of this or fear of that. Fear is a liar. When it tells you to be scared of something, don't get into the "something", whatever it is; but instead feel the feeling of fear itself—the ugly, shrewd feeling—and don't let it take control of you. Let it pass through your body and mind like a sinister stormcloud floats through the peaceful blue sky.

Try this breathing practice when you feel fear: With your eyes closed, feel the breath come into you and bring calmness and strength in with it. Then hold your breath and let it "soak up" all the fear, worry, tension, and whatever else you want to get rid of, and then blow that out with the out-breath. Try this for awhile every day.

It seems like some things have happened to you in the past that have hurt, shocked, and frightened you very very deeply. Your response to it—a very natural one—has been to block it all out of your mind. When that hasn't worked, maybe you've tried to *burn* it away. You know, fire is the great "purifier" of the universe.

I think your gut instincts have been right on, Mary-Jo, I really do. But you've been using the wrong kind of fire, and you've burned down the wrong things. The fire you're aching for is actually a very *gentle* flame—the eternal flame of your own beautiful spirit, your own heart. And what you need to burn in that fire is not buildings or children, but rather the confusion and pain which are buried in the past. You need to burn your pain into wisdom, the impure into the pure. And you can do it now in a new way.

Try this form of meditation for awhile: Sit straight and still, eyes closed, and focus all of your attention on the center of your chest, where you can imagine your spiritual heart is. Picture a small, pink flame there, flickering steadily. Imagine each breath going in right to that spot, feeding the flame. In and out, in and out, right there at the heart-space. As any scary or painful memories come up, breathe them right into that spot and watch them burn up in the flame, making the fire slightly brighter. Anything that makes you feel bad, just offer into the fire and watch it become powerless to control you.

The fires you start with matches can't burn away what you've wanted. But try this new way for awhile every day and night. The more we open our hearts to ourselves, the more we can open them to each other. The more we open our hearts, the easier it is to look at our fear and pain, and then to gradually let them burn away until we're free.

Sita and I both send our love to you. Please feel free to write us anytime; we're your family if you want us to be.

Love, Bo

One has to face fear or forever run from it.

—Hyemeyohsts Storm

Arthur

Dear Bo,

I got out of prison a little over a year ago. I went to Tucson and attended the 3HO drug program. But it didn't work out for me. My father had a stroke and I returned to Michigan. I was in Michigan for only three months when I was arrested and sent to prison again, this time for 20 years with a 10 year minimum sentence. If I don't win my appeal, I'll be here until I'm 39 years old.

I hurt someone I really cared for, that's what put me here.

I can't forgive myself, let alone expect anyone else to forgive me. I can't understand why my life keeps going in a direction contrary to my wishes. I try and I pray, but my ego takes control for just five minutes, and I do something I regret for the rest of my life. Is it really my karmic destiny to be nothing in this life that I want to be?

I appreciate all the help I got from you before. I guess it's time to start all over again. I guess with ten years of lockup to look forward to, I may finally be able to get a grasp on myself. I hope so, I never want to hurt anyone again. I never wanted to this time, but I just cracked and before I knew what I was doing, it was over. I've suffered a lot in this life and I guess I'll suffer a lot more before it's over. It's all because I can't control myself; never have been able to. Any insights you may have would be appreciated.

Love, Arthur/Michigan

Dear Arthur,

I remember you from the last time you were inside. Sorry it didn't work out for you. But I think your image of "starting all over again" is part of what keeps throwing you off. The spiritual journey takes us through a lot of ups and downs. You seem to see it more as a straight climb, and if you're not getting to the top, you must be at the bottom. But that's not the way it goes.

Like it or not, everything that's happened has been part of your journey. Your violence shows you're still stumbling over the same stuff as before. You didn't mention whether you still have a drinking or drug problem, but I'll make a wild guess you do, and that you were tanked up when you blew it this last time. Right?

Changing old behavior patterns requires a lot of work, Arthur. The great spiritual truths you've read don't lessen that work for you; you've still got to do it for yourself just like anyone else. Now that you're back inside, you could slide right back into the spiritual books and philosophies and fool yourself once again about how much you've changed. But then you're a sucker next time you get out and you head for the nearest bar.

It's not your "destiny" to go on like this; it's just an old pattern. Patterns can be broken, and people do it all the time, with enough self-honesty and effort. Part of the self-honesty is to take full responsibility for your life—no talk of destiny or karma or lack of control. If booze gets you crazy, then just never, ever, take another drink again. That's taking responsibility. Take courage, bro, and let me know if I can help.

Love, Bo

Dear Bo,

My last letter was written in a very freaked-out state. But from my earliest memories, I've always been a disturbed person. Things that have carried over into my adult life. I was born with these things and they have gotten worse. I was born with (as my father says) a mean streak; the need to dominate, if not physically, then psychologically. As I grew older I attempted to repress this anger I was born with. I started drug use early but drinking was my downfall. Drinking brought out all my anger and still does.

I'm a lonely person and need to have a woman around me. I fall in love easy but it has never worked out for me. My nature seems to thwart me in everything I do. I try to be a good husband (married twice) or boyfriend but it just never works out.

I had a nice girlfriend this time, but she caught me in the sack with her best friend. Two days later she wanted me to come over and help her fix her car. But actually, it was only to tell me to get my stuff out of her house. We had a big argument and I forced her to have sex with me. After I left, she called the police and told them I had raped her (I didn't hit her, just used psychological force). She lied to them about our relationship and made them think I was just someone she had met in a bar who came over and raped her. There was a very nasty trial and I was found guilty. My case is being appealed and I will probably get a new trial.

The facts are, I did love this woman and I just cracked up for awhile. I have never done this before to a woman. Usually I just get pissed, and I have hit them or slapped them before. What I did was wrong and I know it. I'm sick about the whole thing. What I want to know is why? Why has my life been surmounted with problems since I was a child? Why is it only getting worse? I've thought about killing myself, but damn it, I believe in reincarnation, and my next life will only be worse.

I may be in here until I'm 39. What can I do when I get out with all this hate I'm now growing? I love God very much. I accept what I've done and where I'm at, but I don't see any reason for it. The things I've done in this life haven't been bad enough to account for everything that's gone wrong in my life. I've always been a very emotional person, but now I'm becoming hard and callous. I'm in a rut and I'm burying myself further. I have some awful thoughts going through my head that I can't get rid of even though I try. I'm frightened of what I'm capable of doing. I'm really frightened by what I might do whenever I get out.

I don't want to be mean or hateful. I don't want this girl to hate me though she does. I want to be good and know God. I want His Love. He used to talk to me

189

sometimes through drugs and meditation. But now though I pray every day and try to meditate, it just doesn't happen. All my mind does is run wild on horrible thoughts. There's a reason, I know there is, and God knows what it is, but I don't. I need a helping hand before I sink in my own shit. Thank you for listening to me. I'm sorry this letter is so negative, but I have to get it out. I really have no one else I can tell this to.

Love, Arthur

Dear Arthur,

Definitely sounds like sink-or-swim time for you; congratulations. Really. When we feel the very lowest, that's when we're ripest for some *real* change, the kind that sinks in instead of just staying in the head. So try to have faith in the whole process, even the suffering. I know that doesn't make it hurt any less, but it does help to endure it. Just like it's easier to put up with a terrible toothache if you know the dentist is on his way.

You still need to be more honest with yourself. You say things like "I accept what I've done and where I'm at"; but really Arthur, you don't at all. You just know that you're *supposed* to feel that way. If you really accepted it all, you wouldn't say "But I don't see any reason for it." What does that mean? What accounting system are you using when you say "The things I've done in this life haven't been bad enough to account for everything that has gone wrong in my life."? What accounts for a sweet little baby getting cancer, or nice old people getting mugged and beaten, or a farmer losing all his crops? Was your life "supposed to" be problem-free? Look around, Arthur. Happiness isn't a measure of bad things not happening to you; it's a measure of how you deal with everything that comes down the pike.

If you're really serious this time about unloading your suffering and making some deep inner changes, you've got to let go of all the cop-outs and self-deceptions that you've created about how you were born at a disadvantage and you have no control over your destiny. You're wasting the present by being trapped in the past.

You have all the "right" ideas about God and the spiritual journey, but you're still back in the joint. It's time to stop assuming that you have a harder time than anyone else in *applying* those ideas; it's time to join the rest of us and do the day by day, moment by moment work of getting free: Be simple, be truthful, be kind. Don't run away from yourself by bitching about the past. Meditate without expecting psychedelic talks with God every time you sit down; just develop your own one-pointedness so you don't feel so weak. Pray for patience and courage and openness, not for God to wave a magic wand and take away all your spiritual work.

The work is hard for all of us, really it is. Sometimes we feel like we're just hanging on to the barest shred of faith and we're slipping fast. Nothing wrong is going on in your life; this *is* the journey to God. Take more responsibility and go for it.

Love, Bo

Dear Bo,

Whenever I receive a letter from you I always have to read it quite a few times. The first time my fragile ego freaks out.

"What's he saying?", I ask. "Surely he must have mixed up my letter with somebody else." So I set it down and think for a few hours. When I read it again the truth always rings through. With each successive reading, my ego barriers are splintered and finally my heart opens to what is really being communicated. Thank you!

In 1976 I paid $125 for a mantra from TM (Transcendental Meditation). It was the best money I ever spent. The problem now is I'm kinda hung up on mantra meditation, though now I usually use "Shree Ram" since Ram Dass mentioned it in a lecture in 1980. I've attempted to try Vipassana meditation, but I couldn't get my mind to follow my breath. I just can't seem to get in a calm state. My mind is often filled with thoughts that aren't good.

I still smoke cigarettes. I'm trying to quit but my will power hasn't been up to it. Occasionally I smoke pot or hash in here. I really haven't been getting enough exercise. I need to work on some yoga postures but I don't know very many. Could you perhaps advise me on a few postures and techniques that I should stick with for awhile?

Whatever you think would help me would be appreciated. I often let other people read your material or the letters you send me. Right now, though, I know I need to calm down. I need to relax my mind before I can even begin to worry about where I'm headed. I have always loved God, but I've never loved myself, so I guess that's not really loving God, only fooling myself. I really need to feel better about myself. I do want to be a useful person in society, I really do. I pray that your continued support will help my lotus to unfold, no matter how long it takes or what kind of obstacles I need to overcome.

Love, Arthur

Dear Arthur,

Well, it sounds like things are lightening up a little for you, anyway. But don't slack off on watching for all the old patterns of thinking to come up; keep the self-honesty fresh in your mind.

For example, the problem about being "hung up on mantra meditation" is a smokescreen. Any form of meditation is as good as any other; just pick one and use it without wondering whether it's the right one, etc. It's not so technical; all you're trying to do is focus your mind on one point in order to strengthen your concentration.

Of course, drugs, cigarettes, and various foods like sugar, caffeine, and so forth, may be making it harder for you to sit still. I know it's tough to have self-discipline about that stuff while you're in prison, but someday you're going to have to realize that what you want—spiritual freedom and peace—is a tough goal, and you'll have to get a lot tougher to attain it.

You asked me for some yoga postures, but I think you know enough already. Just *do* some of what you've learned from all these different groups and books; don't keep collecting more.

Jesus said, "In your patience possess ye your souls." Try to patiently apply one form of meditation, a few yoga postures, some breathing techniques, and plenty of self-honesty, to your daily life. That's all you need to do. If the water is 100 feet below the ground, you can't get to it by digging ten ten-foot wells. You have to go all the way without starting over at every interesting new spot. Learning new things is always easier than taking the old ones deep inside your guts. Don't fall blindly into that pattern as you have for so many years.

Let's really get down to it this time; no shit.

Love, Bo

Dear Bo,

Your letters inspire me a lot. This time I want to take it slow and one step at a time. I really want to be a useful member of society, and I want to be prepared for whatever God has in store for me.

I'm now taking 19 credit hours in college and am involved in creative writing. I read a lot, mostly science fiction. I hope to become good enough in writing sci-fi stories to sell some while I'm still in here. I'm working on my spelling and grammar, because as it now stands, someone must proofread my work and then I have to get out the dictionary. Prison life may not be all fun and games, but for a struggling writer it's not that bad. Plus I'm getting a well-rounded education.

I meditate every night but I don't want to burn myself out so I'm taking it slow and easy one day at a time. I will progress at whatever level I find comfortable. No rush this time, I will have a lot of time to work on myself.

Thanks for all your help; I hope the holidays bring cheer for you and yours.

Love, Arthur

[and a few months later:]

Dear Bo,

This term in college was the first perfect "4.0" average I've ever had (for 18 credits!). I'll be receiving my AA in liberal arts pretty soon, and then I enter the BS program in Interdisciplinary Studies. So mentally, I'm planning on a full productive life. I'm still writing, and my writing teacher is trying to get Tate Wilhelm, the 1976 Hugo Award winner for best sci-fi novel, to look over my work.

I get along real well in the college program, and fairly well in population. I'm managing all right and have a lot of outside support I never expected.

I often ask God to guide my path, and ask advice on if I'm doing things right. I'm just acting on feelings anymore; but I must be doing something right, because things are not the way I expected them to be. And I feel like if I keep working on all facets of myself, something good will come out of all this.

Love, Arthur

Life is like stepping onto a boat which is about to sail out to sea and sink.
suzuki roshi

Jim

Dear Friends,

I am presently serving a 25-year sentence for bank robbery, which is not my first incarceration, so it is hardly likely I will be out anytime soon. I cannot avoid my karma. For that very reason, however, I welcome any hints that can help me reinforce my own ideal of yoga, and to live it as best I can in the circumstances which I cannot avoid.

I have learned to live in prison by being extremely flexible, but just to survive is not good enough. Yoga is an intensely personal thing which requires a more rigid honesty than the world requires. To that world, my greatest crimes were those which put me in prison, but those were only surface actions which could carry only surface sanctions. At their worst they could not affect the inner being. "The soul within us does not suffer," as Sri Aurobindo has said.

My real crime was my dishonesty to myself, and it was a sick revulsion to that which finally brought me to yoga. Now I only seek the most effective way to dig out that greater self within. I would sincerely like to know what you have in mind.

Cordially, Jim/Kansas

Dear Jim,

Glad to know you. What we "have in mind", as you put it, is pretty simple stuff—as old as the hills. For everyone in life, there are two ways: The way of appearances, or the way of the Spirit. We're just a connection for the people who want help and friendship in taking the way of the Spirit.

For example, look around Leavenworth and begin seeing what *is* rather than what brought you there or what you need to "dig out" of yourself. Imagine that you just beamed down to this place from another planet, and your job is to figure out the best strategy for living right where you are—that's your mission.

So you look around and decide when and where you can have privacy, who to stay away from, what to do with your time, etc. I get the feeling that you're "resigned" to being where you are and making the best of it. But try to take it just one step further: Try to understand that *every* environment has its traps and limitations. For spiritual work, yours is as good as any other.

Generally speaking, everybody wakes up, has some good and bad times during the day, and goes to sleep. In prison, a lot of it is more intense and scary, but the same things tend to make us feel good and bad whether we're in prison or not. Behind it all are the same human values in your own heart: Calmness, good humor, strength, courage, kindness. These are really what any yoga is ultimately about. You and I are spending our days very much the same, just with different trappings and tests.

Love, Bo

194

Dear Bo,

You mentioned one thing in your letter that rang a bell in my mind. That was about viewing prison from the positive side.
Too often in here, we tend to think it does not have one.
Consequently, we waste all our time and energy in day-dreaming of a tomorrow that will never match our dreams of it.

*Perhaps it is only natural to hate the place that isolates you from all of your accustomed sources of satisfaction. In a sense, we are all monks who have not freely chosen monkhood, and therefore, do not wear our robes very gracefully. But in that respect, I imagine there are very few people anywhere who can cheerfully accept the unpleasant circumstances which their actions, or karma, have brought them. Still less are they able to grab hold of that slim thread of hope, and attempt to change the very structure of their lives. Too often prison takes away all the self-esteem while offering no glimpse of a means to build anything to take its place. The con seldom comes to realize that there is something within him that is better than what he's seen of himself; that the **divine** can be found within him.*

Such a challenge—such a possibility—brings hope even to the negative world of prison. For the Spirit can never be bound even when the body is bound. There has been, actually, only one stumbling block in my life, and that is within me. And every time I make some little victory over despair, or anger, or negativity, I feel that I have stepped beyond the walls of that personal prison; a prison much more oppressive than any of stone and steel.

I have participated in just about every "rehabilitative" program that prisons have thought of, and I realize the futility of all attempts to manipulate the surface being. Even my university training was no more than a boost to my ego. We are too apt to praise knowledge as though it had some miraculous power of its own, and we disregard the source of all knowledge.

What will happen to me personally is problematical. I am fifty years old (1975) and have less than two years served on this 25-year sentence. Moreover, this is the third time I have been in prison. The problems of my life have not been simple ones. There are many actions in life which are simply irremediable. Any reasonable assessment of my chances assures me that it will be many years before this karma is paid. So be it.
Any man should be responsible for his actions. But this is why I am so intensely interested in living the best way I can.

If you catch them young enough, perhaps you will contribute to the making of lives that will give real meaning to life.
Criminals are a hard breed—but all the great saints were hard men, indefatigable in their dedication to a chosen way of life.

God bless, Jim

Dear Jim,

I really enjoy your letters; you have quite a way with words. I don't buy your self-image, though, of being sort of over-the-hill and too late to turn it all around. To the creator of this entire universe, the difference between 50 years old and 20 years old probably doesn't seem like much!

And when you talk about "any reasonable assessment" of your prison sentence, you don't give much leeway to the mysterious divine forces beyond all reason or logic.

Loosen up, my friend. Be one of those "few people anywhere" who you said use the circumstances of their lives to open themselves up to their God-selves. There are as few of those people out here on the streets as there are in Leavenworth; remember that.

Love, Bo

Dear Bo,

Yeah, I guess we all need encouragement. We need to see that God is not just a static force hidden in some heaven, but a force that always responds to the soul that seeks Him. When the world has ostracized you and you find yourself an outlaw, it is easy to forget that God still sees you. But you can never be isolated from God; He always has visiting privileges.

I think part of the trouble is that we cons become oppressed by our crimes. All of us spend too much time looking back. We see how stupid and useless our lives have been, and then it is hard to believe that we might be capable of the tremendous task of the divine journey. We find it hard to believe that God is really within us.

It is easy to use words as I am doing, but setting an example is quite another thing. I hope I'll always be able to stand behind my words, but I also hope I'll be able to live up to them as well. What we need are examples—men who can break away from the little surface being that seems to run the show—men who can plunge into the abyss without fear, and let the divine run the show. It is quite an adventure, is it not?

May God watch over you.

Love to you, Jim

The phenomena of life may be likened unto a dream,
a phantasm, a bubble, a shadow, the glistening dew, or
lightning flash, and thus they ought to be contemplated.

—Buddha (Diamond Sutra)

THE TOUCH OF THE MASTER'S HAND

'Twas battered and scarred, and the auctioneer
Thought it scarcely worth his while
To waste much time on the old violin,
But held it up with a smile:
"What am I bidden, good folks," he cried,
"Who'll start the bidding for me?"
"A dollar, a dollar"; then, "Two!" "Only two?
Two dollars, and who'll make it three?
Three dollars, once; three dollars, twice;
Going for three —" But no,
From the room, far back, a gray-haired man
Came forward and picked up the bow;
Then, wiping the dust from the old violin,
And tightening the loose strings,
He played a melody pure and sweet
As a caroling angel sings.

The music ceased, and the auctioneer,
With a voice that was quiet and low,
Said: "What am I bid for the old violin?"
And he held it up with the bow.
"A thousand dollars, and who'll make it two?
Two thousand! And who'll make it three?
Three thousand, once, three thousand, twice,
And going, and gone," said he.
The people cheered, but some of them cried,
"We do not quite understand
What changed its worth." Swift came the reply:
"The touch of a master's hand."

And many a man with life out of tune,
And battered and scarred with sin,
Is auctioned cheap to the thoughtless crowd,
Much like the old violin.
A "mess of pottage," a glass of wine;
A game — and he travels on.
He is "going" once, and "going" twice,
He's "going" and almost "gone."
But the Master comes, and the foolish crowd
Never can quite understand
The worth of a soul and the change that's wrought
By the touch of the Master's hand.

— Myra Brooks Welch

I see two birds on the same branch;

One eats the sweet fruit,

One looks on sadly.

The first bird wonders ------

In what prison does he live?

The second marvels ------

How can he rejoice?

4. In What Prison?

During the 7-year period which the following letters represent, Mickey and Paul were both inmates at the Oklahoma State Penitentiary in McAlester, Oklahoma. They became close friends and also friends of ours. They're two of the most awakened people Sita and I have had the good fortune to meet in our prison work.

This chapter is about the highest highs and lowest lows, and also a glimpse into the power and pain of deep friendship. It's not a simple or clear-cut story like "I was blind but now I see; thanks a lot." It's more the way life really is for most of us: "I was blind, I saw, I was blind again, I saw again...."

This correspondence is also a good reminder not to close the books prematurely on any of us or our friends, because change often seems to strike as unpredictably as lightning.

The letters start with Mickey:

Dear Friends,

I am a prisoner here at OSP, where I am presently incarcerated on a lock-up unit known as "administrative segregation." I am not allowed yard privileges, and am only allowed out of my cell for approximately one hour a day. I have been "exercising" in this manner for the past eighteen months.

A couple of weeks ago, a friend let me borrow an issue of INSIDE-OUT. Now that I have read it a good many times (and will continue), I can only say that what I saw before as a hopeless situation has now become a blessing to my spiritual growth.

Indeed, instead of spending all of this idle time feeling sorry for myself, I now use it in positive ways. I have a full day and night (with only minor interruptions) to devote to meditation and hatha yoga. It's a perfect setting for doing asanas (postures). I have begun to really dig this beautiful solitude, believe me!

I wish to thank you for the good work you are currently doing and sincerely hope that you will continue.

In spiritual love, Mickey/Oklahoma

[six months later:]

Dear Friends,

Sincerely hope this finds all of the family there in good health and good spirits! I received the holiday card and have it pasted on the wall. It helps a great deal in my meditations.

I doubt that you would remember my last letter to you since it was several months ago and I'm sure you must get a large amount of mail from other prisoners daily. In my last letter I said that I was at that time in administrative segregation where I was awaiting trial for stabbing and killing another inmate, 18 months previously.

Last September I was finally tried, and received a sentence of 10 years to life—to be served after the completion of my current sentence, 28 years.

To say that I wasn't shaken by it would be untrue. I was in fact shaken a great deal, with a month or two of self-pity to ice the cake a bit. But I know where that's at by now. Nothing can be changed one iota through indulgences of the lower self. Grist for the mill, every bit of it. I am in a perfect position to clean up my karma and work on myself, and I intend to continue doing so. Now.

So here we are now, as Ram Dass says. It's ours to do what we want with it. Love, that's the key, I'm sure. Please keep up the wonderful work. Hope to be seeing the next newsletter soon. God bless you. I send love and peace.

Mickey

Sita wrote Mickey and invited him to write a few pages about his life and spiritual journey if he wanted to, for possible use in a book or newsletter. We got this reply:

Dear Sita,

Here is my writing. It may be too long or too repetitious. I know it's dramatic. But if you can use any of it, you certainly may. I would indeed feel honored to appear in your future book, if you feel that my inner changes fit me into it. I feel that I am still just at the beginning of my awakening into the higher realms of consciousness, but I am happy and I am free, which is a great change from the selfish, sad individual of two years ago. And I can love.

Thank you for your beautiful letter and invitation, Sita.
May all of you there be filled with much light, energy, and love!

God bless you, with Love, Mickey

A Personal Drama
I first became involved with drugs at 14. At 15, I had a morphine habit which was very costly. I was continually stealing in order to maintain it. I was arrested on numerous occasions, but since I was still classified as a juvenile, the most that could be done to me was to be placed in a state training school, which I subsequently was, more times than I could remember.

I went from boys' ranches to training schools throughout my early teens. But as soon as I was released from one, it was only a matter of days before I had the needle back in my arm. Life was becoming one vicious circle of: Fix, nod, habit, steal, busted, and once again incarcerated for a few months. Then back on the streets and it starts again...

When I was 16 I was arrested while burglarizing a pharmacy. Since I had now reached the age to be legally considered an adult in this state, I was tried as such. I pled guilty for a two-year suspended sentence on the condition that I voluntarily commit myself for treatment at the Federal Narcotics Hospital, Lexington, Kentucky.

*I was in Lexington for 11 months. I attended group-therapy meetings as well as receiving extensive individual counselling by the psychiatrists there. Their program was a good one for helping junkies to kick their physical habit, but the mental addiction was something else entirely. Although their intentions were to help, it did me very little good. As I have come to learn through experience, the only way to kick a destructive habit for good—**any** habit—is by first wanting, in your own heart, to be rid of it, and then changing your beliefs that you have of it. Will-power isn't enough. You must **believe** that the benefits of not having a habit are indeed better than the effects of the drug itself. Only then can you be entirely rid of it.*

I had the willpower to quit, but not the belief. I wasn't convinced that I needed a better life. In two months after my release from there, I was shooting stuff again.

I developed a habit once again. A few months later, I robbed three pharmacies and was arrested soon after. I was convicted and received three 25-year sentences, running concurrently. I had just turned 18, in June of '73, when I entered the Oklahoma State Penitentiary. Before I could get firmly adjusted to my new surroundings, the July riot occurred. Everything but the cellhouses were burned and destroyed, along with a few lives being lost during the mayhem. It was a bad scene, of course, as everyone seemed to have lost control of their emotions in their desire to destroy. Myself included.

A couple of years later, I was transferred to a medium-security facility. They had several vocational training programs there which were offered to the prisoners. I had no desire to learn a vocation, so I wasn't concerned with that. My only desire was to escape. I had been doing it mentally for most of my life, and I had no desire to start accepting myself now. Without dope there was nothing. I had to get out of there and get back into it.

I attempted to escape after I had been there for two months. While I was climbing over the fence, a tower guard spotted me and began shooting. I was shot in the leg, and that ended my escape. Later, I was transferred back to this maximum-security facility at McAlester, where I am now (I was also sentenced to two more years for that).

*After I had been back about a year, I began regressing even further. There was much—and still is—paranoia, resentment, and frustration seething among the prisoners here. Since the riot, there had been very little "recreational" activity of any kind. Most of the population was on a sort of general lock-down, with nothing but idleness among them. Since I had never really bothered to care or show much compassion for a fellow human being, I was as much caught up in the hatred and self-pity as the "crowd". I was doing nothing to improve my conditions which I had inwardly created, yet I was convinced that **I** wasn't really to blame for my unhappiness. It was the guards; it was the unjust world in which we live; it was my mother because she didn't show me enough love; it was my father because he drank too much. The bastards had all let me down. My God, poor, angry me!! And I just luxuriated in the warmth of self-pity. It is a very soothing trap.*

A few months later, my self-contempt and paranoia were at an all-time high. Wanting some way to relieve my frustration externally, as I certainly didn't want to make the change internally, I began searching for an outlet.

There was an individual on the same run as I, whom I did not like because he was always "looking" at me funny. So I got myself a shiv, went down to his cell one morning, and stabbed him to death. I did not say anything to him; I just started stabbing and stabbing, with no desire to stop until I was sure he was dead. I doubt that he even knew why I was doing it. I did not quite comprehend myself, other than knowing what an immense feeling of power my ego experienced in being able to literally cut down another human being. Since I was secretly very much afraid of this environment, I now assumed that I would no longer be as insecure; that everyone would know I was "dangerous", and would be afraid of me.

I was arrested for the stabbing and placed on administrative segregation. I had very few friends on this unit, as I was (as I had wanted) "feared" by most of the prisoners. But the fear was not of respect, it was of contempt for a psychologically sick individual. I was now more alone than I had ever been in my life.

It was soon after that I began to feel pangs of guilt for what I had done. Why had I killed that guy? I had no right. He had done nothing to harm me. What did his family think of me?

Maybe he had a wife and children out there. The dude had a right to live. Who was I to deny him that right, just because I was too weak to grow up inside and face what I had created? Oh Mickey, Mickey, how worthless you've become! No one loves you, nor do you deserve to be loved. Even God, if He exists, has no love for you.

Thus did I spend my time, locked within my cell, as well as my inner prison, hating and feeling sorry for myself. There was no hope left for me, I thought. So I took a razor blade and slit my throat and the insides of my elbows. I truly wanted to die.

But I didn't die, of course. I was rushed to the hospital, sewn up, given a few blood transfusions, and transferred to the State Mental Hospital in Vinita. I went through the psychiatric evaluation scene, was analyzed, given a host of psychiatric labels, which in essence meant that I was socially and mentally crazy. It was a very heavy drama.

A few weeks later I was back on administrative seg. It was at this point though that my life began to change. A friend came to my cell one day and asked me a question. He said, "I know how it is, you think you've got it bad, bro. But dig: Did you really think you could clean up your karma by killing your physical body?" I was confused by his question; I didn't know what he was talking about. So he gave me a book to read—THE PROPHET—by Kahlil Gibran. The truths contained within that book are what enabled me to open my eyes to much that is within my own being, which I had been stifling through the years by my resentments and guilt complexes. And then after reading INSIDE-OUT and BE HERE NOW, the puzzle was starting to fit together.

202

Yes, there is a higher existence, a higher self within us. And desire does create attachment and attachment is suffering. And life, which does not begin in the womb and does not end in the grave, is indeed as beautiful as you wish it to be, prison environment included. We convicts who complain that life has nothing to offer, should consider, what are we giving to it? It gives us back as much happiness as we put into it.

If all we can contribute to our environment is bitterness and hatred, is it really surprising that bitterness and hatred is what we encounter in return? "As ye sow, so shall ye reap" is not just a Biblical myth. It is a natural law which is infallible. I have found this to be true, right here in this joint.

I put myself through much suffering before I reached this point. And was it necessary? Yes, for me it was. Before I could overcome my complexes, I had to experience their effects. I am not now a perfect individual without occasional upsets; but I am a free individual now, and I know that there are no limitations to what I can do, or what I can become through my own thinking.

I received an additional sentence of ten-years-to- life for that stabbing. That sounds like a long time. It is. How am I going to do it? Wallowing in self-pity for the past, which I now realize was necessary, or dreaming of an imaginary future of when it is over and I am no longer in prison? I am going to do neither. Today, right now at this very moment, is all that any of us can say is ours. I am using my now, not yesterday or tomorrow, as the time to work on myself.

I send much love, light, peace to you all, Namaste.

Mickey

Over the next few years, Mickey was pretty much the ideal of using the prison-as-an-ashram. According to his letters, he was doing his time just as if he were a monk in his cell.

Early in '82, we received our first letter from Paul:

Dear Bo and Sita,

It wasn't but three weeks ago that I received the most beautiful, most meaningful, most invaluable package in the mail from you. I must thank you all from the innermost depths of my eternal being. I not merely thank you for the gift of love you have given me, but also for the gift of love you are sharing with all beings throughout the world! I thank you for spreading the truth that we can all find peace and unity in knowing who we really are, and that in knowing the real Self that we can erase our ego-created sense of separateness and fade right back out of maya back to reality, back to divinity, back home, back to infinite oneness with God and universe! Wow!! It's like, "I was blind, but now I see."

It doesn't take but a seed of truth to set a man upon the path, and you not only provided the seed, you also provided me with the love to nourish it. Well hey, I love you, too! I'm doing hatha yoga, pranayam, and mindfulness meditation every day. Evidently the timing for my contact with these disciplines was perfect, for I'm attaining amazing health and mind control in no time at all. It seems like I've been doing this for centuries—soooo natural does it seem!

Just yesterday I had a meeting with the substance-abuse counselor here. I had written her about starting a yoga-meditation class. Her response to my interest was beautiful, but there is going to be a lot of red tape to go through in order to do it. This particular facility is the tightest in the system; the officials are really down on inmate incentive. We expect great opposition because of what experience has shown us here. The politics are very ugly. The overall energy here is awesomely oppressive; this place is very ripe for riot and massive violence. This substance-abuse counselor here is the only beacon of hope, and she'll be struggling against extreme odds. Is there any way you could help? The prison needs such a program desperately to change the energy.

I'll close for now. Once again, thank you! Shine on!

Much Love, Paul

Dear Paul,

Nice to meet you, too; we feel and appreciate all your love.

Maybe the way I could help get your program off the ground would be to do a workshop there this summer. We have heard from over 100 guys there, so I know there's enough interest. The workshop would be free, no strings attached, so maybe the administration would go for it. I hear what you're saying about the ugly politics and so forth, but don't get stuck in pessimism when you're dealing with a spiritual trip. God is always the wild card, you know. You'd be amazed at the miraculous cutting of red tape sometimes.

Your substance abuse counselor sounds like a real jewel. It's funny, I've noticed that in the very worst joints, there always seems to be at least one bright light working quietly in the shadows. Maybe that's God's way of keeping the whole place from going over the edge.

All the best, Bo

After a few complications and false starts, my workshop was approved. Paul wrote, *Thanks for the advice about my pessimism. I now see the divine workings of **all** events...* He said that my workshop was the first outside program allowed inside since the riot several years earlier. The wild card!

With a total of about fifty men coming together in the hot, stifling gym, we could hardly hear each other because of the bad acoustics and the overhead fans (no windows). But the living Spirit flowed like sap in the springtime, and we all got very high, including Charlotte (the substance-abuse counselor) and a few other staff members. The workshop was great, and it was wonderful to finally meet both Paul and Mickey in person for the first time.

Paul exchanged huge hugs with us, but Mickey seemed strangely uncomfortable. I noticed that during the meditation periods—especially the eye-to-eye meditation with another inmate—he had as hard a time as any of the newcomers; and he avoided eye contact with me and Sita when we spoke with him afterward.

A few months later we received the following letter from Paul about what Mickey was going through:

Dear Bo and Sita,

*For quite a few days now, I've debated over how and when to tell you of Mickey's current predicament. Today seems to be the day. Early last week Mickey cut himself across the neck with a razorblade in what appeared to be a suicide attempt. However, the wound wasn't too bad, and physically he's safe and secure. Mentally, Mickey is in bad shape. I really don't think he was truly wanting to die, because I think he really would have if he intended to—Mickey **knows** how to waste himself, dig? At any rate, I can't say; only he knows for sure.*

I thought he was really doing good, but I knew he was having his "down days" more frequently. I just don't have the chance to be with him very much (only at mealtimes); otherwise maybe I could have helped prevent this. At any rate, I'm deeply concerned with his present state and am praying for him. I've tried to get them to let me go out to the infirmary to see him, but I don't guess they're gonna let me do that.

*I saw Charlotte yesterday; she promised she'd check into the situation and put all her energy into helping Mickey. But I saw her again this morning and she was teary-eyed as she informed me it looks real bad. She said he is on a severe paranoid trip and thinks that nobody cares; that he doesn't have any friends in here. This is not true though! If only dear Mickey knew the love I have for him, he'd know he had a **real** friend. But like Charlotte says, he's just in that frame of mind—he's very confused. And also, he stated that he just doesn't have any energy anymore.*

*I'm mostly in fear of the treatment they're giving him, and the possibility of him being transferred to the state hospital. Charlotte said they were giving him medications to try and balance his "neuro-transmitters"! Hey, don'tcha know that those psych drugs can effect a slow **lobotomy**?! I just don't believe that Mickey requires psych drugs, dig?*

Anyway, Charlotte is good, and her love is real, and she's not gonna let them screw Mickey up if she can help it. She has committed herself to working with him. Fantastic! We can trust her!

Well, if there's anything at all that can befall me, it's the sufferings of others. Yet at the same time, it hastens my own growth, as I see even more the need to become a wellspring for them. Emotionally I went way down when I heard of Mickey's fate, yet spiritually, there's been more fuel added to my fire. I'm just kinda directing all that Grace that God grants me toward Mickey right now. I understand that he's got his own karma to work out in his own way, yet I dream of taking some of it on myself. How can I best serve to help him? What am I missing? Please tell me anything I may be blind to, as I know there are many subtle realms I'm not awakened to.

You know, you wrote me a letter just a couple weeks ago in which you said to enjoy the highs, but expect the lows also, and not be crushed by them. Well, that has helped me to keep flowing through this new happening. I want to assure you that I'm pretty secure in my center. I do not fear any "falls" because I've come to realize the push-and-pull nature of God's Grace. Hard times are lessons for me, and although I don't for wish them to happen, I value them when they do.

I recall my arrival here about a year ago—I had been gone on an escape from here for three years, and had served a sentence in Texas while I was away. You see, my life turned around during that three years, and I totally transformed my life while I was serving time in Texas. Yet I had this Oklahoma time still pending, so I was transferred straight from TDC to here last November. Anyway, when I arrived here, they immediately threw me in a solitary cell and left me alone for about 24 hours.

I had come from being on a huge self-high in Texas, straight to solitary here. It was a **big** change. Everything was going perfectly in Texas, and I had not sinned against myself nor the system in three years.

Well, it was quite a plunge, a very hard fall, to come to find myself in solitary for something I had done three years before. I recall pacing the floor of that cell with pure confusion and torment. I cried and cursed and kicked the door a couple of times, but then all of a sudden, I **stopped**—instantly I smiled to myself and sat down on the floor and did some breathing exercises. I gathered my composure and went in to a deep, conscious rest—I meditated. Soon I was stretched out on the concrete floor with my hands as a pillow and I rested safe and calm and sound and secure for the remainder of my duration in that cell. I found refuge in that space where God dwells, and His Grace humbled me to the limit. I still hold that ability to stay centered throughout it all, and a year later it's now a **lot** stronger.

I know I'll always get hit **hard** at first, but once I go to God for refuge, all suffering will subside because I'll surrender my will to God's will, and if it's God's will for me to suffer, I'll do so joyously in utter humility. Now see here, I'm talking to myself as I'm talking to you, dig? Can you relate?

Thank you for your love and light. Be sure to never hesitate to point out something I may need to see, as I'm a child on this journey and need the guidance of those of you who've matured on the path. I love you both sooooo much!

Peace and love, Paul

Dear Paul,

I'll write to Mickey today. Your letter (as usual) is right on and well put. What else could I "point out" to you in words? The real work is for you and me to stay in the place where we *embody* all the stuff we write and talk about.

And we both have to have faith that we'll be helping a lot just by doing that, even if we never hear from Mickey again. Just keep him in your heart.

I think it's perfectly okay to allow Mickey's pain to rip our hearts apart. At times, the line between compassion and attachment is a very fine one, very subtle, and nobody outside of yourself can know the difference. So don't be too upset about going "emotionally way down." That's part of the ball game too. It's not spiritually unhip or anything.

The psych-drug scene tends to bother me too, but I guess there's nothing we can do about that other than through Charlotte. Just makes faith even more important.

Anyway, much love from here. Let's all keep sending Mickey Light for his difficult journey, and remember that it's all just family business; no accidents or interruptions of our dance with each other. This is the stuff we need to do.

Love, Bo

[same day:]

Dear Mickey,

Just a short note to say hi, and let you know we've heard the latest news. We send all our love and blessings. We've been in touch with Paul, who loves you very deeply as a brother. He tried to get in to see you last week, but they wouldn't let him.

What else can I say when I have no idea where you're at right now? I don't need to lay any trips on you, bro; just to say we're here and we love you. Drop us a line if you feel like it.

Much Love, Bo

Dear Bo,

Charlotte told me that Mickey received your letter. Although he was suspicious at first, he finally showed some light and told her to tell you all, "I'm not totally lost..." He's been transferred to a prison mental health center in another city. Charlotte said she'd write the staff there and ask them to work closely with him.

*I think the statement he made for you is a sign he's still **here**, just going through some conditions to drain old energies, burn out accumulated karma, and re-establish himself in a newer, truer self-image—I feel this will be the outcome. I'd say he's also eradicating pent-up guilt by denying himself his sanity for a time; like a self-punishment trip. But even if none of my perceptions is accurate, one thing is for certain, and you said it Bo: "This is his path up the mountain." That helps me to better help Mickey, as well as to trust God's will.*

*As for me, this past year has been the most meaningful, most **real** year of my life. As I sit here now, I'm really here, and I'm free. Who could ever imagine a man's freedom being found in a prison? There's an unfolding process within me now, an awakening to higher levels of understanding and to purer forms of love and service.*

207

But actually, it's not "higher" or "purer" at all; just a balancing act, a blending-in-with-the-scenery-effect. I've transcended the "elation" and I'm not just "high" anymore. Ha! Can you dig it? I'm just sitting here watching the wheel go round and round without the elation anymore. I'm seeing the Dharma unfold now without tripping on it. Yet my enlightenment level is yet to be clear of all illusion, thus I'm still humanly grounded or "caught"... but it's getting lighter. Keep on shining!

I love you, Paul

[from Mickey:]

Dear Bo and Sita,

I sincerely hope this finds you in beautiful spirits. I received your Christmas card and the beautiful truth of which St. Paul so grandly expressed. How easy it is to become so engrossed in our spiritual evolvement that we lose sight of the very force that gives any of it meaning—the simple act of loving. Without it it's all dry and empty. This love transcends ourselves. Yet try to grab hold and call it "mine" and it loses its magic. Love does what it will, and lets it go at that. To participate in its flow is a holy experience. May we all grow in love and its blessing.

Bo, everything's all right. I chose to be crazy for awhile but I'm back to being normal, or whatever it's called, again. I got real depressed and angry and paranoid and all that neurotic stuff because I wanted to say, "Fuck it, that's it, I ain't dealing with this anymore. It's all got to end. It's all so stupid and empty anyway." And so that's what I wanted to say. And so I said it. Now I can get back to the journey. Love. You said it. The comforter Christ sent us. With it the journey's not too heavy at all.

Dig. This place where I am now is really interesting. IMHU it's called. There are eighty men here, all of whom are into some state of psychosis. They're really neat. Some of 'em are very high but they're afraid to come back down into the grossness of physical reality. Others merely choose to check out 'cause they don't like the rules. Whatever. I don't judge any of 'em for their choices.

I am in a "group" with five other guys who have attempted suicide. It's a psychological therapy thing. I really enjoy it. I love these guys. Some are very tormented from attachments they've formed with the "free world" and have tried suicide rather than give up the attachment. But they still don't really want to die, they're just wanting to make a statement, a rebellious cry for help. I can relate to them. I try to share some of my own experiences in prison. If one of us opens up, the rest will too. I don't try to "tell" anyone how to do their time, but if I can help in the least way, it helps me in the highest way. It's good to feel free. It's good to be aware.

Christ is the Light that dispels the darkness. There can be no darkness where Light is. He said that "Where I am you may be also." It's nearly Christmas, the time of year that we celebrate that Light within where He is. May the joy of this

Light shine throughout each of us, and may we know that peace that says it's okay to love old people, little children, and even strangers. That peace which is total. I wish you both a merry Christmas. Thanks for being who you are.

I love you, Mickey

We had some brief correspondence with both Mickey and Paul. Mickey got transferred back to maximum, and he and Paul became best friends once again. Paul worked up a proposal for a vegetarian/macrobiotic diet program at the prison. He really poured himself into it and got all kinds of support from outside authorities, and then just when it seemed it might get approved, he was suddenly transferred to another prison. The proposal was scrapped.

But just a few days before his transfer, we received the following letters from him and Mickey, one day apart. Mickey's came first:

Dear Bo and Sita,

Discontinue sending me your newsletter. Also your perfumed cards. I don't want to hear anymore from you people. Waste your precious endeavor on your "brother" and his monumental crusade against "sickness". You look for something to be a certain way and that's what you'll see. But like that fellow holed up in that trailer, it's either real or it ain't. I don't really give a shit one way or another. I'm tired of playing this stupid game. Don't write me anymore.

Mickey

Dear Bo and Sita,

Much love to the two of you. Bo, your comment about Mickey ("his path up the mountain") probably saved me from hurting him more than he is, or from hurting myself—as I've come to see that it is impossible to "pin" Mickey or anyone else down at all, and to even attempt in the slightest way breeds pain and suffering. Even now I haven't let go completely. I'm caught.

On one side I'm afraid that to let Mickey go would be a disaster for him, as I'm the only one in here who tries to help him. Just last week I talked him out of suicide. Yet on the other hand, Mickey swings from high to low so rapidly anymore that it seems he would be better off if I let him work it out for himself....

Just yesterday I met a very arrogant, aggressive, and dangerous Mickey. This was a new personality, as before he was either totally high and happy or depressed, withdrawn and suicidal. He came to scare me yesterday. He talked of a desire to catch anyone messing him around in any way, for he claimed he wanted an excuse to hurt someone. He told me that he's not been sick at all, that he's just been playing games, and for me to forget about trying to get him help.

*Bo, his posture was totally different, his gestures were different, his expressions, tone of voice, energy, **everything** was different. This was not Mickey at all. He even managed to spook me a little as I recall keeping a ready distance from him.*

*He told me he wrote you all and told you never to write him again. Believe me,
if he did, it wasn't **him** that did it, do you understand? He said the teachings are
all bullshit, and he got rid of all his books. Well I have no choice now, I guess....
it looks like I **have** to let go. But I can see a pattern, and he'll be high again soon
and wanting help.*

*I've never been in a situation like this, so I need some advice. I love Mickey, but
I don't know what to do unless it's "nothing". I'm confused... but something inside
me says, "just play it by ear and learn to interact with his different personalities
just as if he is completely different people each time." One thing, I think it would
be best if you don't mention my name to him if you do write him. He gets paranoid
and thinks the people who love him are plotting to hurt him, dig?*

Geez, I'm really caught! I love you, may peace be yours,

Love, Paul

Dear Paul,

Just wrote to Mickey a few minutes ago (that letter follows this one). You
asked me for advice on how to deal with him, but again, I encourage you
to trust those intuitive voices in your gut. You've been doing a lot of
spiritual practices in an intense environment for a long time now, and I
think it's time you started to realize that people like me and Sita don't have
any more access to wisdom than you do. Trust yourself. Trust your connection to the same Spirit I turn to for answers. I know it's getting hot and
heavy right now, but these *are* the teachings you've been praying for for
so long.

Your life teaches me at least as much as mine teaches you. However you
handle Mickey's whole scene, you're a pioneer in uncharted territory. If I
were there, I'd have to make my best guesses, and sometimes I'd be right
and sometimes not. I think Mickey is blessed by having you as his friend,
whether you figure out perfect strategies for dealing with him or not. I
send all my support, bro.

Love, Bo

Dear Mickey,

Well, you said not to write you anymore, but my mama always told me
to reply to a personal letter from a friend. And whether you like it or not,
you're a friend of mine. If you never write me again, you'll just be a friend
who never wrote me again.

By the way, we've never owned any "perfumed cards". We're just doing
our thing like you're doing yours. We may well be full of shit, but at least
we're sincerely full of shit. So what are you so pissed off about?

Listen, I hope you decide to keep in touch, even just to argue. We've
exchanged a lot of love and insights through the years, and to me the
bummers are at least as good as the "love and light" ones. Do you think

that Sita and I never get depressed or cynical? We're both tired of "playing this stupid game" too! The problem is, the "stupid game" isn't just the spiritual trip; it's life itself—which includes suicide. I have no desire to find myself in diapers all over again, feeling *really* stupid for chucking a perfectly good body and mind just to start again as somebody else.

The only way to break out—as the wise ones have told us for ages—is to get free. And the only way to do that is to go all the way through; not around or behind or in front of or over or under—but through. If there were an easier way—or *any* other way—believe me, I'd take it in a flash! If you find one, let me know.

All those great highs and clear insights you've had the past few years, have been preparation for helping you to endure this painful karma you've been feeling lately. Just try to hang on to a sliver, Mick; just a fingernail-worth, and you'll make it. Try opening to the pain and fear instead of shutting it out or allowing it to take you over. You can do it; you can do it. I've been there, and I know how cold and scary it can get. I remember times when it took every ounce of energy just to keep from curling up into a ball and going catatonic. You can make it Mick; it may take all the effort you've got and all that you can pray for, but you can do it. You're working out some tough karma. Meanwhile, Sita and I still love you dearly, and we hope you don't chalk us up. We don't need to save your soul; just say hi every now and then.

Love, Bo

[nearly a year later:]

Dear Bo and Sita,

I sincerely hope this letter finds you and your son well and in good spirits. I received your letter a few months ago. Thank you for writing in response to the letter I wrote you, in which I said not to write me anymore. I appreciate the fact that you did anyway.

I am still your friend, of course. I suppose I always will be. It was your message which, in 1975, stirred an awakening in me that probably saved my life, though that is not such a big deal. What is such a big deal is the understanding that came with it, and is still coming as I grow older. Or maybe nothing is happening at all—maybe "understanding" is just another stupid detour from what is Real.

Your message is essentially the same as it's always been. But it's cloaked in a different form now. For awhile it was centered on the "Higher Self" or that "One Within." Now it's mainly concerned with how to cut through suffering and pain. I realize you're not into "how-to" lessons, so maybe I expressed that wrong. But then you can't tell anyone how to get out of their suffering any more than a rock can become a fish. All you can do is tell 'em most people don't give a fuck whether they're suffering or not, because they're too caught in their own private hells, and so they'd best find their own way out.

Yes, I'm sure it would be a good response to say, "Maybe I can't tell them the way out, but I can love them," as if that means anything.

Love. What does it mean? Ram Dass tells us it ain't attachment. St. Paul tells us it's unconditional. But I've never known love that wasn't based on some form of attachment or gratification.

I search my heart. I can find only two people I love. My grandfather, because he does something for me, and has all my life, and a homosexual in another institution with whom I've had a sexual and friendly relationship. I've never met a single being who did not enjoy hearing the words "I love you." But I've not met one either who did not enjoy hearing how great a person they were. Where is the detachment, the unconditionality in this?

The love you speak of is beyond my understanding. And the other love, the attachment stuff, is probably the cause of more pain than anything I ever knew. And you call this "Life". I understand why so many people are afraid to live. Or to "love".

Now you want to tell me that if we don't "get it right" this lifetime, we'll just have to do it all over again. How do you know? What makes you so convinced anybody'll have to do anything again? I've read all the metaphysical stuff on natural laws and what-not, and most of 'em are no more than assumptions. It all comes down to the age-old admonishment of punishment, or the offer of reward, if you think a certain way. Even a white rat in a cage learns to play that game after a while. Or fear it. It's just one more brainwashing technique.

Fear. Let's talk about fear, my friends. Not necessarily fear of bodily harm, but fear of being degraded and humiliated in a world where such things are much more harmful to your chances of getting by than anything else.

Beginning the year before, and continuing up until the late summer of last year, it became increasingly hard to deal with my environment. Long-time "friends" took it upon themselves to play games with my mind. If you've been in touch with Paul, then you probably already know what I'm talking about. If you don't, well, it really doesn't need an explanation. You weren't there. You didn't breathe that shit being sprayed into my cell night after night. You didn't stink of it, while everyone was laughing. You didn't see the pretense. Even my own sister and brother on the streets played the little game. But they didn't ingest the shit, unknowingly, that damaged my liver and intestinal tract permanently, as I discovered at Eastern State Hospital last summer. Nor are they taking seizure medication for a fucked-up brain that resulted from all this shit.

Yeah, I must be a paranoid schizophrenic. And maybe my actions do fit that label, but what happened wasn't any imagination or a hallucination. And the results goddamn sure wasn't.

Now I don't know whether or not you people were, in your own way, playing a game with me or not. And I don't care if you were or were not. I don't believe that you would ever intentionally hurt anyone, especially someone whom you've cared about for so long a time as me. But then, who knows? I no longer try to understand what motivates people. Whenever someone in here would express their pain and I would try to help with words that I thought may enlighten, they would only become further distant and ridicule me for acting like some great teacher, etc. Their ridicule turned to spite pretty quickly.

So fuck them. At the present time I am doing 60 days on the disciplinary unit for assaulting an officer, and "disrespecting" him. I didn't have any motive for doing it. I was just drunk and angry. And a little paranoid. You see, brother, when you ain't got any more friends—if indeed they ever truly were—the only thing left is to be aware of your enemies. Sometimes that's a paranoid situation.

But now I say this: Whoever I am and whatever I am, if anything at all, ain't going for any more games. I'm through with it, brother. I've got just as strong a will to live as anyone, but I also have a life sentence I haven't even started yet. I ain't going to do it being fucked with. And fuck all this shit about punishment and reward. When it's your time, it's your time. The next son of a bitch that plays this game with me is going to find out it's not as amusing as he thought it would be.

I appreciate your letter, Bo and Sita, and I appreciate the years of togetherness we've shared. I'm here, and your friend,   *Mickey*

Dear Mickey,

Boy, are we happy to hear from you again and to hear you call us your friends. We are and always will be.

You said, "Love. What does it mean?", and then went on to say how you can't possibly understand unconditional love because it seems that everybody has their own wants and needs. But the whole point is that Love (capital "L") is *beyond* understanding; it has to be experienced by each one of us directly.

You're trying to deal with it in your mind, and I agree with almost everything you say. No doubt about it, your mind is sharp and your logic is strong. You have great insight. But what you're missing is that the mind is the biggest game-player of all. It's ironic that you're willing to be paranoid about all your friends, yet at the same time you're putting complete trust in your own mind, which has more vested interest in fucking you over than anyone outside of yourself.

I went through a lot of intense paranoia during my acid years; so much so that Sita and my brother were beginning to think I might have to be institutionalized. I do understand how powerful paranoia is, please believe me, Mick. At those times, our minds feed us sweet poison and tell us there's no such thing as nectar; they take our best insights and twist them around to make them seem ugly.

Your mind is telling you the world is chaotic, random and vicious; that it's all totally absurd. But that's because the mind wants to malign what it can't control. Your spiritual work has brought you beyond the mind at various times, which is a threat to your ego. So now it's convincing you to be cynical, and fogging your own memory about what it *feels* like to touch real love, and to *know* about things like reincarnation. These things aren't assumptions or beliefs at all; these are direct experience. And you have had the experiences too; you're just forgetting how clear the feelings were at those times.

I know your lessons right now are hard ones, I really do. I don't know how well I would do in your situation. But none of that changes the basic fact: These are lessons, whether you like them or not. Your life is still a required course, so you may as well once again shoot for an "A". There's no other way out, since you already know too much to flunk. Don't always trust your mind so much!

Love, Bo

Dear Bo,

I received your letter. You said it pretty well. But then, you always have since I've known you. I wish I could put it into such perfect perspective. If I survive this drama, maybe someday I will.

I trust you, bro. I trust Sita, too. Anybody that cares, I've got to trust. And your letter wasn't a bunch of bullshit. That letter came from the heart and from nowhere else. No doubt about that. I've got two friends for life, and maybe even after. There are millions who don't have that much. I am fortunate. I can't throw it away on some paranoid whim. Besides, where would I throw it? I once read that systems of energy contain no garbage. I still believe it. So where could it go?

I know you and Sita are busy, but I'd like to tell you a story. I used to walk the west yard a lot. I walked it for several years; walked it in the scorching summer, the icy snow, the drenching rain, and walked it in the mellow days of May. I could make 350 laps a day easily. Sometimes made a thousand.

One day while I was walking, a fellow convict ambled up beside me and fell into step. After a few laps he said, "You wanna get high?" I said sure, and he broke out five good joints of sinsemilla. I smoked with him and I got very high and introspective, the way good smoke makes you.

I stopped walking and looked around. Suddenly I knew the score. I watched some blacks shucking and jiving like a Fleetwood on blocks, I checked out the poker tables, where guilt-ridden men threw away hundreds as fast as they could read their hands, and the hungry ate it up with relish. I saw the drag queens in their skin-tight pants and dark eye-liner made from magic markers, selling their wares for five packs a shot; I saw the young pretty ones, sitting alone, turned out against their will, and their eyes were dead.

I saw the stabbings, the homicides, and the utter futility of someone making themselves a reputation, as if a brutal act would in some way make them more of what they already was. I killed once, myself, as you know. I stabbed an innocent man 30 times and cut his throat. I felt guilty. I even attempted suicide several times, but the rope always seemed to break right as I was losing consciousness. I began to believe it just wasn't my time, so I blew it off.

Then the friend came by and turned me on to BE HERE NOW and INSIDE-OUT, and he also brought me a great deal of weed. I read the books a minimum of ten times each. Afterward, I would meditate and then smoke a joint. Next I would start my asanas. I got it together for the first time in my life, and had it together for several years after that. In my heart something began to blossom and grow. For some reason I didn't even understand, there appeared an actual feeling of love and compassion.

For the first time in my life, I knew love—the kind you spoke of; the kind Sita spoke of. Yeah, I felt the bliss of forgetting myself long enough to remember my brothers. I was, it seems, in a form of Bhakti Yoga, damn near all the time.

But then came a time when my mother o.d.'d and died. She wasn't only a mother, but my best friend as well, and just about my only link to the outside world.

Not long after, my friend and lover for several years was transferred suddenly to another institution (I'm in the category of bisexuality, if that means anything; or maybe for a lifer like me you could call it "no-choice bisexuality", 'cause ain't nothin' else possible.) And though his departure meant little to most, it was devastating to me. I drew in other lovers, as many as I could, hoping to distract myself from the hurt. And I became attached to each one, and each one sooner or later was transferred away, each time hurting.

I became tired of it all, and very bitter. The blossom in my heart began to fade and become choked. Fuck all of 'em. I figured I had just been used by all those people anyway. Well, now I would use and hurt people, in whatever way I could. I didn't think these exact words in the conscious mind; consciously I was just trying to get numb, trying not to feel anything but indifference, if you can call that a feeling.

I almost succeeded. I talked bad about good people, stole their dope, and just generally violated every convict code imaginable. I had sunk to the very depths of hell, brother. The fact that I am still breathing is only due to some of these convicts' compassion. I know it in my heart. They don't use fifty-cent words or play the psychiatric game, but they care about me, and they are sincere when they say "I'm your friend and it hurts me to see you in this bad state." I know they are sincere, because I've made quite a habit of lying these past three years, and can knock off someone else that's lying. Or at least I think I can.

My bitterness didn't quite work out like I thought it would. I ended up hurting only myself. And I think now I'm glad of that. I don't think I'm glad I'm hurting, but I'm glad I'm not hurting someone else. Not only because I'd feel even more guilty than I already have, but simply because I have a few friends who I never want to see hurt or misused. Could be that I'm learning about love, through the good times and the bad.

Thanks for your help, Bo. I don't know if anyone ever writes and tells you how *much peace and love your words inspire, but believe me, they inspire probably more than you are aware of. You're perfectly attuned with that higher level of conciousness. Yet you don't get so far out that you lose touch with the world. "Render unto Caesar what is Caesar's, and to God what is God's."*

I hope I explained this story right. If I didn't, then just disregard these last five pages and read very closely the following: I LOVE YOU, Mickey

Sita also got a letter from Mickey on the same day, reaffirming his love for us and rapping a little about his times of "insanity". These two letters came on a Monday. On Wednesday, just two days later, we got the following, which is the last we've heard from Mickey at the time of publication:

Dear Bo and Sita,

Well, it is now thought by this writer to tell you that he sincerely hopes that you both will please disregard his two previous letters written the past few days; the letters which he had expounded so much on the trickery of the mind.

It was a good ploy, but it won't do a thing for his difficulties. In fact, his difficulties are even greater than they were then.

Disregard it all as a lie. No, not all of it. When he said he loved you, he still does. Or whatever it's called. He just ain't gonna be convinced that his mind has done anything but be what it is.

This writer will be going back to Eastern State Hospital at Vinita in the next few days. There they will fill his mind with psychotropic drugs and he will forget. He may even forget who he is, until someone says "Mickey". Then he will say "Oh."

He is now on the nut ward, and when you get this letter, he will have probably already be gone.

But he has to say he doesn't feel like he's insane yet. No, but he feels a deep hurt that he has been fooled into something he doesn't believe in.

Mickey would like to die more than anything. But he just doesn't have the courage to do it himself yet. Many people would like to see that occur, though. No, many people would rather just see him experience continual pain. Well, just fuck them and fuck you.

[unsigned]

And so the story goes, toward an end that only God may know. Paul was paroled in mid-'84, and is busy trying to create a new life outside. Mickey has gone back and forth between the hospital and maximum-security McAlester, and Sita and I keep tabs on him in various ways.

The temptation has been to expect some sort of conclusion to this struggle, as if any day now we might get a letter from Mickey saying that his paranoia is gone and his head is on straight once again. But then we realize that such a letter is no more "permanent" than any of the other letters. It could be followed in a matter of minutes by a whole other state of mind.

Isn't that true for all of us?

216

A human being is part of the whole called by us 'universe', a part limited in time and space. He experiences himself, his thoughts and feelings as something separated from the rest—a kind of optical delusion of his consciousness.

This delusion is a kind of prison for us, restricting us to our personal desires and to affection for a few persons nearest to us.

Our task must be to free ourselves from this prison by widening our circle of compassion to embrace all living creatures and the whole of nature in its beauty.

—Albert Einstein

In this place, touching hurts so much.
Love, hate, lust and violence,
all hurt so much;
they overlap, they merge,
then separate again.

What nightmare is this?
My God, when will I awaken?

5. Love, Hate, Lust, Violence

Tom

Dear Bo,

I just re-read your newsletter for March, 1982, and once again your philosophy has touched me.

In 1968, I was beaten, tortured, and gang-raped in a county jail. This took place over a 24-hour period during which, besides the "usual" brutality of such incidents, I was also wrapped up in a sheet and set on fire. My attackers urinated on me to put it out. Although I was released two weeks later, I never really left it emotionally. Emotionally, the clock stopped for me on October 15th, 1968. Few days have gone by since, that I haven't experienced at least a few moments of shame and self-disgust and the wish for death.

For the first few years, I numbed myself with marijuana. But after I stopped using drugs in '72, I slipped into a depression that lasted until 1980 when I finally began therapy. After two years of therapy, my rage is greater than ever. And now my rape may be a factor in the break-up of my 12-year marriage. A therapist has warned me that I may have become obsessed with being heard about my assault because of so long a silence.

For the two years before my rape, I had been a full-time political activist living in the barrios of San Antonio. I published and edited a tiny liberal community paper in Spanish and English.I often marched and demonstrated alone against poverty, against the Vietnam War, against discrimination and injustice of any kind. I was in jail for smashing two closed-circuit tv cameras in a restroom of a factory, to help workers publicize their grievances and win their strike. It was my first offense.

You said, "our greatest acts of violence are how we constantly judge others." I understand these words but I feel so powerless to rid my heart of the desire for revenge. I know how overloaded you are with pleas of help from prisons all over the country, but in your prayers, could you please remember me? I do the same for you and all the brothers and sisters in the Prison-Ashram Project.

On my forty-sixth birthday, February 14th, I began fasting from solid food. On Feb. 22nd I cloistered myself inside my leaky, uninsulated camper. I am also not speaking. I communicate only in writing. I am withdrawing from society and—if necessary—from life, unless I am blessed with justice and/or enlightenment.

God bless you for your wonderful work.

Namaste, Tom/Ca.

Dear Tom,

You're certainly in our prayers, and in the prayers of thousands of people who may read this. I really don't know whether anything I put into words will help you at all, but I'll try. Maybe between the lines we can communicate as if I were sitting next to you in your camper. I wish I could be.

You know that I've been involved for a long time now with people who have gone through the same sort of nightmare as you. I've never met anyone who had an easy time of it, or who looked back and said "boy, I sure am glad that happened!" So I won't try to snow you with any spiritual fairy tales. There are some terribly painful things that can happen to us in life, and you've been through one of the worst imaginable. That's the way things are.

But it's possible to come out of it with both your sanity and humanity intact, and even stronger than ever. Jesus's response to humiliation and torture has endured as an inspiration to the human spirit for thousands of years. Since you describe yourself as an activist, standing up for truth and justice, maybe now you're being given the opportunity to *really* be an activist, like Jesus was. Maybe this is the excruciating degree of compassion, pain, and forgiveness required to bring about truly effective social change; change which lasts.

I know it's tempting for you to say that no one could understand what you've been through. In one sense that's surely true, and it would be arrogant of me to say how I would handle your situation if it happened to me. But in another sense—a deeper one—all of us really do understand the pain, fear, loneliness, shame, and despair that you've described. It just comes in different forms, that's all.

When I was eighteen I had a 100-mph head-on crash with a tractor trailer. I've gone through a lot of operations and intense pain during the past 20 years, and I can remember times when the pain just wore me down so much that I didn't know if I could keep going through it. Many times I squeaked by on the thinnest shred of faith or Grace; who knows which? I became addicted to painkillers, went through periods of denial, over-exertion, depression and oceans of self-pity. And like you, I also heard about things like meditation and yoga and the whole spiritual trip.

I noticed that when I was able to *open* around the pain rather than trying to push it away, every now and then I experienced the "transcendence" that all the spiritual teachers talk about. Pain still hurts like hell during those times (like the Buddha said, "Pain will always be inherently unpleasant; that's just its nature"), but you can get so *big* that you're able to allow it to be just what it is. It no longer takes you over so fully; it no longer plunges you into despair. And the pain brings so much wisdom, humility, patience and other good lessons, eventually we come to appreciate its divine purpose in our lives.

You can say that my pain is different from yours, and yours is different from the young mother whose child was raped and murdered, and from my Canadian friend who fell off a mountain and is permanently paralyzed,

220

and from all the other people in the world who meet an endless variety of suffering during their lives. But pain is pain is pain, if we're willing to open up rather than shut ourselves down. If you look perhaps more openly than you have, you can find in your wife, your therapist, your neighbors and everyone else, a place which understands your suffering more than you've been willing to appreciate.

But what more can I say to you while it's hurting so much? These may sound like meaningless words as you sit in your camper wishing that half your life hadn't happened like it did. I send this letter more as a token of my love and friendship rather than an eloquent argument for or against any point of view. If you do decide to come through this instead of ending your life, just imagine the depth of compassion and understanding you can offer to others who suffer in their own forms of hell. I hope for you, me, and for the world, that you can emerge from this struggle as a true spiritual activist, with a loving heart which has been forged in the hottest fire of pain.

Love, Bo

Dear Bo,

Just received your wonderful letter. It really has brightened my day. What you had to pass on to me is really good and clear medicine.

I have been sweating out a lot of demons in my "cloister". This is the thirteenth day in my truck and the 22nd of my fast. I think I will be leaving the truck and breaking my fast in a few days. For one thing, my family is taking it very hard. They think I want to die, but they are only partially right.

Anyway, I'm feeling much better and clearer, and your letter has really helped. I'll treasure the letter in my spiritual diary and I'm sure that I will often refer to it in the future whenever I'm wrestling with my demons.

I would like to rest now, so I'll close. Thank you and may the light continue shining on you.

Namaste, Tom

To One Who Has Been Done Dirt

Cry or curse or call it unfair, but be grateful 'til the grave
That in this hurt you're the one who received, and not the one who gave.

—Carol Lynn Pearson

Joe

Dear Bo,

Have been in prison now a month and been wondering how I could best continue my two-year-old journey into myself and my spirituality. Yesterday I received a letter from a friend offering your address. Once again, when a real need arises, it is filled.

My crime is child molestation and I have sentence of 10-30 years. For the past two years I have been involved with bio-energetic therapy, a means to expel energy and emotion. I feel it was an attempt to break the blocks in my body and to allow the energy to flow in and out in a natural way. At any rate, it is impossible to continue these exercises here. I still feel a great need to work with my energy, and would like to learn some yoga methods. Maybe you could help me ?

I might add that since my crime I have had two revelations while at Arizona State Hospital. The first was that I have a perverted sexuality. In psychological terms I am described as an anal compulsive. The second (revelation) was re-experiencing my foster grandfather subjecting me to anal intercourse at about five or six years of age. The therapists at the hospital explained to me that they have seen many cases similar to mine. It seems being subjected to that treatment at an early age seems to arrest the natural growth of the individual's sexuality. I believe that happened to me, but not because of what my grandpa did as much as that I did not "experience" what I felt at the time. I simply turned off my ability to feel.

I also refused to accept that what turned me on was "behinds". Something like an alcoholic refusing to believe he wants to drink until he goes on a binge.

I still have erotic dreams about young boys' behinds, but I feel this is good in that I never had them prior to this revelation of my sexuality. I feel that I must accept where I am in order to move ahead.

I am trying to be moved to one of the two prisons that have programs which try to help folk in my situation develop their sexuality in a more acceptable way. This may take several years, in the meantime, since there is no counseling here, I would like to continue to grow spiritually. I would appreciate any advice that you think may be of use to me.

Bless you and breathe deeply, Joe/Az.

Dear Joe,

The materials we've sent you have a lot of useful methods for working with energy. The *pranayam* (breathing techniques) could be very helpful in terms of moving your energy and breaking up energy blocks.

Another method to try is this: Before you go to sleep each night, pray for help in working on these things in the dream state. Ask God to help you develop self-control and awareness by taking more responsibility in your dreams. In other words, you may start dreaming, as you said, "of young boys' behinds", but *in your dream* begin struggling to behave as you know you really want to behave out on the street.

I understand what you said about feeling good that you can finally be honest in your dreams, but now it's time to take it one step further, and begin changing it as well as recognizing it. Most of us allow ourselves free reign in our dreams, but in a way, that's just copping out. Have the erotic dreams, be honest about them, but also work in the dreams to be the person you know you need to become.

I think the combination of meditation, pranayam, yoga, prayer, and working on your dreams, along with whatever psychotherapy is available to you, is a very practical strategy for making the changes in your life which you really want to make. And when you've made them, you may be of great value to others who are stuck in the same painful patterns. Keep the faith, bro.

Love, Bo

Without going outside, you may know the whole world.
Without looking through the window, you may see the ways of heaven.
The farther you go, the less you know.
Thus the sage knows without travelling;
He sees without looking;
He works without doing.

Donny the Punk

[Donny, aka Robert Martin, is a published writer who experienced nearly unimaginable horrors being raped more than fifty times in a 24-hour period after being thrown in the D.C. jail due to a political protest. Some years afterward, while in federal prison, he wrote me asking for help in setting up a network of pen-pals especially for prison punks. Here is an edited version of that correspondence.]

Dear Bo,

*My impression after reading your stuff was that sexuality was noticeable for its absence, and that your readers were living lives of enforced (if not voluntary) celibacy. But this is not in accord with my own experiences and extensive knowledge of prison and jail life, which is **drenched** with sexuality, both consentual and coerced.*

Jail punks are more oppressed than any other group within the walls, living lives of abject slavery, sold and traded among the powerful, forced into prostitution, tossed about as footballs and prizes in racial and other power structures, tormented by conflicts over their sexual identity and role, isolated, humiliated, ashamed, and often suicidal. There's a crying need for someone to reach out to punks, someone who understands oppression.

I am suggesting primarily a network of pen-pals. I believe these should in the first instance be heterosexual or bisexual women, ideally young women, both because women are more likely to be able to deal with rape victims and help them to understand the nature of their oppression, and because it is vital that the punks' need for feminine contact be supported.

I'm 95 days into my solitary retreat now, with no end in sight. The period in solitary has been a real blessing so far, but signs of stress are beginning to manifest. More grist for the mindful mill.

May all be happy! Donny the Punk/Ct.

Dear Donny,

Certainly the problems of punks are terrible, and need to be dealt with far better than anything that's currently going on. But your idea for a network of pen-pals doesn't strike me as workable.

It seems to me that this planet can hardly survive one more special-interest group. A feeling of group identity may feel great and be very valuable at first, but it needs to be quickly expanded to an identity with the whole human race. Instead, what's starting to happen is that in addition to the separateness many of us unfortunately feel due to race, religion, color, or sex, we're now adding whole *new* labels by which we can feel disconnected from the person next door. From where I sit, humanity as a whole is not necessarily being brought closer together by this tidal wave of "you can't understand me unless you're like me" support groups.

The bottom line is, everyone suffers. Everyone truly knows loneliness, pain, humiliation and defeat. I agree with you that we need to open our eyes more to the suffering of punks, but I don't think reinforcing their identity as punks is the solution.

I really do feel your compassion and your desire to serve others. My own instincts are that it would be more useful to remind punks that their "punkhood" is not the center of their lives. If they feel that it is, then *that's* the problem to work on; see what I mean? Let's keep in touch and see whether we can figure something out together.

Love, Bo

Dear Bo,

I am sensitive to the matter of proliferating narrow-issue groups. One important distinction you should keep in mind is that most punks would give their left testicle to escape from that identity. As I envisioned it, the support would facilitate that rather than strengthen the identity. In concrete terms, everyone in his environment treats the punk as a punk. To those on the street who communicate with him, he cannot ever be open about the most important aspects of his life experiences, for fear that knowledge of his "loss of manhood" will spread in his home community. Our hypothetical pen-pal would be precisely someone with whom he can discuss everything, yet know that the person outside sees him as a person and relates to him as a person.

Bo, my writing and working on the rape question and the enslavement of punks (and gays) poses a major dilemma for my own spiritual work, though I am hard-put to articulate it. It is work in the plane of duality, of concepts, and everything I do in it reinforces my own identity as a punk, since I am speaking out of experience. It would be a lot easier to just work on my own invisibility and blur my identities rather than sharpen one of them. But compassion must operate on that level, so in a sense it is the old Bodhisattva dilemma of trying to help beings while not losing track of the reality that there are no beings to help.

Perhaps one reason why I work to help other punks in transcending their punk identity, is that the destructive results of assuming that identity are all too manifest in my own life—where the identity has become so firmly attached as to be part of my own name, "Donny the Punk". Oh physician, how to heal thyself?

May all be happy, Donny the punk

Dear Donny,

I really value your insights and I'm learning a lot from you, though I still don't agree with your proposal. In fact, the last paragraph of your letter pushed me further away from agreement than ever.

You mentioned "blurring your identities", but your spiritual work isn't a matter of "blurring" anything; if that's all it were, you could do it with booze or drugs. The spiritual path is to not *cling* to any identities, but let them come and go as necessary. As Ram Dass puts it, "Grab tightly, let go lightly." It sounds like you've grabbed tightly to your punk identity but forgotten how to let go at all. And this has been my concern about your proposal all along.

The other thing is, Bodhisattvas don't *have* an "old dilemma." Bodhisattvas are enlightened people who stick around to help others become enlightened. You and I are simply not in that league. We're not free enough to "sacrifice" our own development for the sake of others. Anything you do which hurts yourself is not going to be for the good of others. The best thing you can do for others is to get free of all your identities, confusion, and conflicts.

You said that punks need to be able to write about "the most important aspects of their life experiences", meaning their "punkhood". But that's where you and I fundamentally disagree. I don't see victimization, violence, or sexuality being "the most important aspect" of anyone's life. It may be the most painful, the most challenging, the most demanding, but not the most important. The most important aspect of any of our lives is to get free. And I hear you yearning to be free, yet then imprisoning yourself once again by signing "Donny the Punk".

I honestly think the best service you could perform for punks is to struggle free of the stranglehold this identity has on your life. Calling yourself "Donny the Punk" is like somebody calling herself "Susie the rape victim", or "Sammy who always gets mugged". If other cons cruelly call you that, that's one thing; but for *you* to wear it like a badge is quite a different matter.

I really, really feel for your suffering and send you all my blessings for your work. Your mind is sharp and your will is strong, and I have faith that someday you'll be able to cross this ocean of pain, and then be able to help many, many other people across as well.

Love, Bo the human

Anytime somebody fully opens the heart, at that moment there's not a person in the whole world who's unloved.

226

Mike

Dear Bo,

I came to prison in 1970 at the age of 17. I was immediately a target of homosexual pressure. I was assaulted and then locked up in segregation for protection. Then I was transferred to another facility, but the pressure was reasserted, and I attempted to escape out of desperation. I was then transferred to a maximum facility where I was in general population for about two months of constant harassment. I was raped and then requested protective custody.

I remained in segregation for ten months and then was paroled in March of '71. My head was really off and I was back in prison a few months later for parole violation. I was again in segregation for protective custody which then I was subpoenaed back to court where I received more time (1-4 years) for larceny. When I came back, I tried to stay in general population so that I could work and learn a trade. After about a month I was assaulted with a steel pipe and was in the hospital for eight weeks, during which I became addicted to the medication I was receiving for pain. I was given thorazine to kick it.

Afterwards I spent four more months in protective custody until I was paroled in December '72. Once again I couldn't cope—too much stress and things I was holding within. A few months later I was back in prison and went immediately to the psychiatric clinic. I was admitted and stayed there for a year. During then I started getting myself together. I went to college and high school at the same time, held a honor job, was on patient council, etc. My therapist felt I deserved an earlier release.

But faced with the prospect of leaving the clinic to population or to segregation for protection, I made a decision to become homosexual so as to have the protection of another inmate and be able to stay in population and continue my college. I was in population for a month when one night while I was fulfilling my sexual obligation to my protector, a prison guard caught us. My partner just went crazy and tried to kill the guard. I attempted to stop it but my partner threatened to kill me if I didn't get out of the way.

We was both charged with assault with intent to kill. Through fear I simply didn't dare snitch. As it turned out, I was convicted of assault with intent to do great bodily harm less than murder, and was given 5 to 10 years. The assault took place in '74 and I have been in segregation since then (three years).

*But now, peace has taken the place of the bitterness and pain I once felt. I guess it kind of started when I was at the very bottom, at the edge of losing my mind, no hopes—nothing—and then at that time I came to the realization that even in that 6x8 cell, facing life imprisonment with my life in danger, life was still worth living because there **was something more to it**. I could be happy then. I really had no choice—I was forced to seek within for peace and happiness, or else become psychotic.*

That experience of being at the edge left a deep impression on me and left me with the conviction that spiritual seeking is where it's all at. I wonder why something so obvious seems so complicated sometimes?

Love, Mike/Mich.

YOU DON'T BELIEVE IN GOD, YOU SAY

"THERE'S NOTHING ABOVE A MAN"?

HOW CAN A FINGER SAY TO A THUMB,

"I DON'T BELIEVE IN A HAND"?

—Terry Moore,
Lucasville, Ohio

Bill

Dear Bo,

I've been having a lot of trouble with my sexual relationships. I am twenty-one and am in the middle of my fourth year in prison. I am a homosexual.

Since I've been in prison, I've been forced to face myself and my sexual feelings. It wasn't easy but I did it, and worked hard as hell to get out of confusion just to step into more confusion. I solve one problem for another one to pop out of nowhere. It keeps me ticking, but I'm turning to you as a resource for something... something that might help me deal with the problem at hand.

Before I came to prison I thought I was incapable of any kind of sexual relationship. Any I tried to start would last three days at the most because I'd get a deep depression, an empty feeling, and get disgusted. I only had a few sexual contacts in my life, twenty max.

But now I've met someone, and it was love at first sight. It was in meeting this person that I found out sex was empty without love. But I also think, as does the one I love, that I'm too "good" for him. We are deeply in a special love, but there is something contrary between us which is always there in the back of our minds. It's like parts of us are very compatible and other parts are very incompatible. He lives the average American prisoner life: Drugs, food, tv, gets in tangles with other prisoners and the staff, rips people off, doesn't work, etc. (what I call negative and destructive). In this respect, I am the opposite. I've quit smoking, drugs, and a lot of other habits and attitudes that do me no good. I've been in yoga for 2 1/2 years; plan to teach when I get out.

I don't know if he can change in time. Does everyone have that seed of light within them? Should I try to water the seed and hope for it to germinate? Or would it be best to get over this overpowering emotion? He feels "destined" to be a criminal; says I should leave him.

I got him to go to a yoga class and he liked it. Should I cut off the sexual part of our relationship and help him to see the untemporary? I believe no matter what the relationship, it is to help each other progress on the spiritual path. We've learned a lot from each other. He is only aware of the physical world. Is everyone capable of unfolding spiritually?

I care and love him tremendously. Am I too close to be of help? If he needs/wants help—which I'm sure he doesn't think he does. It would be perfect if we would both be on the spiritual path. But only one of us is.

He's 32, and the word "change"—I don't like—because some things don't change. When I hear about people in prison going as far as the 3HO drug program and still repeating.... it's a shot of reality to me. Can I change? I haven't really changed at all. I've become aware of what is... and by not accepting or rejecting I find an inner peace. Not so much conflict.

What should I try? Should I give up faith and hope? Cut him off? Just make a distance—for objectivity? I don't really expect all the answers from you—just your wise point of view.

Love, Bill/Massachusetts

Dear Bill,

I'm glad you know I can't give you answers; I'll be happy to give you what I get from your letter. What I seem to read is that *you* feel you're going to have to end this relationship.

You know, none of what you've written has much to do with whether you're gay or straight or whether you're in prison or out. Mostly what's involved is a 21-year-old guy struggling through his first heavy love affair. Whether you like to see it this way or not, that's basically what's going on.

Nearly everyone has sad love stories, Bill. That doesn't make them any less sad or painful, I know, but maybe it can help you to see it all in a much bigger light. One of the things we discover as we grow up is that not every romance works out. You said "it would be perfect if we would both be on the spiritual path"; I wish I had a nickel for every time somebody has said that to me. But that's not exactly a petty detail, you know!
That's quite a major conflict.

You have neither the right nor the power to "change" your lover against his will. Your mind tells you it would be for his own good, but the bottom line is that your motives are selfish. After all, you're not going around the whole prison trying to change *everyone* for their own good, are you? These are the painful, difficult lessons of attachment and letting go. And they're *your* lessons, from your spiritual guides; these are not accidental detours on your spiritual journey.

You can love this guy forever once you overcome the pain of your failed romance. You can honor him as a big character in your journey even if you never see him again. You can pray for him, not selfishly, but really for his well-being no matter what becomes of him. And he certainly does have the "seed of light" within him, as we all do. But that doesn't mean he'll ever be like you want him to be. He has to do his own time in life, in his own way.

Try to understand that the pain you feel is okay; it's like the breaking of a shell. What happens next is that you open up to new levels of understanding and wisdom based on your own experiences, willingness and faith. This is how life goes. Don't expect this to be the last time your heart breaks open; it may simply be the first.

Much love to you always, throughout your life, Bo

Chuck

Dear Bo,

Hey man how are you? I trust you're fine and enjoying all that's probable. Man, I'm doing pretty good in a lot of ways, but I'm still fucked up in some ways, that I don't really appreciate. I can rationalize some good objectives while in the joint; man I understand a lot of shit, but man, I'm still hurting.

Man, I got some emotional attachment to a little dude here and he's as cold as ice, he's impersonal and insensitive. I've been through a lot of changes with him. You know, looking out for him and sharing my all. All of these things, I like to have done unconditionally. And much of the time it has been. But I'm human, and susceptible to humanistic vibes and affection, etc. This get to be a cold place. I've learned of the advantage of being a loving person. Having a friend, i.e., one that's a verb and not just a noun, is most/very important.

Bo, for some time, it has occurred to me that I need people (and all the more, a deep personal relationship with someone) all to inspire and nurture me, and to be a focal point for reflection. I don't have/haven't been able in the past to execute the type of discipline that would take me into myself (as I wish) nor to accomplish a number of objectives outside of self. I've found a close friend to be very instrumental in these perspectives and areas. Thus much of my motivation—from down deep—was to have this type of person around to help me in these ways. One would think as cold as things are around here, and as good as I've been to the guy, he would—out of intimacy alone—be so inspirational to me. However, the opposite is true. And as a result, I'm left out here on my own, not having enough nerve and discipline to go within, i.e., to breathe and meditate.

My reaching for him is more of a hindrance. I had to tell you this. I got my wires kind of twisted. I got to straighten myself out; got to stop wearing my heart on my hands, begging for love and friendship from someone who don't want to be loving and friendly. I want to break away from this dude, but out of patterns of behavior over the last year and a half, I'm entrapped. It's a mind and emotional thing. And it's hell trying to break away. Please wish me light and love. I need it.

I've been letting too much jive interfere in my ways of desire and higher functions. Bo, I love you and need you. I wish I was out there with you and Sita.

Love you all, Chuck/Alabama

Hey Chuck,

Always good to hear from you, bro, even when you're down. Listen, you were on death row once and without a friend in the world. At that time, the thought of being in general population and having close friends like me and Sita sounded pretty good, didn't it? Well, here you are! But after ten years, it's easy to forget the view from death row; the mind starts wandering again, wanting more things you don't have and taking for granted the things you once ached for. It's human nature, Chuck; so don't get too down on yourself for being down. Know what I mean? Just try to back up for a bigger view again.

This melancholy will pass if you let it; if you try to learn from it and allow it to open you instead of closing your heart off. People on the streets go through all this stuff too, you know. Use it. Work with it. Pray for guidance and strength. It's all a lesson; none of it is by accident. You have to remember that. And the lesson is always a good one if you learn it right.

You already know you can't force this dude to be different than he is, so what more can I say about that? Things aren't the same for him as they are for you. Maybe he's not doing so much time; so the intimacy you long for freaks him out. Whatever the case, you have to let him go. As much as it may hurt, it'll only hurt more later. Maybe he'll come around and maybe he won't. But the next leg of your journey is ready for you; you can't just wait to see what he's going to do. Have faith and let the whole thing take its natural course.

I got a letter from a con in Delaware yesterday that I want to pass on to you. He talks about loneliness too, and I think you can relate a lot to what he wrote. Nice guy; he's been down about eight years this time.

Chuck, you know we love you and you're always in our family and our hearts. Hang in there.

[letter from Don follows:]   Love, Bo

Dear Bo and Sita,

When you asked me for comments or suggestions for your book I was a little frightened. Although I've been stumbling along my path for several years now, I still feel so new that I wonder if I can be much of a witness. When I think of the magnitude of God's love, and the minuteness of my cup, I feel like a transistor radio tuned into a broadcast of Beethoven's Fifth Symphony. So forgive me if my speaker rattles a little.

I think that for people in prison one of the heaviest forms of suffering we experience is loneliness. You can see it in the way we cling to anyone who offers a little caring and concern. When people come in from outside to conduct poetry workshops, to give musical shows, to teach Bible classes, or any number of things, we flock to them like parched men to water. Those of us who have family and friends outside are constantly trying to wrap them up with strings. We lasso them with guilt and all kinds of emotional obligations to try and keep them near. We seek, in any loving, caring being, salvation from our own sense of emptiness. I'm sure you've felt the pull of our inner abyss when you've come into prisons.

We are driven by a belief that if only we find someone who'll accept us, forgive us, and love us, everything will be magically transformed. But—and this is something I'm only just beginning to realize—no one outside of us can do it; the love, acceptance and salvation God gives to those who seek Him inwardly is far beyond anything we may hope to get from another fellow traveller no matter how far along the path they may be. The end of loneliness is this: There is nothing to

232

find outside of yourself except signs pointing inward.

In my own travels I've come to a very interesting place. I recently read THE ART OF MEDITATION by Joel S. Goldsmith. It is a beautiful introduction to Christian meditation. For me the most inspiring thing was the writer's rap on Grace. He says that as we ponder it "It will not be long before we begin to realize that we have heard Grace described as the gift of God, as that which comes from God without our earning it, deserving it, or laboring for it; it is something which comes without personal effort." That blew me away.

I try to keep in mind that God loves me for free; all I have to do is to open myself to it. That's a great comfort when I find myself straining, trying to reach just a little deeper level of concentration, striving just a little harder to do what I believe is right, and generally making everything more work than it has to be.

I find myself competing with some imaginary Guru who is light-years beyond me, who has only to close his eyes and he sees God. All the effort tires me and I'm ready to give up. Then it will come to me that it's nothing I **do** that makes me worthy, it's God's gift of Grace. I'm able to approach enlightenment because that's the way God wants it to be. Then the clouds of depression and despair part and the sun of God shines through. He really loves us a lot, you know, or He wouldn't have created us the way we are.

I hope you have all the happiness you can contain plus a little more.

Love, Don/Delaware

[Chuck's reply to my letter and Don's:]

Dear Bo,

Greetings brother love; wishing you light and love; trusting situations are to your likings/conscious benefits. I got your letter and was very pleased in hearing from you. And as usual, seriously impressed with what you had to say; what you had to reflect on, was on time and was like sweet music to my ear.

I have in fact, scored substantially. For it is when I'm feeling, or embrace, the seat of negative emotions, that my "most thoughts" desert me. And it is that line of thinking that will stress, how all right most things are. Yes, your message was well-received, and I was in fact taking lots of things for granted. I'm not really without anything that I should have; and more than anything else, I'm grateful in having you... I love you and Sita.

That letter you sent from Don was to the point. It spoke of people's attachments/desires to leap on those signs of compassion that they perceive in others—due to voids of loneliness that just seem to surface in prison. I once heard a Buddhist monk on tv tell a student that he should not expect intimacy or go searching for it, nor deny it or its embrace when it come along. I think I was touched by intimacy at some time, liked it so well, and went in search. A hell as an object, but a heaven when it happens without expectation. I'm learning, realizing....

Thanks Bo, I'm going to sign off here. Be cool and keep blossoming; much love to Sita and the young blood,

Love, Chuck

Big John

Dear Bo,

It was with tears in my eyes that I read INSIDE-OUT. I thought I was the only one on this trip. You know, I'm a rare dude. Ex-football player, 245 pounds, 6'3" hitchhiker who stole a car because I was bored with it ALL. President of my '64 high school senior class. And gay.

That always flips 'em out. A 245#, 6'3" fag. It's just me. Maybe that's why I came to the joint, and why I've done five years so far on a six-year youth act. Only one year out.

But I don't let it hold me back. I'm as masculine-appearing as the next guy. I don't have much sex here in prison anymore. So, they follow me anyway. You've probably heard in your prison travels, of Big John (me).

*What do you say about gay folks? I'm pretty sure it's something to clear away. But, because sex has been about the only way I know to show love, and I've gained knowledge **and** love because of some of the dudes I've balled, I find it hard to say it was all wrong or for naught. It was the only way God had left open for me to be whole with others. Maybe that sounds weird, but it's what I've finally figured out lately.*

Love, John/Missouri

Dear John,

I don't see so much importance about the difference between gay and straight, but it sounds like you have a lot of conflict over both your gayness and sexuality as a whole. Your last paragraph defends your outlook although nobody attacked it in the first place—except you.

I think it's a hype to create elaborate philosophies to cover our own actions. For example, you say that gay sex was the only way God had left open for you "to be whole with others". What does that mean? How is it different for anyone else? Why weren't all the other ten million ways open to you?

If you mean that sex is how most of us are loving and open with each other I think you're way off. Look around. There are probably more scams, hypes, and games played between people sexually than in any other way. The person who wants to be open and whole will tend to be open and whole in sex or in just saying hello to the mailman.

I think instead of making sexuality into a wholistic philosophy, you should look at your thoughts and ideas more closely so you can see some places that you may be stuck. You say "sex has been about the only way I know to show love." If that's true, then you need to read books like INSIDE-OUT all over again and try to understand that we can all show love in an infinite number of ways in everything we do. Love comes from the heart; not the balls.

234

Personally, Sita and I *love* getting older and watching our sexuality fade; if anything, we're impatient to see it gone entirely. We most enjoy the things in our lives that time doesn't give and take away. No matter how much you may want to glorify sex, time does lessen the urge. I think it's too bad that the pop psychology of the day encourages elderly people to hang on to their sexuality as long as possible. It's just because of the attachments of the psychologists.

I think you should feel free to explore your sexuality however your best hunches guide you. But don't feel the need to glorify or sanctify everything you do. If you don't have much sexual energy these days, great. Don't let anybody convince you it's unhealthy.

As for the past, you did what you did because that's how the universe moved you at the time. Who do you need apologize to?

Each one of us is a pioneer, and there's really no map to follow other than the inner one we try to find, moment by moment, through faith and self-honesty. Each one of us is "a rare dude" in that sense.

Much love (in a million ways), Bo

...And there are those who give
and know not pain in their giving,
nor do they seek joy,
nor give with mindfulness of virtue;
They give as in yonder valley the myrtle breathes
its fragrance into space.
Through the hands of such as these
God speaks, and from behind their eyes
He smiles upon the Earth.

—Kahlil Gibran

Dennis

Dear Bo and Sita,

I hope this letter finds you safe and in good health. I am great. I have been reading as much as I can on karma yoga. I find it very hard to relax, so karma yoga fits my style.

I have had some problems here for the past month. You see, I can't raise a hand against someone. I have made a vow that for the rest of my life I will live as a humble man. I won't hit or cuss anyone out. Now for the past month I have had some really bad problems here. First I was set up by some people who for some reason just don't like me. Then my life was at stake again. I don't know how serious these people are, but I don't really care. I love everyone. I can hurt no one.

So now I am in the sick bay locked up for my own protection as I won't fight back. I won't argue with anyone. I won't break my word to God and fight. So am I wrong? Why do people have to try me and put me on the spot? I don't hurt people.

As much as I want to blow my top, I won't. I pray and pray. I force myself to stand there and let these people talk about me and if they want to hit me, fine. I shall pray for them. I won't go and break my word with God.

This seems to get me in more trouble. Everywhere I go, people want to put me down and kill me. I wonder what I have done to really deserve it?

For a long time now I have been wanting to tell you this. But it has got really bad in the past month. So now I need to talk about it.

Thanks you for the picture of y'all on the Christmas card. I want you to know that there is not one person I could trust with what I feel and what I fear until I started to write to you. I look forward to your advice and help. I trust God for my health and protection. I am sure that as long as I remain humble and kind I will be safe.

So I will close for now and ask that you take care and may joy shine in your life. God be with you.

Much Love, Dennis/Florida

Dear Dennis,

I've spent a lot of time in my life struggling over this issue of violence/non-violence, so I'll be happy to share some of what I've come up with so far. It's interesting that you mentioned karma yoga, because the main book about karma yoga is the Bhagavad Gita, in which Krishna (God) convinces the warrior Arjuna to fight in a war instead of bowing out in the name of non-violence. Quite a twist, huh? The whole Gita is in the form of a conversation between Krishna and Arjuna. What Krishna tries to get across is:

1) Everything we see or think we see is God. Whatever is real, can't be hurt or killed. Whatever can be hurt or killed, isn't real. So all violence and non-violence is only a part of God's *Maya* (illusion) anyway. It exists for us to learn from, just like everything else. Violence isn't a mistake in the

plan or a terrible detour along the way, as most of us seem to treat it. The violence done to you is part of your journey. The violence you may or may not do to others, is also part of your journey. Nothing wrong is going on; it's all within the palm of God's hand. That doesn't make the struggle any easier, but it might help get rid of the despair around it.

2) People have different paths in life, different "dharmas". There is no one "right" way that applies to us all—even with regard to violence. Arjuna was born to be a warrior, so Krishna tells him to take courage and go into battle so he can fulfill his role in life. Arjuna can rid himself of violence in his heart, and still slay the enemy on the battlefield. I know this is very hard to deal with, but deal with it we must, in our own ways.

3. Krishna explains that what karma yoga is all about, is learning how to act without attachment to the results of our actions. In other words, we read the script as best we can and act accordingly, but we don't keep getting hung up over how the script unfolds. That's God's work.

For example, when you say "I wonder what I have done to really deserve it?", you're questioning the script. Your implication is that somehow all the people around you "should" have been cast in different roles than they are; that somehow God really blew this one. But like Neem Karoli Baba said, "It's better to love God than to try to figure it all out."

So, that's the path of karma yoga which you say you've chosen as your own. You need to ask yourself some basic questions: Was your vow of humility part of God's script or your own ego's? I don't know; *you* may not know. But if your vow was pure, then you need to stop thinking in terms of whether or not you "deserve" these things, and start having faith in whatever powerful trials God is sending your way.

What better way could God grant you humility than to let you experience humiliation? What better way could He grant you peace than to mold it in the hottest fires of violence? Isn't that how all the Christian martyrs died? And didn't Jesus say that whoever loses his life for His sake, gains life eternal?

Dennis, what I'm trying to say is that you took a very heavy-duty vow, and you have to think in much bigger terms than the physical body; much bigger than physical safety or worldly happiness. Injury and death aren't "bad" things along the spiritual path; they're just props, sets, and scenes.

On the other hand, if you don't feel you're ready to open yourself up to such physical danger, then you may want to consider whether the vow was premature. You may want to reconsider your hard-and-fast refusal to defend yourself.

Remember, true non-violence is in the heart.

If you allow yourself to be beaten, but your heart is full of fear, anger, and confusion, then you're not really practicing non-violence anyway. Our greatest acts of violence are how we constantly judge others. If we clear our hearts of fear and judgment, we can meet any situation in life in the most appropriate way. Maybe the true "humble man" is one who doesn't know whether he will be violent or not, but instead lives in faith that God will guide him in every moment.

Please don't misunderstand me—I truly don't know what you need to do. I'm just trying to help you see this problem from a few different sides. You could die a wonderful death and be met by Jesus on the other side, or you could accept yourself differently and start living with the people around you in a whole different way, whether you defend yourself or not. But do try to remember that the game is far bigger than what you see, and even has a lightness and humor about it.

All my love, Bo

Dear Bo,

Wow, I really don't know what to say. I want you to know that I am really happy to hear from you. I hope that this letter finds you safe and in good health. I am fine and every day is a pleasure to live.

I really don't know what to say to you. I guess I should start by going back a few years and begin there. Before I even thought about yoga I had made a vow to be a non-violent person. I did this because I could not stand to see people get hurt. Years later I ended up in prison and confronted with some of the worst and ugliest violence there is. I don't like to argue with people, and I will give away my last dollar if someone needs it more than I do. I am a very easygoing person and have had people come up to me and say I'm too easy.

When I decided to search spiritually I became aware of the fact that more people were coming up to me and trying me. "So you're a Christian," or "so you're a religious person," and many other trials. I tell them I'm a man who wants to learn and live in peace. Now I'm trying to figure out just what type of peace is right. Now I am aware of quite a few things and ways I must reflect upon. Your letter has opened up my eyes and is now giving me a chance to evaluate my path and my spiritual growth.

I picked karma yoga because I want to learn how to work and help people and not do it for my ego. I want to be able to be of complete service to all humanity. I haven't had many books to read on karma yoga. Just the small booklet you sent me. But down deep I have come to the answer that this is the spiritual path I want to follow. I want to thank you. For years people have told me that I'm too selfish. I am now able to look at myself and see what they mean. That's why I picked karma yoga.

But I was not aware of the violence/non-violence part. I can see that I have a lot to learn. You see, you have explained to me that it's a spiritual vow and should be made with certain things in mind. These aspects were not on my mind when I made the vow. I want to reevaluate my vow and what you have wrote to me. I will never break my vow. I want to reflect upon it.

I have been a person who has hurt people and have been hurt. So one day I said that for the rest of my life I won't hurt a single person or animal. I haven't the power to go against my word. I'm so meek or whatever they call it. I don't question people. I don't argue back to people and always have a kind soft tender word to say. If I'm confronted I just sit there and listen and I don't fight back. I hope this will answer some of your questions.

You have a way of hitting the whole thing on the head. You have made me very happy. I will have to say that I do have one fear. But I am trying to put it out of my mind. If I do die today, I pray that I'll be with Jesus. I want you to know that your letter is very powerful and every time I read it I learn more and more about myself. I have to be honest with you and say that you have made me aware of what I was doing wrong. I can and won't raise a hand against anyone, but I am now really praying and spending thought as to what God wants me to do for Him. I get confused at times. I want to make the right choice.

By your letter I feel you have shown me the proper way. I can't break my vow, because I can't stand to hurt people and to feel pain myself. But now I know what to do, what to look out for, and what I have been doing that's wrong. This letter is very hard for me to write. I have tried to think this over before I write you, but I can't. I don't know why.

I do know that in a month I will pick up your letter and will see a whole lot more. That is the way I am. But I do want to say this to you. That's I could never hurt anyone. I could never judge anyone; if I do, I ask for forgiveness. I only want to see peace and harmony in the world. When someone wants to hurt me, I can only forgive them for how they feel and treat them equal as I, and love them as I would myself. I never have different feelings on how I want to treat people. I love everyone.

Take care now and write me back and let me know if I have answered your questions for you. Peace be with you all and God bless you,

Love ya, Dennis

Dear Dennis,

I'm really awed by your letter. I hope I didn't sound cynical about your vow, because it seems to me that yours may indeed be one of those rare vows coming from the heart rather than ego. I hope that God answers all your prayers, and that you realize how safe you really are, dead or alive, in the palm of His hand. Walk with peace in your heart and laughter on your tongue,

Love, Bo

Dear Bo,

Hari Om—Greetings in love and peace.

It's been awhile since I've wrote to you. I'm now at Polk City. I don't really care to be here, but God has used this place to test my inner peace and strength toward

being a humble man. I have gone through a great deal since I've been here. I would like to share with you one of the most degrading acts of violence that anyone could go through.

Since I've been here I have been raped by 12 people and was forced to shave my legs and chest. Can there be any kind of violence as low as this? I wonder. But anyway, I am okay and happy because I can really say I have the type of mind and heart that actually can forgive and forget and say I still love you as a brother; I even pray and meditate on asking God to forgive them for their act of violence.

I explained my reasons for my actions to a guard and an inmate. They both asked me if I were in a dream crazy. I told them if I'm crazy and this is a dream, then this is the most happiest and fulfilling dream I've ever had; that I will continue this wonderful dream until God is through using my physical body. Am I really happy? Yes. This was my choice because God called me to show other people that forgiveness begins in the heart and if it's a true and honest love then it can show forth good works (action) for all humanity.

So now I am again locked up for my own protection. But I am still praying and studying. I shall never quit. I'm not even depressed over all this.

Again I want to thank you for helping me to open my eyes to what's real around me. It makes me realize how much this world needs total peace and love for the earth itself and for each other. God knows what He is doing and He won't fail.

So I will close now my dear friends and want you to know that I love you and pray for you every day. Hope to hear from you soon.

Ever yours in love and peace, Dennis

Dear Dennis,

It tears my heart open to hear what happened to you in there. There's so much darkness in this world! It sounds like your path of non-violence is taking you straight into the agony and ecstasy of the Christ, and Sita and I are really awed by watching it happen.

Your letters remind me how much a beginner I really am. I'm glad you include us in your prayers. You're always in our hearts.

Love, Bo

Buddy

Dear Bo and Sita,

In my life I've never written to a newspaper, newsletter or whatever. I've been getting yours for some time now. Sometimes I read it, sometimes not. The last one I did, and I know the tone of what I'm fixing to say is not at all like where you're coming from.

It seems to me there's a whole lot of letters from guys sniveling about being gang-raped and being on lock-up because they're on protective custody. Most of them are saying they forgive the perpetrators 'cause "they know not better" etc., and/or they re-live that horrible experience over and over. I don't doubt their sincerity about that.

I've been down about eight years out of my 32 years. Prisons are more or less the same the world over. If a guy acts like a victim, he's made one. I don't need to see the results of a Princeton study on how people unconsciously invite rape attacks or mugging, 'cause I've seen them do it with my own eyes. In prison sometimes a punch in the nose is the only way to communicate. It's all some guys understand. Violence won't handle all situations or even one in 20, but sometimes it's the only way. And most of the time winning or losing isn't important. It's whether a guy will stand up for his self.

I've never heard of anyone re-living a punch in the nose over and over every day of his life. I mean, it couldn't hurt as bad as that other thing. Why don't you print this letter as food for thought for the victims and would-be victims? Life isn't a bed of roses. If those guys aren't willing to protect their selves, nobody else will. If a man will stand up, I'll stand up with him. And that's the general consensus in prison. They ain't in polite society. Keep up the good work, y'all.

Sincerely, Buddy/Virginia

Dear Buddy,

Thanks for your letter, which I really appreciate. I especially like your insight about not re-living a punch in the nose over and over. But I don't agree all the way.

You imply that if a person stands up for himself, things'll always work out. Isn't it true that sometimes a guy just like you will stand up for himself and still be beaten, raped, tortured, or killed? It does happen.

Also, maybe a lot of what you call "sniveling" is indeed sniveling. But maybe some of it is somebody who's sincerely trying to put his head back together as best he can. People react to things differently. So please understand that I do value your letter, yet at the same time I ask you to keep your mind open to people who just might be different from you.

Love, Bo

Dear Bo,

I want to thank you for answering me personally. You gave me some food for thought. I'm afraid I was being a little judgmental (of course, a judge put me in here!).

Here where I am there are 500 of Virginia's meanest. I've come to the conclusion that 99.5% of 'em are cowardly bullies. They'll pick up a knife or stab someone in the back, but there's only that 1/2% that'll go against even odds. If it's on equal terms or you're facing them, they won't bust a grape.

The new dudes don't know that. This is the message I was trying to get across in the letter I wrote before.

Yeah, I'll try to keep an open mind. When I wrote you I was in a head where it was barely ajar. It's true a punch in the nose isn't the only way to say no, so don't take my advice to extremes. If your old lady asks you if you want some more peas and you say no and she says "Are you sure?", don't punch her.

Sincerely, Buddy

Many pieces of the puzzle are fitting;
*Some I try to **pound** in,*
but then I calm down and continue.

—Robin Workman,
Moundsville, W. Va.

242

To Touch the Face of God

The quest for perfect union with God
   Is like trying to catch
A butterfly ... without a net.
      Sometimes you can almost grasp it
       And just when you think you got it,
   It sails away.

      But oh the wonder

      When you finally do grasp it!

      You see the beauty, the softness
      and you are filled with

      Such a Love

     That can only come from the knowledge
That you have touched
The face of God.

        John Thompson
        Death Row.
        Huntsville, Texas

We look at man's life
and we cannot untangle this song:
Rings and knots
of joy and grief,
All interlaced and locking.
                    --William Buck

6. Rings and Knots of Joy and Grief

Wyatt

Dear Bo and Sita,

Just wanted to drop a line and say thanks. You know, I sat here this afternoon and re-read the four newsletters from 1983. My copies are long gone, either passed on or lost in numerous cell shakedowns, but another brother who wrote you left his copies with me when he got out of the hole. You folks have had quite a bit of influence in my thinking—even the little "gems" that come through my mind now and then—so I thought it was about time I just said thanks.

I tell ya, folks, it's been one tough year. Things are still pretty heavy here. Lotsa drama! But I have a peace about it all and I'm really having a pretty good time in spite of it all.

When I wrote you initially, we were stuffed three deep in single cells and sweating out the aftermath of a riot/takeover here. Fifty-five brothers drew long-term lockdown and the whole joint was in an uproar for months. Guys were being transferred to other joints, the administration was coming down tough in an attempt to reassert their authority; It was a deep set!

So we all weathered that storm and, though locked down, became a bit less anxious and fearful of repercussions. In December, 10 months after the takeover, the Attorney General's office announced that ten brothers would be charged with holding fifteen hostages and seizing two buildings. Just like that! A real bomb. Turns out that I'm one of the fellas charged and now face 110 years worth of "new" time.

That just floored me! It felt like I was finally getting on the right foot and starting to slow down. I had just gotten a single cell and was starting to pay attention. Things seemed to be coming together and making sense for the first time in quite awhile. The spring and summer had been hell. It was hard on all of us and just knowing that we were all going this together, as shared experience, helped; it did me, anyway. When that failed to pick up my spirits I'd just grit my teeth and count the months left 'til release. I'd focus on that, so the months left at any particular point were like a mantra; "39 months, 39 months, 39 months, 39 months..."

It seemed to help at the time, but in retrospect I see that it just made me all the more anxious and uptight. Not only that, but I was really setting myself up. I mean, when they handed me the criminal complaint with 120 years worth of charges (I've since got one 10-year charge dropped), it was like the world ended right there. Like the object of my mantra was just declared null and void. I had serious doubts about mustering the strength to do what's necessary to fight the tremendous battle before me.

The first reaction was shock, then despair. Still locked down on what amounts to 24 hours a day cell time, I couldn't even get out of my bunk some days. I was hurt and miserable and real close to the edge. Again, I think the shared experience helped. The other bros charged were just as knocked out as I was. A couple of them were within a few months of release. The whole thing just took us completely off guard. The hostage negotiators had promised amnesty, the hostages had been released and the seized buildings returned to the control of the guards. Nobody was seriously injured.... Well, I digress.

*Little by little, anger took over and it became a matter of psyching up for battle and hitting the books to research elements of the case. Every day was a round of case law and note-taking. We all became obsessed with beating the case. That became the focus of existence—nothing else. I was even **dreaming** of case cites!*

*I began to notice how bitter and just mad at the world I felt. Like, some injustice was being done and none of us had this coming. This attitude bled over into my relationships with people—close friends and family on the street, my neighbors here in lockdown, and the guards whom I generally ignore. It felt like some kind of poison was eating me up. For weeks I told myself that this anger was a better place to be than the defeat I had previously felt. Now I see that neither was a "good" place. They are both destructive attitudes. Both weaken you, but one gives you the **illusion** of strength. Struggling with bitterness in the heart will poison you just as quick as surrender to life's problems. There is a point of balance. Getting to that point, or realizing we are already at that point, may not be easy. No, not at all easy, but it is possible. More than possible, it is our right and our responsibility. It's our right because slowing down, paying attention, and being aware, is our natural state. It's where we want to be, what we long for, and where we all end up anyway! It's our responsibility because we do have the choice. We can run as many games and trips on ourselves and others as we want, and for as long as we want. We can goof off, be mad, be scared, be crazy; it's our choice.*

Things seem pretty clear to me right now. I look back over the last year and see that it's all "the path". There was no stopping and starting, no detours. It was all on the way anyhow. Just a matter of paying close enough attention to learn some of the lessons along the way.

I'm still fighting 110 years worth of charges in court. The outcome doesn't seem to be quite so important now. Of course I'd rather not do the time, but that's down the road. For me, it's a matter of how I'm doing it today. That's a teaching, one of many, I sort of first got hip to in the pages of Prison-Ashram Newsletter: The whole thing about spirituality not being what you do, or what disciplines you choose to use, or what teacher you decide is your favorite, has really helped me. Remembering that spirituality is the kind of character one manifests in each moment is a good, sound principle to bear in mind. It's helped me a lot. Like, I don't have to shave my head, take a vow of silence, fast, memorize the New Testament, the Bhagavad Gita, or the Dhammapada to start living clean and light and holy. Maybe some scripture will help, give inspiration, point the way. And some disciplines/tools may be useful for this person or that person. There are things I'm learning and applying, certain tools, that help me and may or may not help someone else. That's not so important. It comes down to what you said in the Fall '83 newsletter, and what you say in so many ways in all your writings, "The only way it's done is in the quality of how we act, how we think,... how we do our time, each and every moment of our lives." There it is!

You know, I was going to wait until I beat these charges to get down and quit messing around. Again, it was something from your newsletter that popped into my mind again and again. Do you remember the page from Spring '83 called "Bullshit of the Month"? Of course you do, right? "I'll be a lot more spiritual AS SOON AS...." I can't think of many excuses that weren't covered on that page!

I thank you for those simple, yet profound, gems, and the way you get them across. And I thank you for being who you are and for caring enough to do what you do. I'm gonna be bold and extend that thanks not only from myself, but from all the men and women whose lives have been touched and made a little lighter by you and all those dedicated to the same type of work. And there are many — of both!

Things are okay now. Still things to deal with and problems to face. I have an awareness now that it's all necessary. It's what is required and it's just the way things are. I made a choice. Just finally decided to let go of the bitterness, to let go of the struggle and to take the time to slow down and to pay closer attention to the things I think, the way I act, the way I react. Yeah, I come out of left field still and I cop some attitudes. I'm not a candidate for sainthood! I'm not even always very nice, but I'm aware of that and have learned how to put myself in check. Instead of getting frantic over my shortcomings and stuffing a load of guilt in my pocket, I forgive myself, pick up the pieces and walk on. Ain't no big thing because when you start thinking in terms of manifesting right character in each moment, you realize that there's always another moment, whoops... there it went and it was a good one.

Don't spread this around, but I'm having a good time here. Naw! It's no secret. Things are unfolding in front of me and making some sense. When I first saw this guy smiling back at me in the tin mirror here in my cell I wasn't sure who it was! Things are just clicking and happening. Life is a great adventure. I could be sailing the seas, or climbing a mountain, but I'm not. I'm sitting in this cell and that's okay too.

Sounds pretty crazy to me, so why'm I grinning?

Seriously, this is a great opportunity. I've said that before and from time to time lost sight of that fact, but it always comes back around. I can't truthfully say I would ever have taken the time to be still and pay this much attention if I were somewhere else. Eventually maybe. Well, I just wanted to say thanx. Thanx!

In love and solidarity, Wyatt/Wisconsin

William

Dear Bo,

I'm a black male, 26 years old, currently serving time for armed robbery (10-15 years). When you were here at the prison, one thing in particular that you said, quote: "This is not a religion or some philosophy teaching; nor am I here to convince, persuade, or force my beliefs on anyone." This touched me. And what also impressed me was my own personal experiences during and after the meditation you had us participating in.

Since being here (40 months) I have had many low points, as this is the prison design. But just for those few precious moments I was never so relaxed and relieved. It was indeed a mind-blowing experience, and I find myself, trying to repeat the same procedure as the one you took me through. Unfortunately, I have not been able to reach the level of consciousness that you brought me aware of. None the less, this is not to say I have given up my pursuit for the truth!

Brother, we are brothers! And I'm tired of trying to fulfill my wants, rather than my needs. Let's stay in touch. For all that you can do in assisting and guiding me in this direction, is helping me, help you.

A brother indeed who's in need, Wm./N.J.

Dear William,

I loved being with you, too. The feeling you describe is simply what it's like not to be playing any games at all just for a few minutes; games of being somebody, protecting your image, feeding desires, fears, memories, plan, etc. Just for a moment being fully alive right where you are. I can help the group to feel it once simply because I catch your ego-systems off guard, but then when you go back to your cell and try to recapture the feeling, the ego isn't going to be as easily beaten.

So, try to remember how good it felt, and that we can all feel that way *all* the time. But between here and there is a lot of patience while we work on sitting quietly. It takes patience, strength, courage, determination; but those are all good qualities to develop anyway, right? And you're going to have to learn how to be firm yet gentle with yourself, all at the same time: Firm enough not to give up, but gentle when you blow it.

Just remember that everything you felt was in *you*, and still is. It didn't come from me. All I did was to trick you into feeling another side of yourself for a few minutes. Now the real work, the real digging, is up to you. That's the same thing I'm doing in my own life. It's the same for all of us. Welcome aboard.

Love, Bo

Jack

Dear Bo,

Whenever I meditate anymore I seem to experience a visualization of the physical world breaking up into light patterns. I cannot understand this. It first happened to me when I was living outside, and at this time my little brother was in the hospital dying of a bullet wound. Anyhow, I asked my brother to try and lose his pain in meditation, which I followed him in. About two or three minutes I started to feel myself leave my body, and had a visualization of a white light that seem to be as a mirror that shoned all the light of the sun but gave nothing that was of the physical world. I tried to get back in my body which I did, but I was blinded for half of a hour.

Since then it happens to me every time I meditate. Will you please give me some advice on this?

Om Shanthi, Jack/Montana

Dear Jack,

Your experience sounds great; I can't tell whether it bothers you, or you're just trying to understand it. I've had many kinds of far-out experiences like yours, and all the teachers I've been with have said basically the same thing: Let the experiences just be what they are and don't get too hung up on them one way or another.

All you really need to do is to keep asking God to take you farther. When you see the Light again, just think, "Thank you, God, and take me farther still." Then leave the whole thing alone as soon as you come out of meditation. The real changes in your life will be obvious as time goes by; it's not important for the mind to always keep up with them. The Light sounds wonderful, Jack, and I'm sure it helped your brother too.

Love, Bo

Just let things be in their own way
and there will be neither coming nor going.
Obey the nature of things (your own nature),
and you will walk freely and undisturbed.

—Sengstan (3rd Zen Patriarch)

249

Alvin

Dear Sita and Bo,

Greetings in the Light, dear ones. I welcome you with love.

Thanks so much for the warm Christmas greetings this year. If I had sat down to meditate it couldn't have been more beautiful. Just the reading of the words, and the assortment of family smiles took me to that place where one in the Light knows so well. I smile, too, as the cosmic joke keeps us light and happy. Surely "everything is everything, and ain't nuthin' nuthin'."

How beautiful it is for us to share on a level much deeper and more subtle than the spoken word. As the holiday season approached and I knew I could not afford to send cards to all my "dear ones", there were fleeting moments of sadness, but ultimately, it didn't matter anyway; as we are never more than a thought away.

Green Haven Prison has an inmate population of about 1850 men. But for 200 of them in particular, New Year's Day was much more than just another day in prison. My block (J-Block) houses close to 200 men. About 20% of these men are on the SNU (Special Needs Unit). Some are crippled, elderly, or just too sick physically to move about the prison. About 50 of us got together a week before and donated $2 or $3 each so that we could purchase some food from the commissary. Would you believe, we had enough stuff to feed the entire block, and even serve seconds to those who wanted it?

The tears that day—including mine—were genuine tears of love and sharing. As I was spreading the mayo (600 pieces of bread!) and some of the men rolled up in their wheel chairs, each had a look in their eyes that was unmistakable. For that moment (to them especially) nothing else did matter, as God spoke clearly in the hearts of all. It was truly a beautiful day, and I just wanted to share that with you.

Perhaps you will remember, but it all began for me right there in Auburn Prison in '78 (yoga class and then Bo's workshop). And now, with just three more years to my release in '85, it's amazing to see how fast the time has gone by. I can never forget the meaning of prison in my life. The judge must have known! (smile)

God's gift to us is love. Merry Christmas to you.

Your very own, Al

[three years later, 1985 finally rolled around:]

Dear Bo and Sita,

This may very well be the shortest letter I have ever written to you. But as the prison jargon goes, "I am rather short myself!" March 22, 1985 is the day that has been chosen for my release. In the words of the parole commissioner: "You have learned how to play the game very well. You may continue to play, but on the outside this time. We're giving you a shot."

I may be transferred between now and March to one of the minimum facilities in the city. For now, I am still here. Until next time, be good and take care.

Yours in oneness, Al

A Moment of Grace
John T. Landin,
Wash. State Reformatory

Once there was a man who lived in a forest. Now, during his youth he was very destructive. He would roam through the forest turning up boulders and rocks, smashing the bugs he would find, pulling up plants and tearing down trees. He would chase the deer and the birds and throw rocks at the bears until they were thoroughly afraid of him.

He began to kill. He killed out of anger, killed for sport, killed just for the sake of killing. The giant trees who had created the forest thousands of years ago were a challenge to him, so he cut them down. He piled up his trophies till they lay rotting on the ground.

As he grew older, he began to use the forest. He built a fortress out of the trees and rocks around him. He decorated his abode with the feathers and skins he hunted. He took all that he needed and wanted from the forest.

As he grew old and realized he was dying he realized that the forest was dying too. He realized that he, like the forest, would soon be dust blown to the wind. He realized that with the death of the forest, all the creatures of the forest would also die. He wept, for he saw how ruthlessly he'd wasted the resources of the forest. He longed so to touch that which he once sought to destroy.

He walked through the brown burning embers of his life's work. The sparse vegetation which remained cringed from the hot sun, which now fell unfiltered by the once lush foliage. The animals, hungry and frightened, fled from the old man as they saw him approaching. He called to them, but his call remained unanswered. He longed to touch the forest creatures just once before he died. He sought to feel love and not fear.

As the days passed he grew weaker, yet he still followed after the animals, calling out after them until he could barely pull himself across the ground. Then came the day when he could move no further, and he knew that his time had come. As he lay there half supported by a mound of dirt, too weak to move even his head, he looked down the arm which supported his brow, down to the hand, now cracked and wrinkled. He looked out upon the remains of his world. And in that moment a sparrow flew down and perched upon his arm.

In that moment he understood Grace.

And so he died, no longer seeking, but simply being in that moment.

Dear Bo, Sita, and Friends,

A man left the stressful outside world to become a monk in a monastery. Upon entering, the chief priest set forth the rules: There was a strict vow of silence, except that every five years each monk would be allowed to say two words only.

After a long five years, the man was summoned to the priest's desk for his two words. He said, "Food's bad."

At the end of his next five years, he was called forth again. He said, "Bed's hard."

The man lasted another five years and returned to the chief priest. "Well," said the priest, "You've been here fifteen years. What do you have to say?"

"I quit!", he said.

"Well good," replied the priest irritably. "You've done nothing but complain since you've been here!"

Love, David/Fla.

Dear Bo,

I attended the workshop you gave here at Florence. At that time I told you about the chest pains I was suffering, and you told me they were a prelude to a beautiful experience. Man, oh man, was that ever an understatement!!

One morning last week my chest seemed to burst open, and everyone and everything was magnificent. People were doing the usual things, but they were doing them so well! The realization that everything was so right, that the love I felt was okay, that the joy was okay for me to feel, that the pain that came from seeing others in pain was just part of the whole; it was all the feelings one could possibly feel.... It felt like the way Christmas was supposed to feel when I was a child (but never quite made it). It can't really be expressed or described, at least not at this time. It was great!

Later, Lonnie/Arizona

Dear Bo and Sita,

Life is really beautiful, isn't it? I don't know a great deal about meditation or yoga, in fact I know very little. But since I've been here I have found a happiness and a freedom unequalled in all my life, also a confidence.

Most of all, I met Love. I've tasted it and liked it and daily I am being consumed by it. Through Love I am learning to control my thinking, my desires, my actions. I pray a lot, almost unceasingly. This power that is instructing me in Love is so wonderful. Sometimes I just want to run around and give to everyone what I've got. I have really found a spiritual treasure house here!

This Love is a most energetic thing. It seems to give me a power; I am filled with it. I guess I am on the bottom rung of this spiritual ladder, and climbing it will be far from easy, but climbing it has become all that matters when I really think about it.

I was very sad and lonely once and I looked everywhere except to God and had nothing. Now I only look to God and He has given me everything. I am rich!

Lem/Minnesota

Dear Bo and Sita,

I hope this letter finds you both well, and happy. I am writing to tell you thanks for INSIDE-OUT and the tapes. They are great.

Things have been happening in my life that is just great. I am not too much with words, but my life has gone in a different direction is all I can say. You know something wonderful is happening to me, I tell myself "You are just getting older, this is what happens." Things keep getting nicer, easier in my head, though I am in prison.

I have been in casts on my leg for over 29 months. The doctor tells me if this electronic treatment I'm getting doesn't work I am going to lose my leg. I have been getting this treatment for over a year, it was only supposed to last 6 months, so you know where that's at. Still with all this shit I feel I am on my way to where I am going.

I have rough days, and I haven't gotten a letter from my old lady in months. I worry about her and still I am so lucky to have found out all this shit, stuff, or whatever the right words are. It would sound crazy to other people but I know you folks will know exactly what I mean. It all started with INSIDE-OUT. Thank you.

Joe/Pa.

Dear Prison-Ashram People,

I wanted to thank you for your book INSIDE-OUT. The only way to say how it has helped me is that it literally saved my life. I'm in the Johnson County Jail on drug charges. In the twelve weeks I've been locked up I've attempted suicide twice. At times the depression and feelings of hopelessness got so great I felt that the only way I could get out was by suicide.

Two weeks ago my depression reached its peak and I was ready for another attempt. Before going to bed I prayed, for the first time in years, for release. When I woke I found your book on my bed. A federal prisoner, with whom I had never exchanged a word, left it for me when he was tranferred. I started reading the book and the effect was instantaneous. Tears came to my eyes and I felt a most unusual shiver — happiness. I began meditating daily and from the first, my thinking cleared. The terrifying confusion left me.

That was a month ago but seems as if it was a lifetime ago. I am happier now than I ever was on the streets. I am freer now than ever before. I can't put it into words. Thanks again.

Praise Maharaj-ji, Keith/Kansas

7. Beauty of the Beast

Maury Logue, #89201 at the Oklahoma State Penitentiary, is a very bright guy and a gifted artist. He's also considered one of the most dangerous convicts in the country. He's stabbed so many other inmates that now he's on 24-hour lockup and is handcuffed even to be led to shower three times a week. He's been on lockup longer than any other convict in Oklahoma, with no end in sight.

We first heard from Maury around 1975. He wrote intelligent, gentle letters and sent us some of his artwork. At some point over the next four years, a terrible bitterness ate into Maury's heart like sulfuric acid, burning a deep, smoking hole which was more painful than he could bear. Now, because of his violence in the past few years, Maury has so much time piled on top of his original sentence, he doesn't expect to ever see the streets again — unless he escapes.

Writing letters of encouragement to Maury, I've had to keep in mind that he spends every day of his life in a cell smaller than my bathroom, surrounded by people who fear and hate him. I've had to remember that the only human touch he ever experiences are the hands which cuff his own.

I have no interest in helping Maury to "cope" or play mind-games with himself in order to survive. I see myself as his second in a duel; just holding his cloak, reminding him of his truest weapons, and wondering, with a good deal of awe, just how well I would fare on the same field of battle.

Here is a taste of some of our correspondence, along with a few of my favorites of Maury's artwork. This chapter begins in 1979, with Maury's first written description of his vicious transformation.

Dear Bo,

*Since as far as I know... you and your family are the **only people** on Earth who sincerely care for the people, the **poor people** who are confined in teeny tiny cages like animals; it is to **you**, I wish to pour out "some" of my pent-up feelings concerning society in general.*

*I stole $25 in an unarmed robbery, I was later apprehended, and sentenced to 25 years in a rusted-out cage...simply to "rehabilitate" me (according to the prison authorities). Society supports these cages which house **only indigent people!** Society is a malevolent mass of morons as far as I'm concerned! I have a friend in here who got drunk one night, thrown in a jail cage, and ended up kicking the toilet off the wall. The courts sentenced him to 12 years in a cage... to "rehabilitate" him! At $10,000 per year, per prisoner, that toilet will cost $120,000... think of all the poor people that money could feed! The state is willing to **waste** $120,000 to get **revenge** on a drunk for destroyin' a stinkin' toilet! You see in Oklahoma a toilet is held in higher esteem than 12 years of a man's life! In a materialistic country* like America it's considered a terrible thing to steal money, but it's okay to put poor people in cages and leave them there until they go mad, and **then** release them on society!

I was a robber when I entered prison, and now after only four years of being "rehabilitated", in a **cage**, I am contemplating becoming a sniper when released. Society has gotten its revenge on me... they've shown me revenge is the righteous, holy, way...that the only way to "rehabilitate" people is to punish, punish, punish! So after completing a four year course in "rehabilitation" I want to spread this "divine rehabilitation" to our wonderful society! Yes... just as the authorities have attempted to ameliorate me by **punishment**... so in like manner, I do wish to ameliorate society by **punishment**!. I have reached the inevitable conclusion that society is insane! They MUST BE EXTERMINATED, beginning with the "leaders".

Now, I can't afford to purchase cages to put society in like they do the poor... instead, I can only afford a high-powered rifle with a scope. I will simply blow the tops of their skulls off... it will be quick and efficient, and it will have an auspicious deterrent effect on all aspiring lawyers, judges, d.a.'s, and politicians.

Perhaps you might even think I'm just "talking", I can assure you I intend to do everything I've said I would, and **then some!**

I love speaking to you, Bo, for you listen, and you **don't** go for the **lie** that society does, that they're too pure, too innocent to associate with us "bad ones". The **only** thing that separates convicts from society is the **fact** that the convicts **got caught!** Society... there's not a single one of those pompous assholes that haven't broken a law or two. **Not a one** of them are innocent!

Hey, the authorities **only** "blew" $40,000 tax dollars to convert a small-time robber into a big-time **sniper**! (me). I'm soooo very very grateful for all the "rehabilitation" they've given me to make this possible! Will the **joys** of incarceration never cease!?

Luv, Maury

Dear Maury,

Sounds like heavy times for you. I really hope you're feeling better than when you wrote. Getting out and killing people is quite a bit different from the kinds of things we seem to have had in common so far. I mean, what is it about my family that you love so much? Whatever you admire and respect in us also exists in you. If you love it in us, then you'd like to be that way too.

Your anger and bitterness are excess baggage that you can no longer afford to lug around with you. I really do understand your pain and anger, and wanting revenge on those people who have made your life so miserable. But if you go kill a few people, then those people will simply check out of this life and take birth again, and you'll probably be killed in the process and have to take birth again too. The world will go on much the same as before, with a little *more* suffering, rather than any less. And then you're born into that world of greater suffering, which means you may have it even tougher than you did this time; and maybe you go to prison again, and get out again, and kill some more people, and get killed again, and take another birth, and suffer more.... Maury, aren't you tired of it yet?

There's really no such thing as "society". There's a bunch of scared, lonely people who *seem* like an organized society, but we're not. And you and I are as much a part of it all as anyone else. So if you're going to start shooting, you may as well shoot me, Sita and Laxmana first.

We're friends, and to me that means we don't have to pull any punches with each other. Take the luxury of being absolutely straight with me, and know that nothing you say or do will change my love for you. You're my brother, even if I think you're full of shit.

Love, Bo

Dear Bo,

Thank you, dear friend, for taking the time to write to me. As for my aspirations of becoming a proficient sniper: You seem to have misunderstood my motive... you seem to think I'm "vindictive." On the contrary, I want to repay society for all the "kindness," "compassion," and "obvious concern" they've shown me. I want to "help" them; do you see?

*You're **wrong** in your assumption that the world will go on much the same as before; after I pick off a **myriad** of "leaders". For it will start a "fad". America will be like Italy... there are many anarchists in America waiting for someone to kick it all off. I shall be that **one**.*

*You're wrong again in your assumption I might be slain and have to reincarnate in this miserable terrestrial realm. By your philosophy I can tell you're familiar with the Bhagavad Gita... Well, in it there is such a thing as **akarma** —action **without** fruitive reaction! It's when you are in KRSNA consciousness, which is exactly what **I'm in**!*

*Bo, why don't you "help me", to "help society"? Take a gun, pick out your "friendly" neighborhood district attorney, or judge, and simply exterminate the ugly body that confines his wretched, unclean soul? DO YOU WISH TO HELP?? **REALLY** HELP?? THEN DO IT!!!*

Luv, the "rehabilitated one," Maury

PS: Definition of a politician—that's a person who's got what it takes, to take what you got!

Dear Maury,

Sorry, but I just can't buy your trip about wanting to kill people. First of all, you and I are very far from being in the state of "Krishna Consciousness". That's the same as being in Christ consciousness; it's a state of pure Love, a love so profound and intense that you see beauty in everyone and everything. Maury, you're angry and bitter and hurt, and your own hatred is driving you up the wall. You could kill everyone in the world, and you'd still be sitting there the biggest loser of all, because you have no peace.

You don't have to keep explaining to me how unjust and unfair society is; I know all about that, I assure you. Meanwhile, when you really come to understand karma you'll see that no one ever gets away with anything. Everyone pays for their unkindness and unfairness, and *you* don't have to be the fool who delivers their punishment. That's just more karma for you.

I know they've done awful things to you, Maury; I really do.
And if you just want to strike back in some way, of course there's nothing I can do to stop you. But let's cut out the bullshit about it being spiritual or holy, all right? Bitterness and revenge are not going to get you closer to God. It just makes you more like the people you hate.

When are you going to let it sink in that what I tell you is for *your* sake, not for the sake of the people you hate? I'm not defending anyone's actions or misdeeds; I'm just trying to help out a brother who's in an incredible amount of pain. All this stuff about love and peace are *not* just head-trips for goody-goodies. It's the heaviest, most revolutionary message in town, only for super-strong dudes who see that they can't let other people's trips drive them crazy. So far, you're just not as strong as you want to be. And you know it, bro.

I love you, Bo

Dear Bo,

*If you think I'm one of those "phonies" who just **talk** big—all you need do is examine my prison records and mental asylum records. Since the last time I wrote you, I've stabbed three reprobates, beaten a myriad of others, and put several on protective custody. I don't like fools, I have no patience or sympathy for them. I haven't actually killed anyone yet, but it's only been because I was drug*

*off before I finished the job. All my life fools have provoked me. I'm quiet, intro-
verted, and a curiosity to them. Thus, they seek to "test" me. They only need test
my mettle **O N E** time and they will immediately realize they made a fatal mistake!*

*I meet their arrogant, bold, stupid, otiose threats with a smile cold as ice. And
when the doors open to the cages I'll still be smiling as I stroll into their cage with
a nice long razor-sharp knife. I grin all the way through the stabbing... their
screams are music to my ears! The horror on their faces is testimonial to their
newfound respect for me. I experience no remorse in eliminating human pests.*

*It's a **law** of the jungle! Only the craftiest, toughest, most dangerous of men is
treated with the deference he rightly deserves. Not only did my dad beat me as a
child, but so did groups of older boys. Since I've been in here, eight big guards
(goon squad), armed with clubs the size of baseball bats, attacked me in my cage.
I hurt three of them, and knocked two completely out of my cage. One was knocked
out and quit his job. I eventually was "subdued"... and **naturally** beaten and
scarred for life. **After** my arms were cuffed behind my back and legs shackled, I
was beaten and kicked again. I was bruised from head to toe. Do you think **that**
will change my mind about exterminating as many advocates of prison that I
possibly can!?!*

No mercy offered, and none shall be given. And my record speaks for itself.

"Love," Maury

Maury obviously wasn't asking for (nor taking) my advice on how to get
his head straight. And yet, it's always been clear that he wanted to keep
our connection going. I didn't especially feel like reading letter after letter
of his violent hatreds, so I tried to slant our correspondence more toward
his artwork and the family stuff he related to like building our house.

He began sending a lot more of his artwork, too. On one envelope, he
sketched this sensitive "self-portrait" of Maury/E.T., which we used for the
cover of one of our newsletters:

But still, in every letter Maury wrote was at least a passing mention of
stabbing or killing people, and a lot of racist jokes. And in my every
response, I let him know that I thought he was a few quarts low. We've
stayed straight with each other right down the line.

Once after reading one of his super-angry letters, I wrote out a short
fairy tale that I asked him to illustrate for me. I called it "The Convict and
the Kittycat," and it must have hit him just right, because he opened up
quite a bit. This was his response; the illustrated story follows.

Dear Bo,

*I'm **very** impressed by the concise, heart-rending short story you wrote about
the kitty cat. That story really "touched home..." It's very prison-oriented, for
many prisons have cats for mascots. We had a **legend** here named "canteen Tom",
one tough ol' **perverted** tom cat (he raped skunks—true!).*

*Bo, you impressed me with your sensitivity. Never since I read Kahlil Gibran have I encountered a **male** who is **"evolved enough"** to express such sensitive feelings! I **really HATE** "men"; they're crude, fatuous, bellicose, vulgar—I regard men as dirty filthy brute beasts which are incapable of rational behavior.*

*You Bo, really surprise me. You're an exception to my opinion of men. You're more **highly evolved**; you function upon a **superior level of consciousness** than the majority of men do.*

*Hey Bo, I felt my ego was dead—but when I got that issue of the Prison-Ashram Project newsletter and saw my envelope art on the cover ("E.T.")—gosh, what a **LIFT!** It copied so well it looks better than my original!*

*I love you folks like you're kin of mine—and that's 'cause violent as I am, I identify with your level of consciousness. Just remember, I'm a reflection of everyone I meet. Those who come to me with sensitivity and compassion, intelligence, receive back the same from me. Those who come to me in ignorance and violence get back the same—**10 times worse**. Y'all take care,*

Love, Maury

ONCE upon a time, there was a convict --- a very mean, tough, nasty bitter convict who hated everyone & everything.

WELL, actually there was **one** thing in the world he didn't hate: A small, black & white funny-looking kittycat who lived all around the prison.

261

BUT of course, the mean, tough, nasty bitter dude had an image to live up to, so he had to hide his feelings for the little kittycat, which he managed to do very easily. He was **excellent** at hiding his feelings.

THE kittycat didn't know anything about images or hiding feelings, though. In fact, she didn't even know the place was a prison, so she walked around every day feeling **purrfectly** free and comfortable, friendly and trusting to everyone except for a very few sicko-types who tried to mistreat her or do wierd things to her.

262

AND SO, one day this funny-looking black & white kittycat strolled over to the bench on the yard where our mean, tough, nasty bitter man sat every day thinking all his **terrible** thoughts, and she began rubbing against his shoes and purring very loudly.

SHE looked up into the convict's face with her light green eyes, which were more innocent than anything he had ever seen. She had two white cheeks and a black raccoon-mask around her eyes, and a ridiculous little tuft of black fur under her mouth, like a tiny goatee on her white neck.

NOW, it's pretty hard to feel mean, tough, nasty & bitter when you're looking at a trusting little face like that. He might have done it, though (because he was **so** good at it), if it hadn't been for the little black goatee. That was just too ridiculous, and his face broke into a wide grin before he could stop himself.

THE mean, tough, nasty bitter convict reached down and picked up the kittycat and put her on his lap, stroking the top of her furry little head while she kept adjusting herself on his lap, as cats will do, purring all the time.

AND all the other convicts, secretly watching from the shadows, smiled & felt new hope for themselves, though none would dare admit it.

THE END
(of our tail)

264

Maury went on to talk about his growing friendship and respect for two women psychologists, Charlotte and Brenda. He refused to speak to any men. However, much to his dismay, Charlotte and Brenda had both resigned by the time I got his letter. He was still in touch with Brenda via mail, but now she was no more directly available to him than I was.

He also sent me a newspaper article from the Tulsa Tribune (June 14th, '83) which featured him and another lock-up inmate under the title "Hate-filled Convicts Become Like Animals". Maury was clearly proud that the article described him as one of the most dangerous convicts in the state. But what struck me more, was the remarkable likeness between the newspaper photo of him and the character he drew for "The Convict and The Kittycat."

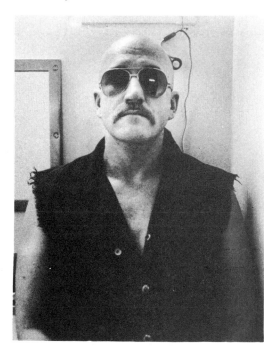

Maury's self-portraits over the years showed us how much his skills were improving.

As we kept writing, every now and then he seemed to be softening:

Dear Bo,

*Mahatma Gandhi said prison is a place for robbers, "but for me it's a temple."
I admire Gandhi—he's **intrepid**! The authorities tried to hire an assassin to waste
Gandhi in prison. Gandhi heard about it—and confronted his would-be assassin—
and said, "I hear you're looking to kill me; so I delivered myself to you." And the
killer turned away shamefacedly from this little 90-lb., toothless, brave little man.
Gandhi's spirit gots **BIG HEART**.*

*Bo, I confess you're right about my needle being stuck on violence. I need to get
my mind off this hole for awhile! Violence is becoming the **total content** of my
thoughts! Bo, I'm really starting to "lose it". I have a permanent anxious/panicky
feeling I've been experiencing lately. I used to get it about twice each year but it
would leave after a couple of days. But this time it's lasted three weeks and is
intensifying. It's the same kind of panic one feels after awakening in a coffin underground. I'm not exaggerating; that's how **intense** it is. I'm introverting more each
day.... once my introversion is complete, I shall mentally ostracize myself from this
entire world and its worthless inhabitants—I shall never speak nor write to
another person as long as I live. My request for correspondence is the cry of a
drowning man reaching out for a little assistance—before the final descent into...
madness.*

Later, Maury

Dear Maury,

I feel bad that you're in such low spirits. You're my friend and I love you.
I just wish you could see that your own hatred-and-violence trip is killing
you; it's not just being in the hole, I swear! I do believe you're going to
succeed in driving yourself crazy if you keep trying so hard. Do you think
it's just a coincidence that you're losing your mind, and your mind is filled
with hatred? When are you going to cop to what's happening?

You've definitely succeeded in making the point that you're a big,
dangerous man. So now what? You're going to be awfully embarrassed
when you die and look around the astral planes and see that the size of
your arms and color of your skin meant nothing at all. You say you respect
Gandhi so much, but then you live exactly the opposite of everything he
stood for. (By the way, his biceps were skinny and his skin was brown!)

Listen Maury, you and I have been friends for a lot of years now and you
have to admit I've never tried to forcibly change you. And even now, I'm
not doing that, so don't get me wrong. The only reason I'm harping on
this stuff is that *you're* the one who keeps writing me that you're coming
apart at the seams. I hurt when you hurt; that's how it is with friends. It's
like I'm watching you butt your head up against the wall, and you keep
crying that your head hurts. You and you alone—not the prison, not the

hole, not your past—are responsible for the state of your own mind. Nobody, including me or Brenda, will be able to save your sanity if you keep up this super-macho, super-bitter routine which you've perfected. You'll just shut me and Brenda out eventually, claiming that we've become "ignorant" or something.

There's an old saying: The only way out is through. You've got so much pain to unlock and let go of; it's going to be tough and scary, but you can do it right where you are. The inner journey is more real than *anything else* you're experiencing, and there *is* relief from everything that hurts so badly.

We're praying for you, pal.

I love you, Bo

Maury replied with some great sketches and a note saying he felt a little better, having found a new (woman) pen-pal and therefore some "escapism" from the hole. He closed with:

*I'm trying to re-adjust to the conduct espoused by you and Brenda—I'm making an **honest** attempt. I shared your letters with Brenda; she cheers everything you say (especially where you said I was a few quarts low when it came to violence and racism). It's like listening to an echo, both of you are giving me the same advice. Between her and you, I'm succumbing to your peer pressure. For I know both of you love me and know what's best for me. I haven't taken advice from anyone in years. But I know you and Brenda are right. Trying to clean up my act. heh heh.*

Love, "too cool fool," Maury

My very favorite of all Maury's artwork is the one on the next page. I wrote him my thoughts about it, and he replied,

I really admire your sensitivity and comments concerning it. My most subtle aspects in the drawing were discerned by you. It pleases me when I realize all the people who will get a laugh out of that picture when you print it in your book. Hey Bo, thanks for taking time in your life to write me.

Love, Maury

In early April, 1985, Maury was stabbed to death by two other inmates while taking a shower. Though this chapter was already in press, the printer has kindly included this note so that we may all take Maury into our hearts and wish him well on his journey.

We love you Maury, and we hope you're enjoying the freedom you longed for. We'll miss you.

We shall not cease from exploration.

And the end of all our exploring

will be to arrive where we started,

Knowing the place for the first time.

--T.S. Eliot

8. The Long and Winding Road

D.J.

Dear Bo,

With all the choices and all the different types of training available, how do I go about directing myself? In AUTOBIOGRAPHY OF A YOGI, Yogananda says that Kriya Yoga is "the" way. I imagine everyone believes their way is the right way, and I'm sure that many are heading in the right direction. But I'm also sure that there are many impostors who seek only the money end of the spiritual journeys of others. I would like some advice, really any you feel would be appropriate. I feel comfortable with the Prison-Ashram Project and the material I've received.

I'd also like to tell you a nice story: My wife has been having some problems with her nerves, high blood pressure, etc. She's been home from work and was even afraid to drive too far from home because of the "attacks" (as she refers to them). The family doctor prescribed some pills. They didn't work, so he prescribed some stronger ones. They made her super drowsy and she felt terrible. I wrote down a breathing exercise for her, and asked her to promise to do this every night, and to pray more and even meditate in the morning.

Now, her letters have changed drastically (as people tell me mine have), and she feels better and better. She has quit taking the pills and what surprises me the most is she isn't worrying like she always has.

I sincerely hope this letter finds you well and in the best of spirits. Please take good care of yourselves.

With love, D.J./NY

Dear DJ,

The story about your wife is wonderful! I'll bet you feel really great about being able to help her so much even while you're locked up. I'm happy for both of you.

About your questions—the main thing to understand is that the *process* you're talking about, that is, how to spot the phony teachers, how to find the teachings that are right for you, etc.—that process itself *is* your spiritual journey! It's not just a nuisance or a hazard.

From deciding on a beginning meditation practice, to confronting our deepest terror, this maze of choices and decisions, *including* our doubts, is the way we develop true wisdom, courage and honesty. So we have to remain open enough, light enough, so that the fear of mistakes doesn't paralyze us from making choices. Our own choices and mistakes are what teach us, gradually, what is right for us and what isn't. Slowly we develop more confidence in our instincts, in our gut feelings, and then the journey starts to feel a little smoother.

I guess what I'm telling you is "Bon Voyage!" Have a good time as you weave through the complicated maze of teachers, phonies, methods, philosophies, and promises. My only advice is to be very skeptical of people who say their way is the *only* way, and the people who try to make you more dependent on them or their organization, rather than more *in*dependent of everything outside of yourself. The genuine teachings don't rely so much on gimmicks, promises, threats, or peer-pressure.

As you've already noticed, these things aren't cut-and-dried. Yogananda was certainly a genuine teacher, yet he leaves you with the feeling that his way is the very best. You've got good instincts, bro; just keep being honest with yourself about them, and don't be intimidated by the people who would tell you to either accept every word Yogananda says or nothing at all. You can pick and choose based on your own heart. You may get very high teachings from a teacher who is caught in his own web.

Just take courage and truth with you, and travel freely in the spiritual wonderland. You're never really moving an inch, you know. You are what you seek.

Love, Bo

My mind is open, my spirit seeking light,
but not so gullible as to embrace
any and every philosophy stumbled across.
Not every light you see is the coming of dawn;
It may be just some bum firing up his stogie.

—Mike Harper,
Reidsville, Ga.

Wisdom is not communicable. The wisdom which a wise man tries to communicate always sounds foolish. Knowledge can be communicated, but not wisdom. One can find it, live it, be fortified by it, do wonders through it, but one cannot communicate and teach it. I suspected this when I was still a youth and it was this that drove me away from teachers.

—Hermann Hesse, "Siddhartha"

Frank

Dear Sir,

We have a group here at Woodbourne, but it seems as if most of the members are more interested in the physical aspect "hatha yoga" than the spiritual aspect. There are only a few of us who are interested in pursuing our "inner selves".

I am a pretty tense person and have trouble relaxing and concentrating. At times I find it frustrating.

*I am searching for the true meaning of life and the peace that comes along with the knowledge. I've been involved with various religions (on the street) and have become more perplexed. I am not looking for a crutch, I'm looking for reality: the truth. If I can't find that, I'd be satisfied to be content with **not** knowing.*

To give you an idea of my situation, I'm 23 years old (1975). I am Jewish by birth. I come from a lower-income family. I was involved with drugs since I was 16. I had a heroin and methadone habit. I'm doing a sentence of one-to-life. My next release board is March 1977.

It's really hard to get people interested and seriously involved with yoga and meditation, because they're doing their own trips, and because most people have come in contact with obnoxious religious fanatics who try to force their beliefs and values on others.

Hopefully our group will grow with inner strength.

Sincerely, Frank/NY

Dear Frank,

It's really nice to meet you. Your own purity is what will really get results, no matter what methods you're using; so don't get too hung up this path or that path; just use what's available.

For example, you said you're a tense person. So do the hatha yoga to get looser. It doesn't matter what anyone else is using it for; *you* can be using hatha yoga in your pursuit of inner peace. Just work on your own tension, your own concentration, your own progress for awhile, and let go of the other stuff.

Besides whatever you do with a group, try to set aside some time every day for your own private meditation. Just sit and become part of the breath of life, feeling it go in and out of your body.

The wisdom and peace you seek are definitely within reach, but not through any group or religion. At some point the whole thing gets down to you; just you and God. Everything you seek is already inside of you. Try to get in touch with your instincts and follow them.

Love, Bo

Dear Bo,

Hi. Thank you; I appreciate the advice. I understand what you said about any paths leading to the same thing, and not to get too hung up in techniques. That is what is hard for me to deal with.

I am very used to being channelled and confined by techniques. In every spiritual path I attempted, I was bogged down by rules, and the emphasis was being placed on this or that, and this being the only and true way. I am glad I am getting away from that.

I am coming along with hatha yoga. I find it very relaxing. I am finally able to sit still while I am meditating. My only problem is my mind wanders crazily from one thing to another and it's frustrating. It discourages me, but I'll keep pushing. I see what meditation does every time I talk to a friend of ours who locks down on my gallery—"Cat" Peirera. He used to be very wild and violent. Now he is calm, and just by speaking with him, my tenseness eases. He is one of the most sincerest persons I have ever met.

This jail is easy—furloughs, work release, edible food, etc. I really don't suffer at all. In fact, I gained weight, and I never looked or felt better in my life. Okay Bo, take care, and may peace be with you,

Frank

Dear Frank,

About your mind wandering during meditation—that comes with the territory, so don't be too upset. If your mind didn't wander, you wouldn't *need* to meditate. Just try to change your idea about what you're doing. Instead of trying to sit there with no thoughts or a perfectly quiet mind, see it as an *exercise* in which you're just trying to bring your mind back to one point no matter how many times it wanders.

As you get better at it, you can catch the wandering mind a little more quickly, so it doesn't wander quite so far. And then you may find it doesn't wander as often, either. But it takes time. Don't "push" too hard; just stay with it.

Love, Bo

Dear Bo,

I hope all is well with you and the project. I'm at Lincoln Correctional Facility now. I'm going to register to a college here in the city or possibly in Queensboro. In the last six weeks, I've moved from Woodbourne, to Ossining (Sing Sing), and finally here. It's really terrific here. The food is excellent, and I go out on furloughs every weekend.

To get down to what's happening, I've been neglecting my spiritual journey. I get lazy and find excuses for not meditating or doing hatha yoga. This bothers me because I don't want to fall back into the same pattern I was in when I was on the street. It scares me because I can see myself falling backwards.

I've even been putting off writing to you.

Well, in about 8-9 weeks I'll be in college. I want to get into the field of ecology/

conservation. I just hope that my present work habits and study habits don't extend themselves into my school work. The courses I'll be taking require a lot of work, and work requires strong concentration, and my concentration is poor.

I am making it a point to get back into the journey. I will wait until everybody here is asleep (I live in a noisy dormitory) and get with the practice. I have to keep reminding myself of my goals (worldly and spiritually) or I'll keep getting hung up in desires and greed. It's hard.

Well, Bo, that about covers it. I appreciate your help and respect your advice.

Love, Frank

Dear Frank,

It's funny how everything comes with mixed blessings, isn't it? It would probably be easier to get back into your practices if you were in the hole in Sing Sing. But here you are, in a "terrific" place, and you're worried about backsliding. This is a really good opportunity for you to realize you can't rely on any environment to force you into a good lifestyle. You have to create one for yourself; a lifestyle that's flexible enough to adapt to wherever you may find yourself.

You were more desperate when you had fewer programs like college, etc., so you turned to meditation and yoga for relief.

You know what? There's nothing wrong with that! Don't be so hard on yourself, and don't let yoga or meditation become one more prison in your life. If your energies are more directed toward college right now, go for it. You don't have to get back into drugs or do anything else that you don't want to do—even if you never meditate again in your life. You have choices, Frank; tell your anxieties to hit the road.

Don't get me wrong—certainly yoga and meditation can help you to stay loose and concentrate on your school work, but just don't let them be quite so heavy in your mind, as if you would be a "bad boy" if you didn't practice. And you certainly don't need to "get back in the journey" because you've never been *out* of the journey. Only the forms change, only the forms. Remember that. Your spiritual growth can be the focus of your whole life whether you're sitting in a cave in Tibet, or watching the tube in a college dorm.

Keep your heart in the present Frank; don't let your many plans get too far ahead of you. Take life one day at a time, and when you feel yourself "slipping", do something about it that very day; don't turn it into a huge anxiety about the future. You're doing fine, really. Relax and enjoy the adventure.

Love, Bo

Russell

Dear Mr. Lozoff,

I am writing to you in hopes to find some of the answers I am seeking. I came to get your name from the Psychical Research Foundation, where I wrote to in reference to an experience I'd had with a force I can only call Satanic. I was trying to find information and some kind of material in the subject of demonry.

At this point I would go into the details of this encounter, but I do not know if that has any interest to you, but if you would like to have me relate the details I would gladly do so. I don't know if the PRF still has a copy of my letter, but I had pretty much explained my story to them. I can't help but believe they were somewhat doubtful of my story because I am a prison inmate. Which I completely understand.

Sir, what I would like is some type of background on demons, their most known habits, and some sure signs of their presence. I would also like to be able to research some past cases of demonic wars with the good forces.

Sir, it is my pure, whole-hearted belief that in some way, although I am not a religious man, I have been charged with the duty of fighting demonic forces. And while I'm not sure as to the true existence of "God", I am sure there is a chief power in control of these forces. The same being true of evil.

Any help you can give me would be appreciated. Sir, I cannot express just how important this matter is, in fact, I fear that the final goal of this presence is my total destruction. And right now, the only defense that seems effective, is the Bible I sleep with. Thank you for your time, I await your reply.

Keep the faith, Russell/N.C.

Dear Russell,

I hate to disappoint you, but I don't have much information about demonic forces. I do however, deal with far greater powers which spring from the absolute power of Love. I know in my heart that *no* satanic or negative force is stronger than you are. Don't allow fear to twist your thinking; fear is just a demon itself. Here's a mantra of protection which you can begin working with in order to open up to your own source of inner strength:

THE POWER OF GOD IS WITHIN ME,
THE GRACE OF GOD SURROUNDS ME.

Just repeat it over and over, silently or aloud, anytime you feel these forces close to you, or anytime you feel fear about the whole thing. When you say the first line, "The power of God is within me," imagine a strong steel rod running right up your spine, making you a powerful spiritual warrior. When you say the second line, "The Grace of God surrounds me", picture a beautiful field of golden light showering down all around you, bathing you in safety and peace, making you completely invulnerable. Now you've calmed down a little, gotten your head straighter, and the pressure has eased up a bit, and so you find it harder to keep doing the practices because you're just not suffering as much.

My personal advice would be to not start studying demonic forces or battles between good and evil. I think that would be playing into its hands. And besides, most of those books are written by people who don't really know what they're talking about.

I'll tell you the greatest weapons we have: A sense of humor, a lot of self-honesty, patience, and openness. I'll be sending you some materials about these "battles", which can be just as tough as the others. Let me know how you're doing, okay?

Love, Bo

Mr. Lozoff,

I received your letter, and was very pleased to hear from you, although I must admit, I was beginning to have some doubts. I know that my letter must have seemed "incredible" to say the least, and I didn't expect to find very many people who would understand, much less believe, its contents. However, I have been encouraged by several people here, including a psychologist, to pursue this matter to the fullest. But nonetheless it has been a problem because of my inability to get the materials I need.

I have taken time to give serious thought to just what you said in your letter and do believe that what you said has a logical and very deep meaning for me. So I will look forward to hearing from you, and to getting the materials you mentioned. Please, if you have any more advice as to finding one's inner strength, please share it with me. As you said, I must keep an "open mind", and maybe that which I thought was pulling, could be pushing. If you understand my meaning. At any rate, I owe it to myself to find out.

I hope to hear from you soon, again thank you for writing.

Keep the faith, Russell

Dear Russell,

Nice to hear from you, and to see that you're a lot calmer about the struggle that's been bothering you. I want to make it clear that I do believe you about these forces; just that they're no match for your true self.

The books I sent you on meditation and stuff might help you to find your inner strength. Just remember that if you want to try these methods, you need to really make them a part of your everyday life; not just read them or talk about them. You'll definitely notice a difference if you start doing meditation, breathing, or yoga every day.

But remember above all else that a light, strong sense of humor is your best protection against all forces of darkness. Worry and fear are just mental garbage that you need to start letting go of (through meditation, for example). Worry and fear are like a rocking chair: A whole lot of motion, but they don't take you anywhere.

Love, Bo

Dear Mr. Lozoff,

*I wanted to write and tell you my address has changed. I would **very much** like to stay in touch with the Prison-Ashram Project. I have been able to handle my temper and moods of depression without any real trouble since I started meditation and the yoga. It's really surprising how much strength we have if we put it to use. People so often say the world will never change; it's not the world that needs it— it's people. If you spend time looking only at what you want to see, for whatever reason, you really don't want a change. Make any sense?*

Anyway, please keep my name around there on a piece of paper, I want to stay involved. I love you and your family, and my thoughts are with you.

Keep the faith, Russell

(one year later:)

Dear Bo,

Had another six-month setback from the parole board recently, but that's understandable; I spent six years building a lousy record, it'll take some time to build a good one. I've had no trouble for some months now, so they'll have to take notice soon!

I guess my biggest problem is in having nowhere to go if I did make parole. My mother has said she'd rather I didn't come around, I guess I'm an embarrassment to her. But, sometimes that works both ways. I really feel I'd be better off away from that "war zone" anyway. I'm so tired of having to compete for love! Maybe it won't come in one place, but there's a whole world out there; and I'm going to find me some! Make sense?

*I still have my temper, but it doesn't have me. I found that in 90% of my "fits", I would have come out a lot better if I had shut up! So many times I'd get mad, act on the impulse, and turn the tide against myself. When I'd **make** myself the bad guy, I always got even madder, and that never helped. So I'm trying to keep things under control, although it isn't so easy at times.*

The depression has been my biggest problem; a couple of times I really went down low. I thought about suicide there for a few days, but that just isn't me. There's always hope, no matter how hard it gets, there's always that! Rather than end my life, I'd rather fight that which causes the pain, but when you fight, somehow you lose understanding of the cause. It's like a puzzle that just won't fit, and you can't force the pieces together. Or like trying to put a model car together without glue, the pieces go together, but won't stay. I think the popular terms for my condition are "nuts, flake, crazy, and bugged out."

I've tried to write poetry to release some of my pent-up feelings. It's good to look at what you feel inside on paper. At least it is for me anyway. I had spoken to a chaplain here who blasted me for trying meditation instead of prayer! (ha ha). But I wrote some poetry concerning the talk we had, now he seems more understanding to what I feel and the way I handle my emotions. Since the heart has a way of speaking in terms that everyone can understand, it helps to make me more understood I suppose.

And now one of wisdom—HELP!! I can't seem to meditate at all anymore. So many things keep cramming my head! I can't get the mood right anymore. Just like my poems, the thought will tumble around, but as soon as I try to apply it, things go crazy. I can't settle down long enough to meditate. I'm always doing something; it's like a drive I can't control. I think it's a deep fear that if I slow down again, I'll run into depression again—and I really get miserable! And I guess I'm afraid that I may not get anything out of it, and I don't handle disappointments very well. I took the parole setback in stride, only because I had to!

If you can give me some sound advice I'd be grateful! Take care, and by all means,
Keep the Faith, Russell

Dear Russell,

First of all, it's *wonderful* to hear from you. You know, reading all your letters from start to finish, I can hardly believe you're the same guy who wrote me about fourteen months ago for help in battling demonic forces. Maybe you're losing sight of how much you've grown and how much strength you've gained since then. It's remarkable though, so lighten up on yourself and enjoy it!

Look at who you are right now:
1) You no longer sit around worrying about forces that might possess you;
2) You're gradually taking responsibility for your problems;
3) You're developing creative talents and means of expression;
4) You're genuinely interested in quieting your mind so you can do deeper spiritual work.

You sound like quite a guy, don't you? But nobody ever said you'd be able to do it in a day; or that it would be a snap.

Just be patient, and above all remember that you've already come a long way. Have faith that you're not a spineless pawn of depression or misery, as you fear. Fear pretends to be the voice of reason, but it's the nearest enemy we have. It's fear that says "Watch out for the demons!" And when that no longer works, fear says "Hey, if you get off into meditation, maybe you won't come back." And if that one fails, then it's "What if you open your mind up to depression?"; or "You know, you may die inside these walls," or any of a million other little bits of "caution" or "concern".

That's why it's important to learn how to sit still. If you can make your body sit through all that bullshit, then your mind will start getting clear, and eventually you'll understand what Jesus meant when He said "Resist not evil." All we have to do is to allow it to rant and rave and tempt and taunt, without budging us in mind, body, or soul. First comes stillness of body; stillness of mind and soul will follow. This is part of what the Buddha called "right effort"; not "right" as opposed to "wrong", but "right" more like "skillful".

Anyway Russell, it's great to hear from you, and as far as I'm concerned, you're a powerful warrior along the spiritual path. So when your fears and depression and anger come up, just sit still and tell 'em to stuff it!

I love you, Bo

True Knowledge is not attained by thinking. It is what you are; it is what you become.

—Sri Aurobindo

Dan

Dear Bo,

I've been able to see things a lot different through my reading. I have come a long ways, and have a lot further to go yet. The feeling that I get now that I can see clearer: The sense of feeling as when you notice a butterfly not as a butterfly but as a living pulsating energy, and I can feel that energy as it flaps its wings, as I breathe. Without caring, only doing what God created it to function. His purpose. I believe I am on a wondrous new way to a very high spiritual enlightenment.

It is hard when you live in a four man cell, and the others don't get off on what I do. I am praying I can go into a longer meditation. Can you possibly give me some examples of better ways to close out all sound? It is hard. It is really noisy. Some people have no consideration for someone else. Perhaps you could give me a few other suggestions or pointers.

I have a French mantra: "Mon Dieux est avec moi." It means "My God is with me." I feel it is wonderful I can take advantage of this time and make it work for me, not me to suffer of it. Thanks again for tools to help spurn me onward upward....

Love, Peace, Dan/Washington

Dear Dan,

I love your description of the butterfly; yes, I too think you're on a "wondrous new way".

About working with noise, I have three suggestions:

1) Change the way you see it, like a sprinter would have to change his attitude about hurdles if he entered a hurdle race. To the sprinter, hurdles get in the way; but to a hurdler, they're part of the event. Noise is a part of the event you're in, so don't think in terms of trying solely to "shut it down". Your own resistance just creates more noise.

2) When you try to meditate while it's noisy, let your mantra *surround* and *include* all the sounds you hear. In other words, sit there thinking "My God is with me", and let all the noise just be part of how God is with you; let it all fall into the lap of your mantra, just being what it is. Keep thinking the mantra, and then you don't have to get involved with details of conversations or music or whatever the sounds are.

3) Try to train yourself to wake up in the middle of the night, when everyone else is asleep. I used to get up at 3 A.M., do about two hours of yoga and meditation, and then get another couple hours' sleep before the day began. You can do it, too, and after a short while of getting used to it, it may become your favorite part of the day. You don't even have to get out of bed or make any noise. Just sit up and do some quiet stretching or breathing methods to get your juices flowing, and then bunch your pillow or blanket under you as a meditation cushion. You may have trouble at first—like falling asleep in meditation, but that'll change before long. This could be your own "secret life" that no one else has to know about. It's

a very powerful time for prayer, too.

Try any of these approaches for awhile before giving up on them. It always takes time to adjust to anything really valuable. And by the way, at the end of every meditation you should spend a minute or so picturing all the people around you, and silently offering them a loving blessing for their own difficult, noisy journeys. You could gradually change the whole place for the better without anyone ever knowing how it happened.

Much Love, Bo

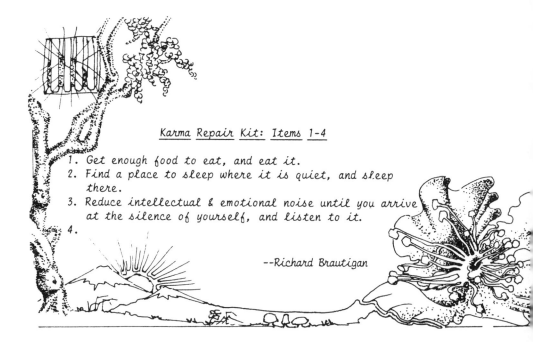

Karma Repair Kit: Items 1-4

1. Get enough food to eat, and eat it.
2. Find a place to sleep where it is quiet, and sleep there.
3. Reduce intellectual & emotional noise until you arrive at the silence of yourself, and listen to it.
4.

--Richard Brautigan

David

Dear Bo,

I truly enjoyed your presentation at Auburn Prison. And I'm highly interested in truth and consciousness.

You mentioned drugs a few times. I'm very attracted to using these, as well as electrical induction (biofeedback), toward consciousness expansion. I've read Carlos Castaneda and feel strongly pulled in that direction.

Please advise me or relate any material concerning these matters. Also, I'd like to read your latest book.

Thank you, David/NY

Dear David,

You can use drugs, biofeedback, therapy, yoga or anything else, but at some point they lead right back to the simplest recipes—quieting the mind, deepening your sense of God, doing good deeds, etc. Remember that there are traps in *any* method. If you seriously want to use psychedelics as a method, you have to understand that the traps are dangerous and very tricky. Consider the differences between you and Castaneda:

1) He had a guide (Don Juan); the whole thing would have been very different if he hadn't.

2) The drugs didn't *do* any of his spiritual work. They just set the stage. All his progress was made by facing his fears and finding the courage to see himself clearly.

Being a middle-class intellectual, maybe Castaneda needed to eat a magic mushroom to see some of the scary, horrible things he needed to face. But you're in prison. All you need to do is look around. The spiritual part is what you *do* with it, not the source of the visions.

Since neither biofeedback nor pure drugs are available to you inside, my advice is to work with what you've got. Right now Auburn Prison is your method; believe me, it can be as powerful as peyote.

Much Love, Bo

Horace

Dear Bo,

Thanks for the books and magazines. Within one of the magazines you sent, a question was raised to which I would like to find the answer. The question was how to combine the search for higher consciousness with social and political action. This is a question that has been dogging my mind for the past few months and occurs most frequently whenever I discuss my spiritual quest with my Afro-American brothers.

I would sincerely appreciate it if you would send me some advice that would aid me in understanding and resolving this troubling question.

Have a happy day, Horace/NY

Dear Horace,

I read you loud and clear. This dilemma comes up for most of us who want to be spiritual seekers and yet have a social conscience. The only problem lies in seeing the two as somehow being in conflict with each other. They're not. In fact, social/political action *needs* a personal spiritual basis; otherwise, each "new order" quickly becomes as corrupt and insensitive as the one it replaced.

Let me give you an example. In 1967, Sita and I were helping out in a labor strike in Blue Ridge, Georgia, against Levi-Strauss and Co. (Levi jeans). It was a classic "company town" situation: Levi had come in with promises of jobs, revenue, etc., and so the county had given them a building for their factory and all sorts of tax cuts. Once they had gotten established, Levi operated under the philosophy of taking as much as possible from the people and town, and giving back the least possible return.

After a few years of broken promises and management abuse, the women got up the courage to strike, and it was a violent one. Levi goons even burned down the union steward's home and ran over a picketer with a car. But everyone pulled together. They rebuilt the steward's home in a matter of days; they welcomed my brother and Sita and me along with other civil rights organizers to give them advice and strategies. In their struggle, these all-white mountain people opened their minds and hearts to blacks, Jews, and hippies (some of them had met blacks in their lives, but they had never even *seen* a Jew or hippy!).

But then a funny thing happened in Blue Ridge, something we had never before experienced in our years of marching and organizing and boycotting: Complete success. The women got a large grant from a New York philanthropist to open their own co-op sewing factory, so they kicked Levi out of town and took over the factory. My brother stayed for a year to help train the women in how to manage their factory. Everything was absolutely perfect.

When Sita and I came back occasionally to visit, we noticed that the women seemed jealous of one another's position in the co-op; we heard snickering and snide remarks about long hair and beards; we even heard racism re-emerging from the very people who seemed so "radicalized" during their struggle. We heard conversations about color tv's and stereos and new trucks. We no longer heard any mountain wisdom about how all people are equal; or how people of all colors and regions need to band together for mutual support. In short, the strike was over.

We had to face the fact that what we *thought* we were doing is not what we were actually doing in Blue Ridge. The fault wasn't with the people of Blue Ridge, it was that we wanted to change the world, but we didn't have much wisdom in how to do it. We helped the people to become uptight, greedy middle-class Americans. All they had wanted in the first place were better pay and working conditions; it was *our* assumption they would become revolutionaries if we helped them to get those things.

Before Blue Ridge, it was easy to be noble freedom-fighters battling against tyranny; easy simply because we knew we'd never really *win*. We never had to face the possibility of becoming the people in power. Blue Ridge forced us to look at ourselves and our movement brothers and sisters, and ask whether the world would be any better off if we suddenly got all the power we fought for.

Look around where you are, Horace, and ask yourself that question with regard to your revo brothers. Do you think they'd run a good prison? A good country? Do you think they'd be able to wrestle with the incredibly complex issues of fairness and justice and power to *all*?

Look at what happened to the Russian revolution. Look at what's happened to the American labor movement. When there's no personal, spiritual growth accompanying political change, the oppressed become the oppressors not long after their victory. It's happened all through history, and we can look at some of the African and South American nations and see it happening every few years.

Spiritual work is important for all of us. It's *most* important for people who are trying to change society. Sitting alone in your cell to meditate, you're not copping out on the "struggle"; you're taking responsible steps of preparation.

To shoot his arrow north, an archer has to draw the bowstring south in order to create power. Same thing with a spiritual activist: In order to create external change, we first have to develop the internal power and wisdom so that the change we create is good and lasting. Angry minds don't understand this.

Love, Bo

Dear Bo,

May the peace and blessings of God be upon you. I received your beautiful letter, and as a consequence I have the needed clarity and light for the journey ahead (or should I say for the journey that is always now?). I will forever be grateful to you for taking the time to share your insights with me, and a part of your life, too.

I will continue to move toward that clear innerspace that you wrote about so eloquently. It has not, and I realize it will not, always be easy. What perhaps has been most difficult for me is the actualization of all-embracing love. It is not easy or even possible for me in this place, at this time, to look with loving understanding at every individual's dance. For I know that if I am not careful someone would try to dance on me. When neither love nor understanding avails, distance is usually the only way that I can deal with the situation.

There is much resistance here to the Light. The change in attitudes and perspectives that are prerequisites to the beginning of a self-realized life is just too much real work. But I have enough to do in dealing with my own weaknesses to try to change the direction of someone else's trip. We each have our hour to awaken, and no one can rush or delay it. Thanks for the kind and loving Light,

Love, Horace

Dear Horace,

Maybe you're not as far from that "all-embracing love" as you think. I can feel it even as you describe the people you find you need to keep at a distance. You don't have to walk around hugging everyone to be in love.

If you can just remember your own words, *"we each have our hour to awaken"*, that might be the key. Just look at all those people around you whose hour hasn't yet come, and love them for who they really are—the self they don't even know about yet. You can be fully cautious and fully loving at the same time; no conflict. There's an old saying, "Love the tiger, but at a distance."

So I think you're right on, bro. Keep on truckin'.

Love, Bo

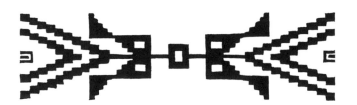

Keith

Dear Bo,

Lately in my meditations, I have been experiencing a feeling of total "nothingness" while at the same time, I am aware of every sound, movement, touch, smell and taste. Sort of an ultra-awareness. By "nothingness" I mean, it feels as though I am not attached to my body, but rather, am just a consciousness. It is very exhilarating, yet frightening. I think this is a state I have been striving for, yet I am scared to continue with it in fear that I will get lost in it or it will control me.

I quite honestly don't know where to go from here. I hope you may be able to explain this and advise me.

Sincerely, Keith/Kentucky

Dear Keith,

Your meditation experiences sound great; seems like your fear and curiosity are the only problems.

If the experience were really "nothingness", then who is it who could be afraid? So either you're not as non-attached as you've been thinking, or else it may be that your fear happens right *after* the experience. Either way, your fears and thoughts are just noise of the mind. Fear is always a hype; so is the thought, "where's all this leading to?" Just watch those thoughts come, and let them go; don't get sucked in by them.

Whatever it is that's happening in your powerful experiences, it'll happen better if you just allow it to be, without analyzing it to death. However "far out" you think your meditation has taken you, you're never outside of the palm of God's hand. There's no "out there" at all, really; you're just experiencing various parts of yourself as you grow. Observe and enjoy it, but don't blow it out of proportion. You're simply touching a tiny, tiny tip of the Great Mystery. Be happy about it.

Love, Bo

Of what can we be sure, except that whatever we have will soon be gone?

—Ramayana

Emmett

Dear Bo,

Thought I'd drop ya another line. Wrote a couple of weeks ago, but the mail has a strange way of disappearing into the dark corners of this prison (if ya understand...)

I'm very interested in the ashram project. I'm on death row with two death sentences, over the killing of someone I loved very much and also a stranger. I've spent two and a half years trying to hold on to my sanity. I tried to drop my appeal, yet was not able to, because the first round of appeals are mandatory and automatic. I've lived with nightmares, too.

I grew up in a deeply conservative Pentacostal Church (Assembly of God). From there, I spent two years at the Freeman Bible Institute in Wylie, Kansas. If you've ever heard of it, you know that it is considered one of the most staunch, hard-line Christian schools in the country. The lifestyle on campus is paramilitary. I used to suspect we were secretly being readied for some Holy War. I was taught that all other religions and views were of the devil. The ashram project would be considered as a false prophet. Even as I write this letter somewhere deep in my mind, little alarms are sounding off telling me, I'm flirting with the enemy. Ha!

There were so many questions in my mind—eternal hell, heaven, one physical life, etc., I started to go nuts and I got off into dope and in the end, I hastily packed and left one day, before I was expelled. That was in '78. I really got off into the drugs and in April '82, I was charged with murder. Here I am.

*Now, as I begin to reach out, twenty years of teachings hound me even though I have so many questions about those teachings. Do you see what I'm up against? Because of my death sentence, I feel I must find what is right. As of now, I don't know. I'm starting to meditate and **truly love it!** So that's me in a nut shell!*

Take care, Emmett/Virginia

Dear Emmett,

I hear the conflicts you're talking about between your questions and your "paramilitary Christian" background (I love the way you put it!). It sounds to me like maybe you're already beginning to see your way through. I can feel a healthy sense of humor, open-mindedness, and your underlying wisdom about the one truth behind it all. It'll take time, sure, but I think your meditation practice is a good key to overcome the built-in biases from twenty years of "hellfire and brimstone" teachings.

The religion you describe is what I call the religion of fear: Fear of evil, fear of self, fear of fun, fear of new ideas, fear of people who feel differently; you name it, you're supposed to fear it. That view sees the world as one big, wicked trap. It may be sincere, but that doesn't make it true. The aim seems to be to scare you into living "right". But you know from your own painful experience that it doesn't work out that way. It produces either repression or rebellion, and in the end, people often wind up as tragic examples of the very qualities they were trying to destroy.

So, have some patience with the old voices and teachings, and keep following your gut. That's the best any of us is doing on death row or out here on the street.

Love, Bo

Our laws of Men change with our understandings of them.
Only the Laws of the Spirit remain always the same.

—Hyemeyohsts Storm

Mike

Dear Bo,

I've been in quite a bit of confusion lately and I fell down and went "boom!" I studied a book—THE KNEE OF LISTENING, by Franklin Jones—and ran into seeming contradictions, which are only now gradually dissolving.

His book appealed quite strongly to my intellect, and I seem to have used that to create conflict. My schedule of spiritual practices went out the window, got lazy and tensed up, and wasn't sure about meditation, which I basically stopped doing. He says to stop struggling, but that was quite a struggle! My understanding of understanding seems to be a misunderstanding. Help?

Love, Mike/Michigan

Dear Mike,

Jones' book (he's also called Bubba Free John or Da Free John) is about *his* journey, not yours. Yours is between you and God. Of course, part of your journey is to read the book, fall down, get back up... so everything's still fine. I think you did exactly the right thing: You opened up to a teaching, tried it on for size, and then let it go when it didn't seem right for you. Don't worry about the enthusiastic claims that his way is the highest way or any of that jazz; just keep following your gut.

Many people are attracted to his teaching because it sounds great to let go of all structure and effort. But as you observed, that's quite an effort! My own feeling is that we can't pick and choose our spiritual paths quite so easily. I think we each *have* a path already, and the real job is to discover what it is, then follow it.

Jones makes perfect sense, as you noticed (too bad sense isn't the whole ball game); but it looks to me like his followers spend just as much energy, devotion, and effort as we all do, and then *define* it as non-energy, non-effort, non-devotion. A path by any other name....

Love, Bo

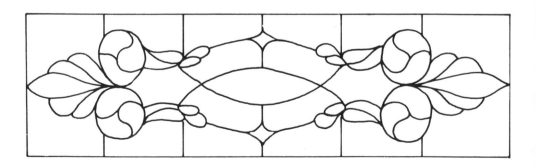

Dear Bo,

It is difficult to find words to express all that your visit to the Prison for Women means to me. I'm still bubbling over with the joy that simple evening represents. I experienced a validation of myself and the women I am living with in the unusual combination of inmates that ended up coming. I was delightfully surprised by the whole event and how effortlessly it evolved. I mean really, how absurd, who ever heard of life just living itself?

I am a drop-out from TM (transcendental meditation) after 3 years, as well as a variety of other "self-awareness" institutions which I grad-ually gave up as I became more self-confident and self-reliant. Prison has been my most recent "technique" and most powerful perhaps because it forced me to strip away to the bare essentials. I like your meditation because it has that simple purity that my experience tells me lies at the core of all things that I deem essential to me. Perhaps you could say that even living has become a sort of meditation for me, or perhaps just perversely pleasurable. Oh well....

In this supposedly regimented atmosphere, I've allowed myself to become more spontane-ous and everything is becoming increasingly easier and more enjoyable. And now it doesn't concern me anymore—whatever the Parole Board decides—I know my growth will not be hampered.

Of course, I'd prefer to be with my family, who I've come to value more than ever, but I have to admit that I've gained from my separation more than I've lost, and that I've dis-covered an endless reservoir of "family" to share my love with.

Thank you for sharing some of your time being with us here at Prison for Women. I thoroughly enjoyed myself.

Sincerely, Jane/Canada

Dear Bo,

I had all the answers given to me one day and they were so unimportant they weren't worth remembering.

Your friend, Doug/Ky.

Dear Bo,

Things are well with me. I study constantly and once in awhile I even think I'm learning something. I'll never get a gold star for accomplishment, but just cleaning some of the mud out of my mind is a powerfully warming experience. I may not run but I crawl well.

Love to all of you, Jim/Kansas

Dear Bo,

I've been writing you for days in my mind; ana came to realize I was writing me.

And I thought I was repatterning my life, and came to realize it was God who is repatterning it.

My practice of fasting has returned. My dreams are more vivid. My meditation is more meaningful, and I sleep better. I am beginning to understand.

Yours 'til the wheels fall off, Mo/Texas

PS: And a girl is returning to my life.

photos by

James Szulczewski,

W.C.I.,

Waupun, Wisconsin

Dear Bo and Sita,

Received the Christmas newsletter '81 a couple of days ago. Always wondered when someone would say what it does. So many of us get caught in the trap/travesty of the religion we happen to be into at the moment—we never see/experience Spirit. Being religious versus being spiritual.

I met you guys in '75 and over the years our talks have been sparse.

Mostly at times when I needed to talk with myself as well as with you. Now it's down to 9 months and then I get to feel some grass under foot and sun over head again.

This time has been hard... forced solitude isn't like voluntary solitude until you learn how to volunteer; and learn about the voice that makes misery as well as joy until it too volunteers to be quiet. Just can't bullshit these walls and steel nor can they be escaped—you always seem to return to your seat, and no matter how hard it's pushed away, it's there.

Has been interesting watching you guys grow. You're no longer naive. We can produce a lot of crap along the way, and your hip-boots probably topped out a few times wading through.

Thanks for your company and love... it's been felt and has pulled me through.

Love you, Gary/Florida

Hi Folks,

Thank you for all your good energy. This time of incarceration is a time for growth, outer responsibility minimum, inner maximum. Kind of enjoying all this time to meditate, do yoga, contemplate. This vehicle may be locked in the garage, but the driver feels free. I'm getting the idea that freedom isn't on the other side of these concrete and brick walls, it lies quietly waiting to be found in the center of every being.

Wish you happy, Kim/Michigan

Dear Friends,

Please send me a copy of your spiritual manual for prison life.

"Central Casting" has assigned me to live in a prison for three years. I was on my way to the nut house from an overindulgent cocaine habit. Thanks to the Lord I have been reassigned here. I got into being "Tom the Cocaine Dealer" too deeply. I was beginning to think that was really me.

Thank you for whatever help you can send my way.

Love, Tom/Florida

Dear Bo,

Two years awaiting trial in a county jail were not in vain.

Freedom from worldly cares, plus some kind but firm spiritual guidance from a distant friend, allowed me to open my heart and let God be at my center to replace the narrow selfishness that had been there....

The best to you, Tim/Minnesota

Dear Bo and Sita,

I want to thank you for your love and warmth; here's a couple of poems I'd like to share.

Love, Yogijesus (Don Penrod)/Oregon

God Gave a Party

God gave a party and no one came,
God gave understanding and no one changed,
God gave happiness and everyone cried,
God gave life but everyone died.
God gave Spirit and no one cared,
God gave Love but no one shared!

The Trip

What happened to Love? It took a plane.
What happened to Grace? It took a train.
What happened to Sunshine? You know, it had to rain.
What happened to the world? It went insane.

Bo & friends, Death Row
N.C., 1974

My friends in the prison, ask unto me:

"How good, how good, does it feel to be free?"

And I answer them most mysteriously,

"Are birds free from the chains of the skyway?"

-- Bob Dylan

9. Letters From Outside

Donna

Dear Prison-Ashram folks,

For years we have witnessed the fine work done through you all. We thank you. Now I find myself coming to you for something directly connected to my own life and family.

Our daughter, who's four, was kidnapped last summer by a two-time rapist. The police found them in 4½ hours and she was remarkably all right though much darkness went her way.

Those hours were an incredible test of our work of these past years. Between the streams of terror and panic and tears, we did all we could to surround the two of them with love, to pray, to meditate. And we found, then and afterwards, that many many people hearing of the kidnapping were stopping doing what they were doing, and doing as we were.

Police, hospital, strangers, all were surrounding us and our daughter with love. And when we got her back, she was still whole and filled with innocence, in spite of the violence and sexuality she was subjected to. She had spent most of the time talking to him, of right and wrong, of her understandings of the order around her. "I loved him a little and hated him a little" was one of the first things she told us.

Then came months of assimilating and sorting the great pain. And all that still continues, though quieter now. And during that time, the legal issues were being drawn into it. We could not find any peace in the "Catch-22"-ness of it all: Having our 4-year-old testify and be torn apart by defense lawyers; dropping the case, which was threatened if she didn't testify; sending this man back to jail which had not done him any good before, etc. etc. We were all victims.

Finally, we fasted and prayed for three days and came to a peaceful relationship to it all with this understanding: The proper responsibility in the guilt was in his hands and demanded a public confession. He did plead guilty and it was settled out of court. He was sentenced on the violated probation and on the new sentences. He stood up in court and said, facing my husband, that though he has no memory of the incident (supposedly he has blocked out the whole thing), he was sorry for all the pain he caused to our family.

So now, the children ask what he does in prison, how long he'll be there, how old they'll be when he gets out, and on and on. We wonder if our relationship to him is done. Do we have any more responsibility now than to hold him in our hearts and prayers, and do our own work to come to a full forgiveness? I still wonder if I should personally go to him or write him, to tell him all the specifics of what went on so he can come to some peace with what he did instead of spending all those years in jail for an offense he has no memory of.

All I've come up with so far is to pass his name on to you. From what I understand, he has a very mild and inward nature unless he's drinking. Maybe medita-

tion would be a door for him. Would you send him whatever you have, and just know that he's there in case you go to his prison?

Thank you from the bottom of our hearts for all the fine work you've been doing.

In Love, Donna/New Mexico

Dear Donna,

Sita and I thank you deeply for sharing your ordeal with us. Your letter is awe-inspiring for the compassion and consciousness you've brought to such a nightmarish experience.

I'm sure your process of "assimilating and sorting the great pain" will go on for awhile, but it sounds like your faith and vision are remarkably unclouded. It's through such pain that many of us discover what the spiritual life is really all about. The opening, deepening, pain, and wisdom all go hand in hand. Sometimes God's blessings are excruciating, but blessings all the same. It seems that you and your whole family have been given one of those.

You asked for my advice about your relationship to Oscar. I can't think of any "shoulds" or "shouldn'ts" that wouldn't sound stupid after all you've been through. Oscar has already been greatly blessed just by the fact of you being his victims. Your forgiveness and concern are profound contributions to his spiritual journey, like Jesus forgiving those who nailed Him to the cross.

My only advice is to try to be as self-honest as possible, and make sure that whatever you do is what you're *able* to do from the heart—not what your mind thinks you should do in order to be "good". If you're ever able to truly open to Oscar and offer him your kinship, I think that act could do more for world peace than a hundred summit conferences, because this is really the nitty-gritty of bringing God-consciousness into our worldly lives.

Our love to you all, Bo

But I say that even as the holy and the righteous cannot rise beyond the highest which is in each one of you,
So the wicked and the weak cannot fall lower than the lowest which is in you also.

Kahlil Gibran, "The Prophet"

The Nashville Bomber

Dear Bo,

Good news. I've done very well, and now have freedom with pay. I'm now a telephone installer and make $10.60 an hour. The catch is, I never know how long I'll be working in any city. But I may get to stay here about a year.

I've been enjoying the freedom, the travelling too. But it can be inconvenient at times. I have a lot more worldly possessions now than I did my last time out.

No more excitement, and I hope to learn more of the normal life, but I still find it hard to accept all this prosperity and money I now seem to have. But my prison days are over, and I have the right to count my chickens now. On the average I make $300/week take-home pay and am a very good installer of phones.

I just wanted you to know that the help and faith in me was well-founded. I've done all I can to go straight, and I remember my past so I can live my future a lot better. I don't allow my temper to get the best of me anymore. Give my regards to all; they too can make it.

With love, John/N.C.
"The Nashville Bomber"

Dear John,

Can't tell you how good it is to get your letter. Yeah, I'll just *bet* you're a great installer of telephones! It's a lot easier without dynamite.

Listen, there's no reason in the world you should feel uneasy about making good money and enjoying yourself. Maybe all you need to do is to start tithing a little to charities, or volunteering some time in worthy causes around the community. That kind of stuff helps you to feel a nice balance in your life and a healthy connection with people who don't yet have it so good. But relax and have a good time, bro. We're with you all the way.

Love, Bo

Skillfulness in action is called Yoga.

—Bhagavad Gita

Janet

Dear Bo,

I work in a juvenile facility here in Toronto. It's extremely depressing, and I've found myself close to quitting more than once. Unlike what you probably find in the adult prisons you visit, these young people don't seem open to positive change. Ideas like meditation and yoga—except among a very few individuals—would seem to be out of the question; and yet they need it so badly!

What do you say to someone who needs to listen, but won't?

How do you reach someone who's bent on destroying his whole life? Or do you just let them do it, and then work with them ten years and ten miles down the road, in the adult institution?

Most of the staff here are really good people, and would love to find a program which would create more effective change. They care a lot, but can't seem to find the right key. Do you have one handy?

Sincerely, Janet/Canada

Dear Janet,

The key to working with juveniles is right under our noses; it's so simple that we keep looking too far for new programs and philosophies. But the key won't be found in any program; it's found in the example we set.

Whether juveniles like to admit it or not, they're *extremely* impressionable to role models of the adults around them. That's how many of them got into trouble in the first place. In an adult prison, the guards aren't seen as role models. But in a juvie facility, the inmates are constantly—even *sub*consciously—checking out you and the other staff members to gain more understanding of their options; the range of possibilities for what kind of adults they might become.

I did a workshop at your institution a few years ago. I was invited to speak to the staff (I guess it was before you started working there). I looked around the room and saw a group of very dedicated, very caring people (as you said) but they were also chain-smoking, nail-biting, coffee-guzzling, harried, and disorganized. No matter how loving their intentions, what young offender is going to be impressed with that example of adulthood?

I really don't mean to be coming down hard on you or your colleagues, because believe me, I admire all of you tremendously. But the age is past when we can separate our own well-being from the work that we do; we know too much to be that way anymore.

The frenzied social worker who's always trying to catch up to yesterday and subsists on baloney sandwiches stuffed down in the hallways is old hat. We know now that what people really get from us is more a measure of who we *are* than what we say or the things we give them.

In a juvenile facility, a staff person who's calm and strong and happy is worth his or her weight in gold. People who are living examples of truthfulness, good humor, patience, and courage are going to change more lives—even if they're employed as janitors—than the counselors who can't get their own lives in order. I can't possibly stress this enough.

So, I do agree with you about the difficulties of working in a juvie prison, but at the same time I think there's not only a key, but a very exciting one at that. Just by doing your own work on yourself; by continually striving to be a shining, happy example of whatever you believe in, you will *become* the most powerful program the facility could ever offer.

Not all kids are ready for change. But a large proportion of them are; and you'll begin to attract them like moths to a flame, as your own light shines brighter and brighter. Much love to you and blessings for your inspired work with these children of God.

Love, Bo

The greatest disease in the world today is loneliness.

—*Mother Theresa*

Keep on sowing your seed, for you never know which will grow. Perhaps it all will.

—*Ecclesiastes*

Alan

Dear Bo,

I am a member of a Christian community. Since last spring, a co-worker and I have been working with a group of inmates at Auburn Prison. We have discovered that working as white do-gooders with a bunch of ghetto blacks is tough. Our problem right now is what to do to really help them, so we are going back to square one and re-evaluating our program with our admission that we know nothing and need help. Thus this letter.

Our first step has been to link up every inmate with a member of the Christian community on a correspondence basis. Now we have more people with a stake in our program, so it doesn't just rest on the shoulders of the two of us. Please send us any information and advice. We want both to help them on a spiritual level and work on a practical level to aid in their ability to operate in the world, etc.

Many thanks for your fine work; am looking forward to hearing from you.

Yours in Christ, Alan/N.Y.

Dear Alan,

A couple of ideas right off the bat:

1) Come to a clearer idea of what you can best offer. The possibilities for helping prisoners are almost unlimited, but no one person or even a community can bite off the whole range. The pen-pal connection is a good idea. You also mention spiritual stuff—what form? Classes inside? Other speakers and teachers? You could organize a fellowship group among the cons themselves; you could hook up with other spiritual groups around Auburn to sponsor classes besides your own for non-Christians; etc.

The first thing you may want to do is to find out what all the community resources already are, so you can understand the bigger picture of how you may best fit in. You can ask the inmates to come up with a list of ideas for needed community support, and then see whether you're able to help fill any of them. In the course of doing your homework, the answers you're looking for may start popping out from every direction. You just have to scan the situation and decide to do a few things really well, rather than a lot of things half-ass.

2) About being white do-gooders among ghetto blacks—I hear where you're coming from, but you have to expand your vision if you want to be of any real use. Yes, you're white do-gooders on one level, but on another level you're disciples of the Christ—*way* beyond petty details like skin color or age.

Your passion to help others is the most ancient, universal will-to-do-good that exists. If you were green or yellow, and lived in 400 BC on another planet, it would feel the same. The fact that you're white right now and the cons are mostly black is just the least detail. Think big. Be big. Otherwise, you'll just keep getting caught where some of the inmates are stuck, and then you'll all be jiving each other instead of journeying down the path.

I guess that's the bottom line that I want to emphasize to you: *You*, ultimately, have to decide what it is you're able to do. Don't fall into the classic "naive liberal" trap of being so intimidated by race and personal history, that you just become a doormat for the people you wish to help. You'll burn out that way, and you won't really help anyone in the long run. You have to do whatever you do with joy and interest, and you can't let the cons define who they want you to be to them. You have to figure out who you *are*, and then share yourself with love.

Love, Bo

Dear Bo,

A few weeks ago I began a meditation group in our local jail. (I meditate on a regular basis, and attend weekly sessions with the Seattle Dharma group.) Although the jail is not the quietest or mellowest place to meditate, I find that I have my best meditation of the week there. I'm not sure why, but perhaps it's because when you are in the joint there isn't anything else you can lose, and therefore it is easier to let go. Freedom comes when fear leaves.

And compassion seems so absent on one level inside, but it only takes a little caring and so much of it pours out. My heart feels like it is going to explode sometimes with giant outpourings of love.

May all beings be happy,

Glenn/Washington

John [resident of a yoga community]

Dear Bo,

I'm writing to ask for your assistance. For about the past two years I've been coordinating sending out books and our yoga courses to those who ask—also providing a spiritual pen-pal as either myself or someone else in the community who is interested.

I'm very open to any ideas you may have through your experience of how this can be done with more love—more skillfully. Doubts come up in my mind about just being totally naive—not really understanding what people "inside" are going through. I wonder—am I in over my head? I guess I also have to admit some fears about violence. How to let that go?

Simply to be willing to start someplace...

Thanks for sharing the inspiration and love you share.

In divine friendship, John/Ca.

Dear John,

Yeah, I've certainly wrestled with these things over the years. Writing to prisoners is just as much (if not more) of a spiritual practice as any other form of yoga you do. If you can remember that; if you can stay in the space of working on yourself as you write each letter, then it's an incredibly valuable discipline.

Frankly, most pen-pal relationships are little more than an exchange of attachments. After awhile both sides lose interest because it feels dead. But you know in your heart that you have fears and problems and wondrous questions in your mind; so share your real life with your pen-pals—not just a recitation of yoga methods or spiritual affirmations or philosophies. If you're afraid about violence, then write about that to your pen-pal. *Ask* for help as well as offering it. Many prisoners have quite a bit of experiential wisdom when it comes to things like violence.

This letter I'm writing to you now becomes part of my self-work today. Actually, this is the second draft, because when I read the first one over I realized that I hadn't given you my full attention while I was writing it; and that's just not good enough for the precious work we all have to do with each other. Everybody counts. Anytime we slough somebody off, we've missed the point of why they came into our lives.

Believe me, I know that a prisoner's story can be very grabbing, and that his or her situation is sort of intimidating right from the start. But just a little bit deeper in, we're all so very much bigger than our bodies or our past histories or the walls which enclose us! It's just as important for you and me to realize this as it is for a prisoner. If you think of yourself solely as who you see in the mirror, then that's the prison you live in. In this sense, you and I and your pen-pals *all* share the same journey from bondage to liberation, and that journey is what you're trying to correspond about.

Keep your letters very personal; as intimate as you're able to be. Keep them absolutely straight; don't let honesty slide due to attachments on either end. Stay clear about what you're able, and not able, to provide; don't let a pen-pal define who you must be to them. This is our work on ourselves, and it's very powerful stuff if we keep doing it as best we can. Of course, it won't always work out, either. But then sometimes it'll really blow our minds and change our lives.

Good luck and love, Bo

Tomorrow, tomorrow, and tomorrow
creeps in this petty pace from day to day, 'til the last syllable of recorded time.
And all our yesterdays have lighted fools
the way to dusty death.

Out, out brief candle; Life is but a walking shadow; a poor player who struts and frets his hour upon the stage, and then is heard no more.

It is a tale told by an idiot;
full of sound and fury, signifying nothing.

— Shakespeare

Pam

Dear Bo,

At the beginning of my letter, my own motives for writing it are not clear, but I hope that they will unfold as I continue.

My husband Danny has been paroled from the federal prison to the halfway house as of July 15th. Since he has been away, Danny has written to me a lot about yoga and meditation, and what it has done for his life. After seeing him for a few days on furlough, I can see for myself the changes that he has made. I am very pleased and happy for him, but very deeply disturbed within myself.

I am wondering how I will have to change to blend back into his life once he is released. I am writing to you in hopes that you might help me. Since Danny has been away, I have been through very many hard times. At the time his incarceration began, I was six months pregnant with our first child and literally penniless. I was forced to undergo serious mental changes that were not to my liking. I gave birth without him here, and since that time, I have become increasingly depressed and disillusioned with my life.

With a 2½ - month-old son, it is hard for me to do much of anything for myself, but I have the desire to begin down the path. My husband wants very much for me to develop an interest in yoga and meditation because he feels that it might help me break out of this self-made prison of self-pity and depression. After reading your book, INSIDE-OUT, I agree. He also brought me BE HERE NOW.

I was wondering if you might be able to help me begin this journey. It is very important to me to learn meditation and yoga because I love my husband very much and I want to do all that I can with the reconstruction of his life and of my own. Your help and prayers would be appreciated.

Also, let your readers know that while in prison they may feel loneliness and pain, but they are not alone. There are millions of women with souls like a butterfly that can be crushed at the slightest touch. We are the silent ones who sit lonely and wanting, night after night, waiting for their loved ones to return. Praying for a change such as my husband has made, makes the wait worthwhile. Lucky are those who find it. But determined and steadfast are those women whose prayers have not yet been answered.

Thank you very much for helping my husband to find his purpose. Your works are greatly appreciated by many of us that you will never know.

May God be with you, Pam/N.C.

Dear Pam,

It's a pleasure to meet you. You're a very beautiful and sincere lady, and Danny is a lucky guy. You've long ago begun the journey you're asking about, so don't worry about where to start.

I'm sending you some material with instructions for various practices, but don't confuse the teachings with the truth. You've discovered a lot of truth and strength just by figuring out how to get by day-to-day. If yoga and meditation have helped Danny find strength, courage, honesty, patience, etc., these aren't different qualities than the ones you've been developing by waiting for him and raising your two kids all by yourself. There's nothing simpler than the deepest truths.

I surely agree that meditation might be a good way to loosen your grip on self-pity and depression. Don't feel guilty over it; everybody has stuff to deal with, and this is yours. Over a period of time of daily meditation, you can begin seeing the self-pity and depression arise in your mind, and you can just sit there watching them do their dance—as if you're studying them for a school report or something. Gradually you see they have no power over you other than the power you've always given them. Try not to be so worried about "fitting in" with Danny in his new head. If he's really gotten something good from yoga and meditation, then he'll be *easier* to get along with—not harder. This isn't some sort of secret society with handshakes and passwords. These are methods, nothing else. Keep your mind focused on the *aim* of the methods, which is as old as the hills: living a balanced, happy life with faith, strength, and an endless sense of humor. The two of you should be able to work things out just fine.

Love, Bo

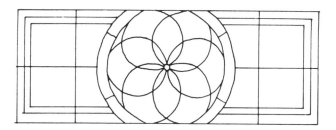

If a man speaks or acts with a pure thought, happiness follows him, like a shadow that never leaves him.

—Dhammapada

Larry and Yusufu

Dear Bo,

My name is Larry, and I have been pen-pals with Yusufu for six years. His was the third name I got from you, the first two did not respond to my letters. Yusufu did answer, and has continued to for six years. We write about once a month, sometimes more, sometimes less. He has been an inspiration to me on many occasions. To be in jail and to work on your consciousness and spiritual development is to plunge into a cleansing fire daily. His commitment hasn't wavered as far as I've ever seen. Getting a letter from him usually makes my day.

Last year I visited him for the first time. The person who I met face-to-face was authentic and true to the person in his letters. Truthfully, I was surprised. Surprised at his willingness to expose himself in front of other prisoners, and that there wasn't a different person in person than in correspondence.

I'm not sure what I want to tell you. My life is richer for having known Yusufu. He has allowed me to peek into a world hidden away from my normal surroundings. His example astonishes me, because I doubt I'd be so strong or open in his situation—and if he can do it there—I can do it here.

He has given me the honor of touching his life. He has shown me how one can rise above the most corrupting influences, and learn to love in an unloving place. I think the only real teaching one can do is by example, and so, you have allowed me to hook up not with just another spiritual seeker (and certainly not a Sunday-morning seeker), but with a spiritual teacher. I thank and honor you for your work.

Larry/California

Dear Bo and Sita,

A month or so ago, I suggested to a close friend of mine, Larry, that we both write you a thank-you letter for bringing us together about six or seven years ago. We have continually written one another throughout this time, and we've grown very, very close. We write about once or twice a month, covering a variety of topics, the most important of which has been our spiritual journeys.

It has not been easy for me—I'm in my tenth year and I've had many personal tragedies to affect me—but the worst parts of my life are only minor by comparison to my righteous spiritual friendship with Larry.

In 1982, he stopped in here for a surprise visit. He lives in California; the prison I live in is in southern Illinois. We had exchanged pictures and talked deeply about ourselves, but nothing was more beautiful than our first meeting in the flesh in the visiting room. He is white and I am black, so you can imagine how we must have looked in the visiting room with other visitors, who were all white. The Larry I had come to know in my letters was the very same Larry I met then; we had a very beautiful and delightful time.

310

Larry has really sharpened my spiritual practice, and has shown me most accurately that it's not words that counts so much as deeds. Many guys are always looking for someone to write, but it's always a female, not a male. Admittedly, I'd like to be able to write a female too, but as Larry has shown me over the years, I can grow to/with a male just as easy as I can with a female.

It has been a real loving, caring, sharing and growing experience, and I am certain that it will last a lifetime (and beyond). And it is all due to your willingness to step outside societal prejudice and connect the seekers of this world, inside and out. I thank you and the ashram project very deeply for your work and bringing Larry into my life. The gifts of peace, happiness, and most of all, love, be with you all, always.

Yusufu

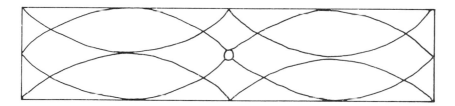

Dear Bo,

This evening I watched the sun fading behind my parent's farm in Canandaigua, and I was thinking about the brothers in Attica, and wondering whether they too were watching that same sun. I felt compelled to write you and thank you for the workshop at Attica that I, as their yoga instructor, was able to attend.

I've been doing a lot of reflecting about different turns my own path has taken, and I've learned a very important lesson. The Ananda Marga organization had been a useful vessel for me, I had flowed along nicely under that direction. However, even prior to your lecture at Attica, I started to feel differently, like people were asking me to commit myself to that path and strictly adhere to that one way. I began to feel trapped, yet I felt scared... would backing off from Ananda Marga make me "ineligible" to continue along spiritually?

Not so at all. As long as I live simply, meditate, love, and try my hardest to clear the noise from my head, I know now that I don't have to be in line with any particular ritual or organization. As long as I work towards God the best I know how, I know now that I'll do well.

The words you spoke reassured me that the various paths all blend together anyhow. The brothers and I came to that conclusion simultaneously at our next yoga class, when we were discussing your workshop. They especially loved the experience when we did the eye-to-eye searching exercise — God looking into God. That blew them (and me) away.

And so the Dharma continues. We'll all survive beautifully as long as we forget the packaging we're in, and remember the internal substance of ourselves.

Shanthi, Kathy/N.Y.

Tammy

Dearest Bo,

My husband went before the parole board Dec. 13th. He brought them 18 months on a 10-year sentence, a parole plan to Long Beach, Ca., and several letters of support. The results were excellent. He got paroled onto his one-year consecutive sentence. His release date is Aug. 23rd.

What I really need is some advice or insight into why my husband and I are going crazy fighting ever since he got his parole date. It will be a miracle if we make it for the next eight months, without separating. I think that knowing he's getting out is making him a lot more touchy and protective and possessive. I don't know why.

*I finally got a job and am working my butt off five days a week. I used to visit him four times a week, but can only see him Sat. and Sun. now. You'd think our two visits a week would be more special and joyous, but we fight. We fight **so** much it's killing me, and him too.*

I'm crying out for help and surely hope you can give me some assistance. I've been waiting for this man for two years and don't want to end up in divorce. Thank you for your open heart and loving involvement. I anxiously await your reply.

Love, Tammy/Nevada

PS: My husband is on PC (protective custody). He was on the yard until August, but administration got word of a contract out on him, so they pc'd him.

Dear Tammy,

Sorry to hear about your rough times. Marriage isn't easy these days inside or out, so try not to panic; problems come up, and you can deal with them. It happens to everybody.

Bill may be feeling the tension of PC as well as all the understandable anxieties about getting released. He may also feel threatened by how independent you've become and he may be trying to test his old dominance over you for the free world. This is really a perfect time for you to start in a brand-new relationship with each other—as best friends, equal partners, and trusted advisors.

With the strength you've gained over the past couple of years, you may not be able to live in any other way, but this may all be new and scary to Bill. He may have to let go of old images about you being his "chick", because now you need to be much more. And believe me, he needs you to be more than that, too, if he's going to make it on the streets this time around.

You need to have as much patience as you possibly can, but don't give up your new strength and independence. He may be freaked out about sex with you, or whether you've been unfaithful to him; he may be terror-stricken by having to ask for your advice or help, or having you drive him around until he gets back in action. He may have anxieties about handling money, balancing a checkbook, getting a driver's license, and in general keeping a worldly scene together. Prison tends to strip people of those skills and then turn them out on the streets with the parole officer as a constant threat if they don't miraculously remember how to do it all.

But the marriage bond is worth a lot of time and trouble. Try to appreciate all these hidden causes behind your fights so that you don't keep getting caught up in the words and details. As a long-married couple (1966) who have been through our share of pain with each other, Sita and I both wish you well in this difficult, painful adjustment period. Try to see it as a process rather than a problem, and just do the best you can.

Love, Bo

Dear Bo,

How nice of you to write such a wonderful letter! Thank you. It's sad to say, but I really don't know why we're still together. When we are getting along there is a lot of love between us. BUT it takes only a word or sentence to start a fight, for either of us to cop an attitude, for a lot of hate to surface. It's been like this since he got his parole date a few months ago.

Actually, I've never been an angel, and the first two years I was in Carson City I got caught in lies, put Bill in switches, and he won't ever let me forget it. Bill is a thrice-published short fiction writer, and if words could kill, I'd be dead a long time ago. Because we are forced to have only a verbal relationship, our fights have developed certain patterns which I'd so much like to break. I can't do it alone, though.

*Maybe he's going nuts because he's only a few months short now, and for the past 14 months he's been locked inside a pc unit. Maybe freedom will greatly help our relationship—maybe it will help **end** it. I don't know. It's a sad statement.*

We both have loving family, but we basically have only each other. I often wonder if we stay together because of unhealthy need and/or dependence on each other.

Patience and tolerance has not been the name of our game lately. Well Bo, I hope I didn't bring you down with my troubles. I don't have anyone to talk to about this, so I guess I just dumped it all on you. Sorry—but thank you for being there!

Love to Sita,
Tammy

Dear Tammy,

You didn't bring me down; that's what I'm here for. I'm your friend. But you know, it's very hard to give advice from a thousand miles away. I can only play hit-and-miss with my best guesses, and hope you can separate the wheat from the chaff for your own situation.

Words can often be more harmful than helpful—especially if one of you is better at words than the other. You could try some nonverbal communication like sitting opposite each other for 10 or 15 minutes without saying anything; just looking straight into each other's eyes, with no smiles, gestures, touching, — nothing but total honesty and true feelings. Let each other see your deepest fears, highest hopes, and the love that you really do have in your hearts. Get out all the secrets between you in that way; just "say" them through your eyes and ask for (and give) forgiveness for the ways in which you've both hurt each other.

Sometimes when we've been locked in battle, Sita and I have used this reminder: "What's it all about, anyway?" In other words, don't we really want good things for each other? Don't we want to help each other as best we can? Sometimes it's important to put petty arguments into a bigger perspective.

Take courage, my friend. I know fertilizer stinks pretty bad while you're swimming in it, but Lord, how it makes the garden grow! I offer you much light for the growing season ahead.

Love, Bo

Dear Bo,

Thank you so much for your letter. It touched me deeply.

Bill has been out of prison now for two weeks, and we've already moved (to California) and found our own apartment. He is really driving himself (and me) so much that at times I feel he might explode. The saying you and Sita use, "What's it all about anyway?" is easier said than done, especially when one or both of us is in the middle of hurt feelings or high-powered emotions.

Sex is beginning to become a problem — not too much, but hardly any! For 3 years while he was in prison he used to tell me how much... and yet now he almost has to be begged, manipulated and conned into it. Yes, I know how tension, stress, and pressures can lessen his desires, but why do I have the capability to separate the two and also use sex as sort of an outlet?

He warned me that he'd climax too quickly when he got out but said that with "continual practice" he'd be over it in a few weeks. He does come fast, but we don't even do it enough for him to change. I am very unselfish and understanding, so I don't think he feels so inadequate that he doesn't want to have sex. I use the words "have sex" rather than "make love" because there is no tenderness, passion, or expression of love from him (other than telling me he loves me) when we do it. I feel so lousy about this. I was led to expect more and different than what it is. I, as a result, feel unwanted and undesirable.

With very good reason, Bill is always uptight. His sister, brother-in-law, and their close friend, and his mother are always calling, and even though they feel they are only trying to help, they put a great deal of pressure on us. Always inviting us here and there — we don't want to go, yet feel obligated to. We never get a chance to spend any quality time together. If we are eating, he's either reading or watching tv; after dinner he gets absorbed in his writing, and by the time he comes into the bedroom, he's asleep before his head hits the pillow.

I am expected to sit by, watch, and absorb all of this and never open my mouth. I'm just supposed to clean house, cook, clean after him, drive him everywhere (he has no license yet) and ask for no affection, nothing for myself. Sometimes I want or need him to just put his arms around me and hold me, but I dare not ask. There are so many people and things pulling him in different directions that my requests become only extra added burdens for him. When I've had it "up to here," and do come out with something he doesn't like, or feels is out of line, he blows up, takes EVERYTHING out on me, and will actually go to the extreme of telling me to get out of his life.

I can see how this is all a tremendous lesson in patience and self-control for me. It's clear at times, but usually I'm too caught up in this melodrama to see clearly — and that's when all the pain sets in.

I have no one but you to express myself to. When I tried to express these things to Bill he gets down on me for "bitching, moaning and sniveling." I can't even express my pain through crying, 'cause he gets mad at me.

I had him read your most recent letter to me and he made no comment. There isn't even time in our lives for us to sit down and do that non-verbal practice. I'd love to have 5 minutes to look into his eyes, to feel him through his eyes. But I think to him, there are more important things to do. Ain't that a kick in the ass?!!

Anyway, that seems to be the dilemma. I hope you can offer some consolation or advice. I oftentimes feel like I'm going to SNAP. Thanks Bo, just for being there — for being my friend.

Love, Tammy

Dear Tammy,

I *know* that "What's it all about anyway?" is easier said than done, but the fact is, you guys are going to have to do some not-so-easy work if you hope to somehow pull through this period together. It sounds like there's no way Bill would see any sort of counselor with you (I suppose the idea has come up?); and I'll tell you, it really feels like groping in the dark trying to give you advice from 3,000 miles away. I think you need to start considering some things for yourself — like counseling, meditation practice etc. — before you *do* "snap".

If Bill is unwilling to make your marriage a top priority right now, you have to take a clear look into your reservoir of patience, and figure out whether you're able to handle it for awhile longer. Maybe you can, and maybe you can't; it's something only you can determine.

Sita and I went through a rough period once when the only way we could hang in there was to have separate bedrooms and stay pretty much out of each other's way. We had separate rooms for almost a year, but we gradually softened up in little everyday ways, and then sort of "dated" each other now and then as our love and trust slowly built back up. What we had was worth the struggle.

I'm very strong on marriage; I think few people appreciate the deepest possibilities of it. If you can, by all means hang in there with your mate "for better or worse." But you'll have to shift your viewpoint in order to do it with love; you can't keep getting stuck in the surface issues or the question of your rights versus his.

Since you said Bill was willing to read my last letter, maybe he'll read this one too. Let me give you an example of what I mean about the depths of the marriage bond: When I was nine, my father was paralyzed from a massive brain hemorrhage. The doctors and all our relatives tried to convince my mother to put him away in an institution instead of taking care of him at home. They urged her to get married again (she was only 33!); that it would be unfair to her four kids to revolve our lives around a cripple who might not even recognize us ever again. They told her he'd only live about a year anyway, so why go through the considerable trouble?

Thank God my mother found the strength to resist all those perfectly logical arguments! Within a few years, my father knew us all again, and was able to get around the house with a brace and cane, and later in a wheelchair. Although he couldn't speak in whole sentences, his mind was clear and bright, and he became the sweetest, kindest, most innocent person I've ever known.

After *fourteen years* of being humbled and purified, he died in his own bed with my mother, me, Sita, and the whole family gathered together for his final days. His last words, as he looked into my mother's face and smiled, were "Pretty, pretty!" He loved her so!!

When Sita and I say "What's it all about, anyway?", it's with the recognition that if either of us were to be crippled tomorrow, the other would find it a *privilege* as well as a duty, to love and care for that one the rest of our lives. Marriage can become sacred in ways which last far beyond the world we see around us. Marriage can take us all the way into enlightenment.

If you and Bill feel you really belong together, you just have to find a way to stop fearing and punishing each other. Even if it's only you who's willing to stick it out right now, you need to do it in a way that helps Bill through this painful period of his life, rather than doing it in a way that keeps building your anger, hatred, and self-pity. If you're unsure whether you can stick it out in the right way, maybe you should set a time limit for yourself, and if things don't seem to be getting any better by then, you can make plans to leave before you destroy each other.

I only wish I could give you more of a magic wand, more of an easy answer, but please know that Sita and I offer you all the support and best hopes from the center of our hearts.

Love, Bo

Frank

Dear Bo and Sita,

I have just read issue #73 of the SUN magazine. I was very pleasantly surprised when I pulled my copy out of the mailbox and found that this issue was dedicated to your work. It brought back many happy memories.

Let me explain why your work means so much to me. In 1975, I was sentenced to 7-10 years for armed robbery. At that time I was a very confused, unaware being. Short-ly after my incarceration, I found a tattered copy of INSIDE-OUT #1. I wrote you, and we began a relationship through the mail that lasted for the next two years. During that time, you helped me to become aware of my own potential. I came to see clearly that we are all one, and that all is as it should be.

After my release, I stopped writing you, but never forgot the lessons that you helped me to realize, I knew all along. I came out of prison with a completely new outlook on life. I understood that I had complete control of my life, and I decided to try to make my light shine as brightly as possible. I went to college and received a B.S. degree in mathematics. I then took a job as a high-school equivalency instructor in (of all places) prison.

I have been here for a year now, and I feel very deeply that all of those years of suffering and pain were prerequisites for my present position in life. Since taking over this job I have had the opportunity to share your ideas with several of the inmates here. I have also been very adamant about helping these people to better understand their situation, and how to handle it.

I want you both to know that I love you very deeply. There will always be a special place in my heart for you. Because you have helped me, I am now able to help others to help themselves. As you said about karma, "What comes around goes around." May you know only love and peace forever.

Your friend and brother, Frank

Here on the mountain I have spoken to you clearly. I will not often do so down in Narnia. Here on the mountain the air is clear and your mind is clear; as you drop down into Narnia, the air will thicken. Take great care that it does not confuse your mind. And the Signs which you have learned here will not look at all as you expect them to look, when you meet them there. That is why it is so important to know them by heart and pay no attention to appearances. Remember the Signs and believe the Signs. Nothing else matters.

—C.S. Lewis, from "The Chronicles of Narnia"

Whoever you are, wherever you are, however your life is going right now—as your eyes fall upon this last page of my book, you're a big part of my life, and I want you to know that. I thank you for being with me. I wish you every good thing. It's a privilege just to be here together, stumbling toward the Light. Take heart; we'll make it.   I love you, *Bo*

The Prison-Ashram Project will continue to send this book and other materials to prisoners free of charge for as long as we can afford to do so. The project is always in need of donations, grants, or bequests. If you'd like to help support this work, please send your tax-deductible contribution to:

Prison-Ashram Project
Rt. 1, Box 201-N
Durham, N.C. 27705